NEW WORLD HASIDIM

SUNY Series in Anthropology and Judaic Studies
Walter P. Zenner, Editor

NEW WORLD HASIDIM

Ethnographic Studies
of Hasidic Jews in America

edited by

Janet S. Belcove-Shalin

STATE UNIVERSITY OF NEW YORK PRESS

The system for transliterating Hebrew words into English is based on standard Hebrew orthography as detailed in the *Encyclopaedia Judaica,* vol. I (New York: Macmillan, 1971), with allowance made for more readily recognized spellings of certain words. Certain terms that are far more identifiable in Yiddish than in Hebrew are used and are based on YIVO transcription guidelines. In some instances, variant spellings are employed with respect to dialect or common usage.

Published by
State University of New York Press, Albany

© 1995   State University of New York

Production by Susan Geraghty
Marketing by Fran Keneston

Printed in the United States of America

For information, address State University of New York Press,
State University Plaza, Albany, N.Y., 12246

Library of Congress Cataloging-in-Publication Data

New world Hasidim : ethnographic studies of Hasidic Jews in America /
    edited by Janet S. Belcove-Shalin.
        p.   cm.—(SUNY series in anthropology and Judaic studies)
    Includes bibliographical references and index.
    ISBN 0-7914-2245-3 — ISBN 0-7914-2246-1 (pbk.)
        1. Hasidism—United States.   2. Hasidism—United States—Social
conditions.   3. Jews—United States—Politics and government.
4. Habad—United States.   5. United States—Ethnic relations.
I. Belcove-Shalin, Janet S., 1954-. II. Series.
BM198.N38 1995
305.6'96—dc20   94-300
                                                                CIP

10 9 8 7 6 5 4 3 2 1

For all Hasidim
who aspire to Hesed

CONTENTS

ACKNOWLEDGMENTS

I wish to thank a number of people whose help and goodwill made this volume possible. I am grateful to the volume contributors, who took in stride my repeated requests for revisions. I would like to note that work on this volume afforded me the opportunity to personally get to know many of my colleagues whom I had heretofore known only through their work.

I owe a special debt of gratitude to my colleagues Veona Hunsinger and Donald E. Carns. Veona saw the manuscript through several revisions and helped prepare the final text. Donald encouraged me in my work and provided me with the extra time and resources needed to finish this project.

I would like to thank Rosalie M. Robertson, Walter P. Zenner, and Christine E. Worden of SUNY Press for guiding this volume through its many incarnations.

I also wish to thank two family members: my father, Allan S. Belcove, for his keen eye at proofreading; and my husband, Dmitri N. Shalin, for his faithful support of this project and readiness to shoulder a greater burden of household duties to expedite its completion.

I think I speak for all contributors to this volume when I extend my heartfelt thanks to the many Hasidim who generously offered their time and insight to the odd, often inscrutable, and sometimes annoying lot of ethnographers. It is to the Hasidim that I wish to dedicate this volume.

FOREWORD

Samuel C. Heilman

Among Hasidim, all of whom trace their origins to the movement begun by Israel Ben Eliezer, the Baal Shem Tov, distinctions are commonly based upon which rebbe or charismatic leader one follows and the customs associated with that group. For anthropologists and sociologists, however, another kind of difference might more usefully be drawn. Here, the crucial contrast is between the Hasidim of the imagination, those who people fiction or whose exotic figure adorns works of art and walks the corridors of nostalgia that lead to the palaces of collective memory, on the one hand; and the Hasidim of real life, those who actually fill the synagogues and yeshivot, who follow this or that rebbe and live in a community of believers, on the other. For those who have encountered real Hasidim, hoping to find incarnate the mystic who finds meaning in kabbalah that informs his every movement, or who fills his days and nights singing and dancing to melodic tunes, punctuating them with pithy proverbs filled with the wisdom of Hasidic tales, the result is often a disappointment. Romantics turned on by Buber's *Tales of the Hasidim* often find the Hasidic realities of an Orthodox Jewish community, frequently insular and deeply engaged in a political and cultural war against what they perceive to be the corrosive forces of contemporary secular society, hard to bear.

The role of the ethnographer, informed by the dual disciplines of anthropology and sociology, however, is to make the real comprehensible, to capture as much as possible all the dimensions of the people in question, to make this encounter with reality sensible. Interest in applying this approach to Hasidim—admirably pursued in the pages that follow here—has grown over the last two decades, as exhibited in a number of books that have taken an unsentimental and complex measure of Hasidim. These studies have revealed a deep structure to Hasidic life that is influenced very much by the forces of contemporary culture, by political change, by technology, and by the real events of history. Hasidim are more than picturesque reminders of yesteryear, Jewish grand-fathers and grandmothers caught in a bubble of time. Although they survive from the past, they are not identical with it, as the papers in this book demonstrate. In fact, the ethnographic record shows that today's Hasidim are very much part of the modern world, struggling in a variety of ways against powerful social forces that threaten to either sweep them away or else transform them into something radically different from what their founders conceived or their leaders perceive.

In a sense, it is precisely the process of cultural and social sur-vival that has led to this change in the real life of today's Hasidim. To understand this development, one needs to realize that in effect Hasidim are today survivors in a double sense, having come through both an ideological and a physical assault. The ideologi-cal force that threatened to wipe them away came in the tremen-dous wave of religious reform and secularization that for two hun-dred years has swept ever more powerfully across world Jewry. As fewer and fewer Jews define themselves through religious practice and tradition, as ritual life is largely abandoned in favor of an absorption into secular modes of life while cultural assimilation into non-Jewish Western civilization has become normative, Hasi-dim have stood out as cultural registers, remaining stubbornly contra-acculturative. In the process, these erstwhile radical mys-tics and religious revolutionaries who challenged the rabbinic sta-tus quo when they first emerged in the late eighteenth century have become redefined as among the most conservative elements in Jewish life, the ultra-Orthodox or—in the increasingly popular Hebrew term *Haredim*—those whose attachment to ritual and religious tradition is anxiously maximal. As Haredim, they are a minority of a minority, approximately 25 percent of the nearly 10 percent of Jews who call themselves "Orthodox." But they are a minority that has been, at least on the surface, able to maintain their alternate lifestyle and values in the face of the secularizing and acculturative trends. Long after they were expected to disap-pear, they have continued to exist. And they do so boldly and in public, their attachment to traditional religion and the past flying in the face of modern secular America or Western Europe and contemporary secular Israel where they have largely concentrated. Still to be standing when you have been counted out in advance by all observers is of course a triumph, and that is what has often attracted the attention of the rest of the world to this tiny fraction of Jewry.

Hasidim are also survivors in a physical sense. Reluctant to leave the European heartland of Jewry and their rebbes, even when the dark clouds of Nazism loomed on the horizon, in part because their leaders warned them against emigration to the *treyf medinah*, America, where Jews might survive but Judaism would die, or to Israel, the Zionist heresy established by unbelievers who wanted to reinvent Jews and Judaism, they remained in Europe and were constantly ravaged by the firestorm. Entire Hasidic courts and dynasties were turned to ashes. Only a few survived, traumatized and shredded from their past. But those few reestablished themselves, often with a survivor guilt and compulsion to give a more powerful life to the past than it ever had. They determined to establish even larger followings with institutions that were stronger than before the Holocaust. They would root themselves in the very soil they once believed so hostile to them and their way of life. They would discover new strategies for survival. One crucial feature of this reborn Hasidism was that Hasidic customs of the past, once marginal, were raised to a level of sanctity and centrality that sometimes made them indistinguishable from laws established at Sinai. Yesterday became a point of reference for tomorrow. All this is the cause of survival. Yet the challenges faced in the new worlds where Hasidim now found themselves were different from those they faced in their formative years in Europe. Yesterday had to be constantly reinvented, even as it was endlessly revered. Today had to look like yesterday even as it served as a prelude to tomorrow. The Satmar Hasid who sold computers had to look as if he still lived in a European shtetl. The past was the cover under which the present could be engaged.

All this was because in the new world, the outside world and new ways beckoned endlessly. In America, especially, instead of being faced by hostile host societies that kept Jews at bay, Hasidim of the post–World-War-II world found themselves in societies that made belonging easy and even attractive. America was a place where Orthodox insularity seemed out of place, or alternatively where even the Orthodox Jew could enter into the mainstreams of contemporary existence. Exile felt different here. As for Israel, which promised all Jews a share in their own sovereignty, exile and insularity had to be redefined completely if they were to make sense there. In these two new great centers of Hasidic life, keeping the faith and the followers now required new strategies and new institutions. And it raised the ante for being a Hasid.

To be a Hasid today means more than simply following a rebbe. It means spending extended time in a yeshivah, plumbing texts and insulating oneself and one's family (especially children) from the attractions of the world outside its walls. It means staying away from the rough and tumble of making a living or else investing it with ontological inferiority—with the inevitable compromises that engenders. In Israel, it means staying out of the army with the erosion of religious authority and the mixing of secular and religious, boy and girl, that occasions. And it means expending much energy finding economic support for this lifestyle as well as focussing much concern on attracting and holding followers who could easily drop out and flow into the mainstream culture of contemporary society. Much of this requires not only ideological vigilance but political savvy. All this is a far cry from the mystical vision of the Baal Shem Tov and his disciples.

This new world of Hasidim is not an easy one to sustain. Life in it has made the Hasidim anxious Haredim, even as they point with triumphant pride to their continuing survival. Some have responded to their anxiety by going on the offensive, hoping that by changing the world, or at least the Jews in it, into Hasidim, they can insure their survival or even hasten the coming of the Messiah who will solve all the problems of contemporary existence and usher in a new age of promise and hope. The Lubavitcher Chabad Hasidim stand out here, but there are others—the Breslov Hasidim, for example—who also have tried to remake the world in an effort to insure the future.

Other Hasidim have taken a defensive posture and turned away as much as possible from the outside world to insure the future, building high the walls of their voluntary ghettoes with a separate language (Yiddish), separate neighborhoods and schools, distinctive and esoteric customs, and even special buses that carry them in and out of the dangerous outside world with a minimum of contact. Satmar and Skverer Hasidim are prominent examples.

Still others have responded by trying to amass money and political power in the hope that they will be able to protect themselves and their way of life with the dollar bill and the ballot box. They have often sought to make the Hasid the image of the quintessential Jew. Every time a political candidate or public figure has his picture taken with a Hasidic figure or lends economic or political support to a Hasidic cause on the assumption that by doing so an act supportive of *all* Jews has been undertaken, these Hasidim count a victory. They want the earlocked and bearded Jew to be the image of the authentic Jew and his voice to be the only voice of Jewish authority. They see themselves as defenders of the faith.

Which, if any, of these long term strategies for survival will succeed cannot be known. Yet the series of papers that Janet Belcove-Shalin has assembled in the pages that follow will give readers a better understanding of what is at stake in this survival. Focussing primarily on the Hasidim of America, this last best Jewish enclave in the diaspora, these papers flesh out some of the complexity of contemporary Hasidim and offer an opportunity to see Hasidim unmediated by romantic imagination and nostalgic visions.

INTRODUCTION:
NEW WORLD HASIDIM

Janet S. Belcove-Shalin

Hasidism has come of age in the New World. The controversies that surround Hasidic Jews command headlines, their parochial ways capture the artistic imagination, their Old World values surface in popular culture. A good example of their prominence is the publicity occasioned by the ninetieth birthday of (the now-deceased) Rabbi Menachem Mendel Schneerson, the Lubavitcher Rebbe—spiritual leader of Lubavitcher Hasidim. One can readily understand why the event was covered widely in Lubavitcher publications and parochial Jewish newspapers, but what about the *New York Times Magazine* lending its cover page to the occasion (Asnin 1992)? Stories about the Rebbe and the messianic fervor surrounding his birthday appeared all around the country, including such unlikely places as the "Society page" of *Newsweek Magazine* (Woodward and Brown 1992) and feature page of the *Las Vegas Review-Journal* (Davis 1991; *Las Vegas Review-Journal* 1992). In my own community of Las Vegas, a city not renown for its piety or *Yiddishkeit*, the Mayor enthusiastically proclaimed April 14, 1992, the Rebbe's ninetieth birthday, as "Education and Sharing Day" (*Las Vegas Israelite* 1992:3).[1]

The Hasidim's influence has been rising steadily, reflecting their high birthrate and growing political savvy. Hasidic Jews can

This chapter has benefitted immeasurably from the helpful comments of Dmitri N. Shalin, David R. Dickens, Zalman Alpert, and Ira Robinson, as well as Joel Schwartz and his colleagues at the Council of Jewish Organizations of Boro Park.

1

be heard delivering benedictions to the United States Congress.[2] Their leaders caucus with presidents and serve on blue-ribbon panels.[3] Hasidim enjoy much political clout in Brooklyn, where many of their groups are headquartered. Thanks to their extensive lobbying efforts, the community has benefited handsomely from federal and metropolitan programs, including CETA (Comprehensive Employment Training Act) dollars, Headstart and HUD grants, and Sections 8 and 202 housing assistance (*Forward* 1992a; Winerip 1994; Hoch 1993). Since Hasidic Jews vote in high numbers, they are courted by candidates running for political office. The Lubavitcher Rebbe alone commanded anywhere between 15,000–20,000 votes in his corner of Brooklyn.[4] It is also widely believed, though Rabbi Schneerson denied the rumors, that the Lubavitcher leader's political influence extended beyond his Crown Heights neighborhood all the way to Israel. In April of 1990, the Labor Party failed to form a coalition when two of their members suddenly withdrew their support after placing a phone call to Lubavitcher headquarters in New York. Public outrage over the Lubavitchers' perceived interference was widespread, and it was roundly deplored by *Yediot Aharonot*, an Israeli newspaper, that lamented the plight of a nation whose lot is "in the hands of a rabbi who lives in Brooklyn, who has never set foot in Israel" (Mintz 1992:358).[5]

Once a little-known religious sect, Hasidim are known in and outside of the Jewish community. Hasidic Jews emerge as protagonists of Hollywood films and T.V. movies.[6] "A Stranger Among Us," the Disney production picture starring Melanie Griffith as a detective operating undercover in a Hasidic community, is but the latest example of Hollywood's fascination with the subject (Koltnow 1992). Hasidim have long been popular characters in short stories and novels. Nobel Prize winners I. B. Singer and Elie Wiesel have written extensively about Hasidism. Philip Roth, Chaim Potok, and Woody Allen have popularized the humor and pathos of Hasidic Jewry for readers who might not have recognized a Brooklyn Hasid from a Pennsylvania Dutch Amish. For many of their nontraditional Jewish brothers and sisters, the Hasidim's lifestyle has come to symbolize "authentic" Judaism. In the attempt to lead more meaningful lives, scores of nonobservant Jews, known as *baalei teshuvah*,[7] have joined the ranks of Hasidim. Perhaps the most unexpected instance of the Hasidim's influence on American culture—"I thought someone was putting me on," exclaimed Assemblyman Dov Hikind, who represents the Hasidic neighborhood of Boro Park (Associated Press 1993)—is the discovery of Hasidic garb by the haute couture fashion industry. Inspired by the "'elegance and purity'" of Hasidic Jews (Newsweek 1993), Italian fashion designer Fabio Inghirami recently unveiled his "Hasidic-theme men's collection"—"Talmudic scholar with panache," as he described it (Associated Press 1993). Inghirami's Hasidic line has been a hit with fashion critics and will be sold in stores around the country.

To be sure, not all portrayals of Hasidim and Hasidic life have been favorable. Just in the last few years, Hasidic communities have been rocked by controversy and scandal: accounts of child and drug abuse (Dugger 1992; Haas 1991), fraud (Nordheimer 1992; Hays 1991; Malnic and Chazanov 1993; Goldberg 1993a), racism (Treadwell 1991; Hevesi 1991), violence (Goldberg 1992; *Forward* 1992b), kidnapping (Myers 1993), succession battles (*Forward* 1993a; Goldberg 1993b), and debates on the separation of church and state (Greenhouse 1993a, 1993b; *Forward* 1993b; Savage 1993) have found their way into the media. One particularly tragic event occurred in the summer of 1991 when a vehicle driven by a Lubavitcher Hasid accidentally struck and killed a Black child (Lee 1991; Kifner 1991b, 1991c; Barron 1991).[8] The strife between the Black and Lubavitcher residents of Crown Heights precipitated a prolonged period of strife that was reported on for some time (*Las Vegas Review-Journal* 1991; Kifner 1991a; Gonzalez 1991; Logan 1993; Tabor 1992a, 1992b; Beck 1991; New York Times 1991a; Barbanel 1991; Finder 1992).[9]

To understand American Hasidism, its lifestyle, religious precepts, and influence on our nations's culture and society, it is vital to have a sense of the Hasidim's historical roots and present-day community life in America. In the sections that follow, I will try to convey the richness of the Hasidic tradition, the diversity of contemporary Hasidic life, and the ethnographic scholarship that illuminates it.

HASIDIC ORIGINS

In the long history of Judaism, Hasidism is a fairly recent phenomenon. It sprang to life in mid-eighteenth-century Eastern Europe as an alternative to traditional rabbinical Judaism:[10] The Hasidic movement sought to transform rabbinical Judaism from what was perceived by its followers as a rigid, overly scholastic faith into a teaching and lifestyle based on egalitarianism, charismatic leadership, and ecstatic devotion to God. Hasidism arose from the ashes of eighteenth-century Poland, where Jewish culture and society had deteriorated into political anarchy, financial impoverishment, and spiritual malaise.[11] As such, it can be best understood as a revitalization movement, or "a deliberate, organized, conscious effort by members of a society to construct a more satisfying culture" (Wallace 1965:504).

Hasidism was by no means the only charismatic Jewish movement in Europe of this period. A number of false messiahs, notably Jacob Frank and Shabbatai Tzevi (in the seventeenth century), sought to wrestle the mantle of leadership from traditional Judaism, promising their followers the world to come. Yet, these attempts at salvation only led Eastern European Jewry (also called Ashkenazim) further down a ruinous path. By contrast, the Hasidim, or the "pious ones," were remarkably successful in their goal of rejuvenating Jewish life. The Hasidic movement had its share of disappointments and setbacks, but in the end it emerged triumphantly as the first major Jewish current since the diaspora to create a distinctive ethos and world view.[12]

Hasidism was founded by Rabbi Israel ben Eliezer (1700–1760), the Baal Shem Tov (the Master of the Good Name), also known as the Besht. A renowned storyteller and popular healer, he had a special appeal to the simple folk. The Besht taught his fellow Jews that God was omnipresent and that the Divine could be served not only through study and prayer, but also through an uplifting melody, a spirited dance, or an inspiring story, if the Almighty was praised. Hasidism radically democratized Jewish worship by legitimizing nonscholarly forms of communion and upgrading them in importance to the level of formal Torah study. The highest Hasidic ideal was *devekut*—communion or attachment to God. According to the Besht, devekut should not be seen as an esoteric domain accessible to only the mystic, but as the spiritual precondition for all religious observance, in other words, as practical mysticism to be mastered and performed by each and every individual. Authentic spirituality, taught the Besht, could be attained by the common folk, the *am haaretzim*,[13] provided one is willing to worship the Almighty with humility (*shiplut*), joy (*simchah*), and enthusiasm (*hitlahavut*). These spiritual qualities could endow human activity with sacred significance, turning seemingly mundane exercises into a genuine *mitzvah* (good deed, divine commandment).

Under the Besht's successors, his teachings were systematized and new social forms patterned. Dov Ber of Mezeritch (1704–1772), the Besht's immediate successor, was an erudite Talmudic scholar and charismatic individual who devoted his life to codifying the master's teachings and inspiring followers to proselytize on behalf of the burgeoning movement. The ensuing proliferation of Hasidism marked a novel form of religious leadership hitherto unknown among Ashkenazic Jewry—the Hasidic rebbe. The ascetic mystic or Talmudic scholar was no longer regarded as the sole exemplar of religious virtuosity. First and foremost, a rebbe's authority was based on his piety and charisma; his key task was to bring Hasidim to God and God's grace to Hasidim.

The rebbe's authority grew more routinized with time and eventually became dynastic, as the mantle of leadership was passed from father to son.[14] By the third and fourth generation of Hasidic leaders, a colorful array of personalities had come forward to propound imaginative world views. In the Northeastern part of Eastern Europe, where Rabbinism was predominant, Lubavitcher Hasidim made strong inroads. The founder of this Hasidic branch, Shneur Zalman, undertook to synthesize the Besht's principles with traditional Rabbinic teachings. He originated the school called *"Chabad,"* an acronym based on *Chochmah* (wisdom), *Binah* (understanding), and *Daat* (knowledge), which reinstated rational Torah study on par with ecstatic prayer, an emphasis still central to Lubavitcher Hasidim. In the South, Hasidism evolved in a different direction. Two types of Hasidic communities and leaders came into prominence here, one emphasizing humanism, the other, the miraculous (Dubnow 1971:750). Both schools accepted the role of the rebbe who intercedes on behalf of his Hasidim with the Almighty. The former type of Hasidic role model is Levi Yitzhak of Berditchev, who is best remembered for his tireless appeals to God for the benefit of humanity. Barukh of Mezhbish, the Besht's grandson, is better known for the splendor of his court and his ability to perform miracles. The Bobover court today reflects these qualities to a considerable degree: elegant garb, elaborate ritual performances, and aesthetic flair are among its most prominent characteristics. The Hasidism that sank roots in Poland had still other prominent features. Faithful to their origins, Polish Hasidim eschewed abstract theory for simplicity of thought and action: "Attributes of modesty, love among Jews, and the essential ethical virtues became integral parts of the Hasidic personality" (Lipschitz 1967:53). The present day Gerer community exemplifies these ideals.

As Hasidism gained a following throughout Eastern Europe, it encountered resistance from "normative Jews" who dubbed themselves "Misnagdim" or "opponents," of the Hasidim. Misnagdim accused the Hasidim of many a sin, including the latter's insular lifestyle, contempt for the Torah, unseemly shouting, singing, and dancing during prayer, excessive feasting and merrymaking, the "cult of the rebbe"—as well as of the frivolous innovations in the liturgy, prayer sequence, and the method of ritual slaughter. The Misnagdim fought the Hasidim tooth and nail. Some sought support from gentile authorities, burned Hasidic books, flogged and jailed their supporters, excommunicated them, and drove Hasidic leaders from town. Economic, political, and kinship sanctions were levied to further isolate the pariahs.[15]

The staunch opposition to the first generations of Hasidic leaders was one factor that drove their successors closer to traditional Judaism. In Poland and Lithuania, Torah study was reinstated as a prime religious virtue. The most cogent synthesis of Hasidism and Rabbinism was developed within the Chabad school by Shneur Zalman. Conceding that Torah study was equal to the observance of all *mitzvot* combined, he recast Jewish learning as the Hasidic ideal of devekut. Moreover, in a complete aboutface, some Hasidim joined forces with the Misnagdim in criticizing their own leaders for their opulent courts and outlandish ritual displays. Hasidism had turned full circle. By 1830, writes Schatz-Uffenheimer,

> the main surge of Hasidism was over. From a persecuted sect it had become the way of life and leadership structure of the majority of Jews in the Ukraine, Galicia, and central Poland, and had sizable groups of followers in Belorussia–Lithuania and Hungary. (1971–72: 1394)[16]

Hasidism has been rightly perceived as the first Jewish religious movement with a distinctive lifestyle and mode of worship since the destruction of the Second Temple (ibid.). Its sovereignty, however, was shortlived. Unlike traditional Rabbinism, which evolved for three quarters of a millennium in a Polish cradle of political tolerance, the Hasidic movement had very little time in which to mature. After revolutionizing Jewish life in one corner of the diaspora, Hasidism assumed a more conciliatory stance. Hasidim closed ranks with their once mortal enemy, the Misnagdim, to combat a far greater foe—secularism—which was threatening traditional Judaism under the banners of the Haskalah,[17] and later, Zionism, Nationalism, and Socialism. Many of those individuals who had withstood the forces of assimilation later became victims of Europe's world wars—unmitigated disasters for Hasidism. During World War I, the communities lying in the paths of warring armies were destroyed, their inhabitants scattered throughout Europe, isolated from their coreligionists and deprived of spiritual guidance. The Holocaust dealt a final blow to the remaining Hasidic centers of Europe. Some Hasidim managed to survive the Nazi death camps only to emerge from the ashes with the embers of their heritage still smoldering. These survivors resettled elsewhere and struggled to reclaim the glory of the old European courts. The new habitats, Elie Wiesel reminds us, are inextricably bound to the old Hasidic masters and extinct Hasidic communities:

> They live in America but they belong to Lizensk, Mezeritch, or Rishin. There are no more Jews in Wizsnitz, but there are Wizsnitzer Hasidim on both sides of the ocean. The same is true for the other Hasidic branches or dynasties. Ger, Kossov, Sadigor, Karlin—these kingdoms have but transferred their capitals. Lubavitch is everywhere except in Lubavitch; Sighet and Satmar are no longer in Transylvania but wherever Satmarer and Sigheter Hasidim live and remember. (Wiesel 1972:38)

COMMUNITY LIFE IN AMERICA

Hasidism today is a global religious phenomenon. Sizable Hasidic communities can be found throughout Europe (particularly in England, Belgium, Switzerland, Austria, and France), South America, and Australia. The Lubavitcher Hasidim, known for their missionary zeal, even boast of a "Chabad House" in Kinshasa, Zaire (Lubavitch International 1992a).[18] While Hasidim can be found on all inhabitable continents, the centers of Hasidic life are located in Israel and North America, most notably in metropolitan New York.

The history of Hasidim and Hasidic communities in North America begins in the late nineteenth century. Contrary to common wisdom, writes the historian Ira Robinson, "Jewish immigrants from Hasidic areas were lacking in neither spiritual leadership nor organizational elan" (1990:4). Congregations of Hasidim were well served by those whom Solomon Poll (1962:63) has termed *"shtikl rebbes"* (the Yiddish expression for "a bit of a rebbe")—persons claiming a distinguished ancestry or descent to established Hasidic leaders, or in some cases, noted for their charismatic authority. The historical record reveals that as early as 1875, Rabbi Josua Segal, known as the "Sherpser Rov," arrived in New York City and subsequently became the "Chief Rabbi" of some twenty Hasidic congregations known as "Congregations of Israel, Men of Poland and Austria." Toward the end of the century a few more Hasidim emigrated: A rabbi from Moscow, Rabbi Hayyim Jacob Vidrovitz, arrived in New York City in 1893 and proclaimed himself "Chief Rabbi of America" while ministering to a handful of small Hasidic congregations (Robinson 1990:5); in 1896 Rabbi D. M. Rabbinowitz, one of the first Lubavitcher Hasidim to have come to the United States, made the city of Boston his home when he became the rabbi of Agudat ha-Sefardim (Robinson 1990:4).

At the beginning of the twentieth century, minor rebbes and emissaries from established Hasidic courts emigrated to America. In 1912 a descendant of Rabbi David Twersky, the Talner Rebbe, settled in New York City. A year later Rabbi Yudel Rosenberg, the Tarler Rebbe, arrived in Toronto (Robinson 1990:6–7). In 1903 a nephew of the Lelover Rebbe, Rabbi Pinchas David Horowitz, was directed by his uncle to come to America. After a number of mishaps and detours, he established the first "American" Hasidic court in Boston in 1916, calling himself the Bostoner Rebbe (Teller 1990:13).[19] After World War One, yet another wave of Hasidic leaders arrived in North America, settling in communities along the Eastern seaboard and in the Midwest.[20]

Robinson points out that the remarkable success of an American Orthodox community transformed this continent, in the eyes of many Hasidim, into a logical place to settle, or in the very least, to visit. Such distinguished rebbes as Rabbi Israel Hager (the Radutzer Rebbe), Rabbi Joseph Isaac Schneersohn (the Lubavitcher Rebbe), and Rabbi Mendel of Visheff (son of the Vishnitzer Rebbe), made extensive tours of North America in 1914, 1929, and the 1930s, respectively, when they visited with their followers and other Jews. "A prewar North American community," writes Robinson,

> did exist and did enjoy a spiritual leadership....When, during World War II and its aftermath, the surviving remnants of Hasidic life in Europe took refuge in the New World, they did not find a tabula rasa. Hasidism and Hasidic leadership existed already in North America. The prewar Hasidic pioneers had provided a base, upon which the new Hasidic immigrant would proceed to build their communities. (1990:17–18)

It was not until after World War II, however, that Hasidim and their rebbes massed upon these shores. The revered Satmarer and Klausenberger Rebbes were among those who settled in Williamsburg; the Lubavitcher Rebbe sunk roots in Crown Heights; the Stoliner Rebbe along with others took up residence in Boro Park (Mintz 1968:37); and the Bobover Rebbe settled on the Upper West Side of Manhattan. By the mid-sixties, the Hasidic population in New York was believed to be between 40,000–50,000 adherents strong, with Satmar at 1,300 families and Stolin, Bobov, Klausenberg, and Lubavitch having between 100 to 500 families between them (ibid.:42).

Thanks to the Hasidic community's high birthrate (the average family has about five or six children)[21] and a growing number of new adherents, the Hasidic population has doubled in the last twenty years. It is estimated that there are 250,000 Hasidim in the world, of which 200,000 live in the United States, with 100,000 residing in New York State alone (Harris 1985:12).[22] While one can point to a handful of *shtieblech* (Hasidic prayer rooms) in Manhattan,[23] the majority of American Hasidim reside in Brooklyn, particularly in the neighborhoods of Crown Heights, Williamsburg, and Boro Park.

Crown Heights is the capital of Lubavitch Hasidism, its supporters there claiming 15,000 members (ibid.:13). Lubavitch is perhaps the most visible Hasidic group, famous for its aggressive outreach campaign that was spearheaded by the world-renowned rebbe, Menachem Mendel Schneerson. Lubavitch runs several schools for baalei teshuvah, "returnees" to Judaism, in Crown Heights and New Jersey (Alpert 1980). They also maintain a fleet of "Mitzvah Mobiles"[24] that troll the streets of New York and other cities with large Jewish populations to encourage Jewish men to don *tefillin* (phylacteries) and Jewish women to light *Shabbat* (Sabbath) candles. At 770 Eastern Parkway, where Lubavitcher headquarters are located, the celebrated *farbrengen* (gettogether) attracts the faithful as well as the just plain curious who come by the thousands to hear the Rebbe discourse on *Hasidut* (Hasidic philosophy) and partake in the singing and good fellowship. Outside of New York City, Lubavitch is known for its Chabad Houses (community centers/synagogues) whose mission is to "turn-on" Jews, mainly college students, to Judaism.[25]

Some three miles from Crown Heights, across the Williamsburg Bridge from the Lower East Side, is the community of Williamsburg. With a Hasidic population around 45,000 (ibid.:12), this neighborhood is home to most of the city's Hungarian Hasidim. While Sighet, Pupa, Klausenberg, and other communities maintain synagogues there, the area is dominated by the Satmarer Hasidim, one of the largest Hasidic communities. Satmar has built an impressive organization: it operates a *Bikur cholim* which arranges visits to the sick, an employment agency, the largest Jewish school system in the United States, a clinic, and a pharmacy (Alpert 1980). In addition to its main synagogue on Rodney Street, Satmar supports seven branches in Williamsburg, with additional ones in Boro Park; Lakewood, New Jersey; as well as in their own village of Kiryas Yoel in Monroe township, New York.

The Satmarer Hasidim are well-known for their virulent anti-Zionism, which has pitted them against the more moderate Lubavitcher Hasidim,[26] as well as for their insular and uncompromising lifestyle. Until 1979, the community was lead by the late Rabbi Yoel Teitelbaum, whose self-appointed mission was to preserve the law and customs of his forefathers in all their pristine purity.

In the southwestern part of Brooklyn lies the neighborhood of Boro Park. The newest among the three major Hasidic communities, Boro Park is unmistakably middle class: Its relatively low crime rate, comfortable environment, and affluent veneer make Boro Park an attractive settlement place for Jewish residents. Although a few rebbes (e.g., the Trisker, Chernobler, Skverer) settled in the neighborhood as early as the twenties and thirties, the masses didn't arrive in Boro Park until the mid-sixties. The burgeoning Hasidic population here is estimated at just under 50,000;[27] it supports more than three hundred synagogues and several dozen yeshivahs and day schools (Schick 1979:23). Among the rebbes who have built their courts in Boro Park are the Bobover, Stoliner, Bostoner (of New York), Blueshover, Munkaczer, Kapishnitzer, Novominsker, and Skolyer. Quite a few Hasidim from the renowned Polish dynasties of Ger and Belz have also settled here, even though their rebbes are headquartered elsewhere. No one community dominates the neighborhood, though Bobov, which is estimated to be the third largest Hasidic dynasty in the United States, has achieved considerable influence.

Because of Boro Park's popularity, the cost of affordable housing has skyrocketed and is now out of reach for most young families. Many have chosen to move to nearby Flatbush, with a few settling further away in Staten Island. By the turn of the century, Flatbush might well evolve into a major Brooklyn Hasidic enclave.

Outside of New York City, in Rockland and Orange Counties, are the Hasidic communities of New Square, Kiryas Yoel, and Monsey. All were pioneered by Hasidim who desired a more sheltered life from America's acculturative influences. In 1954, Rabbi Yaakov Yosef Twersky, the Skverer Rebbe, purchased some land near Spring Valley as the site of the Village of New Square. After years of struggling, New Square numbers over 450 families with some 2,100 members (Mintz 1992:202). In the early seventies, Satmar established a satellite community here, named after their revered rebbe who is now buried there. "Kiryas Yoel," situated in the Township of Monroe, is a thriving village with a population well over 8,000 people (ibid.:214). It is home to the yeshivah where the young men of Satmar study, and to the Rebbe's eldest son and future leader of Satmar, Rabbi Aaron. In Hasidic circles, however, it is well known as the residence of the late Rebbe's widow, Feiga, whose disputes with Rabbi Moshe Teitelbaum, the reigning Rebbe, have polarized the community.

In nearby Rockland County is the community of Monsey. Monsey emerged as a sizable Hasidic enclave in 1972 when Rabbi Mordechai Hager, the Vishnitzer Rebbe, settled there. Monsey is the most diverse of these communities. While largely Vishnitzer in composition, Hasidim from Ger, Belz, Lubavitch, Satmar, and other dynasties also reside there, having built the more than 50 shtieblech (prayer houses) that make this community a desirable residence (ibid.:201).

To the north, in the city of Boston, one finds the Hasidic communities of Boston and Talne. Talne is a small Hasidic enclave, distinguished by the fact that its rebbe, Rabbi Dr. Isadore Twersky, is the Littauer Professor of Jewish Studies at Harvard University. His congregation is not typically Hasidic either, for it counts among its members the Rebbe's graduate students. Boston is also home to the New England Chassidic Center that was established by the Bostoner Hasidim under the spiritual guidance of their rebbe, Rabbi Levi Yitzhak Horowitz. It is one of the oldest Hasidic dynasties on the continent, having been founded in 1916 by the Rebbe's father. It is also distinguished for being the first dynasty to have adopted the name of an American city. Like Lubavitch, Boston is well known for its accessibility to outsiders: All Jews are welcomed to experience a *Shabbaton* (Sabbath get-togethers at the synagogue) with the Rebbe and his Hasidim. In the Hasidic world, Boston is recognized for its medical service program, called ROFEH.[28] This agency provides medical referrals for patients who come to Boston for treatment, as well as lodging, transportation, and interpreters for their family.

Outside the Atlantic Seaboard, Hasidim and rebbes are scattered throughout the continent. Montreal is the home of the Tasher Rebbe. In Milwaukee, Rabbi Michel Twersky, son of the late Hornistaypler Rebbe, maintains a synagogue.[29] The Denver following of his late brother, Rabbi Shlomo Twersky, is currently led by the Denver rabbi's son, Rabbi Mordehai Twersky (Alpert 1980:242). Lubavitch is the most widespread Hasidic community, with one or more Chabad houses in most states. Touting it as their "Northern Exposure," after a popular television program, Lubavitch has recently founded a Chabad House in faraway Anchorage, Alaska (Lubavitch International 1992b:12).

The largest Hasidic communities outside of metropolitan New York are found in Montreal, Chicago, and Los Angeles. Shaffir estimates that there are some 4,000 Hasidim in Montreal, Canada's largest Jewish community. It is comprised of ten dynasties, with Lubavitch being the largest at 225 families. In Chicago, most of the Hasidim are either Lubavitch or Hungarian Hasidim who are led by a number of shtikl rebbes. Los Angeles is home to the largest Hasidic community west of the Appalachians. Not surprisingly, Lubavitch is the main Hasidic presence. One exuberant Lubavitcher Hasid recounted to me more than twenty Lubavitcher institutions in the city, including Chabad Houses, schools, synagogues, and a drug rehabilitation center, as well as Iranian, Russian, and Israeli outreach programs. Coexisting with Lubavitch are a number of Gerer and Satmarer families, estimated to be about thirty each, and various shtikl rebbes.

THE SOCIAL SCIENTIFIC STUDY OF AMERICAN HASIDISM

Although Hasidism has been the subject of historical, philosophical, and popular accounts dating back to the nineteenth-century *Wissenschaft des Judentums* school, the social scientific study of Hasidism is far more recent (Belcove-Shalin 1988). As late as 1958, the sociolinguist Joshua Fishman lamented, "What about the recently formed Hasidic enclaves in sections of Brooklyn? They are still virtually unknown to the American social scientist" (1958–59:98). A few years after this observation, and little more than a decade after the Satmarer Rebbe settled in Brooklyn, George Kranzler (1961) and Solomon Poll (1962) published ethnographies on the Hasidim of Williamsburg.

Studies of Hasidic community life came into their own during an important paradigm shift in the social scientific study of Jewry, and, I hasten to add, in turn helped establish a new trend in the social sciences. Until the 1970s, an implicit theme of American ethnography was society's inexorable march toward assimilation and ethnic homogenization (Heilman 1982:141; Zenner and Belcove-Shalin 1988:24). This perspective is well articulated in *Protestant—Catholic—Jew*, a classic study in the sociology of religion in America by Will Herberg. Herberg writes:

> Insofar as the "Americanness" of religion in America blunts this sense of uniqueness and universality, and converts the three religious communities into variant expressions of American spirituality...the authentic character of the Jewish-Christian faith is falsified, and faith itself reduced to the status of an American culture-religion.(1955:262)

For ethnographers of Jewish life, the secularization/modernization thesis was based on the assumption that as American Jews evolved into Jewish Americans, Judaism would eventually be superceeded by a civil religion. Seymour Leventman succinctly characterized this transformation from *gemeinschaft* to *gesellschaft* as the move from "Shtetl to Suburb" (1969). Orthodoxy appeared from this vantage point as a "residual category" (Mayer 1973), a "sub-cultural system within the larger Jewish order" that had become sectarian (Sklare 1972 [1955]:46). Its only appreciable value was that it "functioned as a cultural constant in the life of the disoriented newcomer, as a place of haven in the stormy new environment" (ibid.:44). European Orthodoxy, it was believed, would have to be supplanted by less parochial American religious brands. According to Marshall Sklare's classic study, *Conservative Judaism*, Orthodoxy's failure to take root in America could be understood as "a case study of institutional decay" (ibid.:43). Poll's early study of Williamsburger Hasidim, by contrast, was more balanced; the author described Hasidim as a fledgling but committed community, well adapted to the New York City landscape and the capitalistic economic system, cultural and religious diversity, and democratic institutions of their adopted homeland (1962:264). Yet even he could not help but wonder if Hasidic youth in America could withstand the temptations of the secular world (ibid.:x). Similar doubts were expressed by Kranzler, who surmised that the external symbols of Hasidic traditions, the *kapotehs* (jackets), the *shtriemels* (holiday hats), the *peyot* (side-curls worn by men), could not possibly endure: "They will not be able to make the proper adjustment, and will break completely, if the strain becomes too strong. Only a small minority will cling to the extreme pattern of their parents" (1961:240).

Poll and Kranzler's foreboding proved to be unfounded, while Sklare's predictions turned out to be altogether wrong. The secularization paradigm has been rendered obsolete by more recent studies that document the resurgence of Orthodoxy. Especially influential in this respect has been the recent research on the baal teshuvah (Aviad 1983; Kaufman 1985, 1989, 1991; Davidman 1990, 1991) and on thriving Hasidic and Orthodox communities (Mayer 1979; Heilman 1976; Lowenstein 1988; Belcove-Shalin 1989; Shaffir 1974). Chroniclers of Orthodoxy have taken note. In his 1972 edition of *Conservative Judaism*, Sklare conceded that "Orthodoxy has refused to assume the role of invalid. Rather, it has transformed itself into a growing force in American Jewish life and reasserted its claim of being the authentic interpretation of Judaism" (Sklare 1972 [1955]:264).

American Orthodoxy today exemplifies a rich and variegated belief system. In their book *Cosmopolitans and Parochials* (1989),

Heilman and Cohen distinguish three wings of American Orthodoxy: the traditionalists (ultra-Orthodox, contra-acculturative);
the centrists (adaptive acculturative, modern Orthodox); and the
nominally Orthodox. These communities differ primarily in their
commitment to ritual observance and by the degree to which they
are willing to accommodate to secular life. As a group, the traditionalists, centrists, and nominally Orthodox make up approximately 10 percent of America's six million Jews (.3 percent of the
total U.S. population), some 600,000 strong—and growing.

Hasidim fall into the traditionalist camp. They distinguish
themselves from the *Yeshivahlite* (yeshivah people) traditionalists,
whose orientation is molded by a network of rabbinical colleges
that includes Chaim Berlin and Torah Vodaath (Brooklyn),
Mesifta Tiffereth Jerusalem (Manhattan), Ner Israel (Baltimore),
the Telshe Yeshivah (Cleveland), and Midrash Govoha (Lakewood, New Jersey), all of which are affiliated with the Agudath
Israel of America[30] (Heilman and Cohen 1989; Alpert 1992b).
The Hasidim and Yeshivahlite differ in a number of ways, most
notably in the social structure of their communities, patterns of
leadership, array of customs, and ethos. Yet they share an
unswerving commitment to scrupulous Torah observance and are
of the opinion that all knowledge of importance (save for vocational training) lies solely within the Torah.

HASIDIC STUDIES TODAY

Since the pioneering studies of Kranzler and Poll, research on
Hasidic life in North America has grown and diversified immeasurably to include a wide range of Hasidic communities and topics.[31] When only a few years ago I reviewed the ethnographic literature on Hasidim (1988), the popular approaches—charismatic
leadership, recruitment practices, cultural performance, self-identity, tradition, and social change—were few in number and traditional in their treatment. Urgently needed were new lines of
inquiry reflecting the latest developments in social theory, such as
feminist theory and the anthropology of religion. The present volume of original ethnographic studies helps fill the lacunae. Our
undertaking serves to accomplish several objectives: it illuminates
the beliefs and practices of a vital religious community; it capital-
izes on and gives fresh impulse to the current surge in scholarly

and popular interest in Hasidism and Orthodoxy; and it shows how innovative theoretical perspectives can inform contemporary ethnography.

A few words about the authors and their research topics are in order. Among the contributors to the volume are pioneers in the field of Hasidic ethnographic scholarship, as well as a younger generation of scholars. The volume's focus is on the Hasidim of North America, although the article by Loeb, which documents the influence that American Hasidim exert on Jewish communities elsewhere (in this case, the Israeli Yemenites), underscores the international appeal of contemporary Hasidism. The Hasidic communities discussed in this volume encompass the wide spectrum of Hasidic life. Loeb, Shaffir, Morris, Koskoff, and Kaufman analyze the Lubavitcher Hasidim, key exemplars of Lithuanian Hasidism, currently headquartered in Crown Heights, Brooklyn. Kaufman includes in her study the Bostoner Hasidim. Epstein and Belcove-Shalin examine the Bobover Hasidim, whose roots extend back to Galicia and who are based in Boro Park, Brooklyn. Kranzler familiarizes the reader with the Hungarian Hasidim of Williamsburg, centering his attention on the Satmar dynasty.

In the past, most studies of Hasidim dealt with the Hasidic beliefs and practices of a particular neighborhood or dynasty and tended to avoid comparisons with other religious communities, Hasidic or non-Hasidic.[32] By contrast, the works of Shaffir, Kaufman, and Davidman and Stocks are comparative in their main thrust. Shaffir describes the boundary-maintenance devices used by three Hasidic communities in Montreal. Davidman and Stocks analyze the gender experience and family dynamics which mark the relationship between Lubavitcher Hasidim and fundamentalist Christians. Kaufman shows how feminists and newly Orthodox Hasidic women frame their lives in "woman-identified" communities. While Kaufman focuses on the Lubavitcher proselytizing among modern American women, most of whom are Ashkenazim, Loeb explores the effects of Lubavitcher proselytizing in a traditional Middle Eastern community in Israel.

Several authors draw attention to the postmodern age in which Hasidim are forced to coexist with other groups. As Hasidim establish "traditional" nuclear families (Davidman and Stocks), homes (Belcove-Shalin), and clear-cut gender-identities (Kaufman), they work to offset the postmodern crises of values dominating our culture.

Traditional ethnographic studies of "Hasidim" typically portray Hasidic men to the exclusion of women. A number of essays in this volume explicitly redress this imbalance. Koskoff writes about women's musical performance. Davidman and Stocks explore gender roles as they relate to marriage and sexuality. Kaufman and Morris enable the reader to hear the authentic voices of Hasidic women.

The papers collected in this volume assist the reader in overcoming the popular image of Hasidim as an insular community, bent on reinventing the shtetl in America (Freilich 1962). This misconception is laid to rest in those studies which examine the political, social, and cultural links that Hasidim forge with other communities. Loeb, Kaufman, and Morris show how Hasidim work to attract newcomers; Shaffir demonstrates how they negotiate community boundaries; Koskoff offers an insight into the deliberate ways in which Hasidim appropriate alternative cultural forms; and Kranzler and Belcove-Shalin document the political and social activism among Hasidim.

If there is one theme that pervades the volume, it is the interplay between tradition and modernity. This focus is particularly central to the works of Shaffir, Kaufman, Morris, and Davidman and Stocks, who highlight a tension between the desire to maintain a distinct identity and to adopt the ways of modern culture, a tension that is endemic to Hasidic life. Each author takes issue with proponents of the secularization thesis, which casts religion as antithetical to modernity and progress.

Shaffir makes deft use of the symbolic interactionist perspective to sort out the conflicting impulses that inform Hasidic politics in the city of Montreal. The most common strategy employed by Hasidim, according to Shaffir, is that of cultural insulation. Shaffir singles out three dimensions distinguishing boundary-maintenance practices employed by the Hasidim in their interaction with secular society: institutional control (specifically in the area of secular education), negotiation strategies (useful in various public controversies), and proselytizing (among nonobservant Jews). Contrary to common wisdom, according to Shaffir, the Hasidic identity is fortified rather than diminished through encounters with the non-Hasidic world. The very necessity to clarify boundaries in the face of the indifferent or hostile world reaffirms what is unique about Hasidism and Hasidim.

The waning years of the twentieth century have been marked by a worldwide religious revival. The resurgence of religious fundamentalism in the far corners of the world as well as on Main Street U.S.A. encourages the reappraisal of traditional values and rediscovery of one's spiritual roots. Acknowledging this trend, Davidman and Stocks explore how Hasidim and fundamentalist Christians successfully construct religious societies in the postmodern world. The authors compare the diverse communities, the disparate ways in which they construct gender, marriage, courtship, and sexuality, zeroing in on the more general sociological question of how newly flourishing "traditional" religious communities create a place for themselves in the muddled context of a postmodern society. The authors argue that secularization is hardly a monolithic phenomenon. They bring to the fore the uneven impact of postmodern society on these religious communities and the alternative strategies the Hasidim deploy in maintaining tradition.

A typical study of Lubavitcher recruitment practices depicts an encounter between a Lubavitcher Hasid and a secular young Jew, usually of Ashkenazic extraction. Loeb's paper, by contrast, delineates Lubavitcher proselytizing activities among the traditional Habbani Yemenites of Israel. The author follows the Habbani on pilgrimage to the Rebbe in Brooklyn and shows how this experience fosters the rediscovery of ancient customs and the enhancement of religious observance: In the Habbani world view, the Lubavitcher Rebbe embodies the religious ideal of charisma which contemporary Habbani associate with their forbearers. Moreover, the New York community of Lubavitcher Hasidim symbolizes the triumph of religious living in a secular society.

Issues of gender crop up in various studies at the interface of tradition and (post)modernity. Kaufman and Morris's work challenges the common wisdom of secular Jewish women who view their Orthodox sisters as subordinate, second-class citizens. The authors amplify the voices of women that were muted by their conservative environment and antifeminist appearances. Kaufman, an active participant in the nascent dialogue on religious feminism, explores how *baalot teshuvah* (newly Orthodox women) use patriarchal religion to enhance their positions in society and acquire the high status that eluded them in secular society. These new converts to Orthodoxy may disavow the feminist movement but they remain open to the feminist discourse that they use (albeit selectively) to filter their newly found experience and knowledge of Hasidic life. The apparent hostility to feminism that marks their pronouncements, Kaufman maintains, is not so much an antifeminist stance as an attempt to keep at bay the jarring proclivities of postmodernity that threaten their religious identity. In a similar vein, Morris provides us with an ethnohistory of Lubavitcher women's religious activism from the 1950s to the present. At a time when American society severely limited women's rights and freedom to chose, argues the author, Lubavitch was a hotbed for women's activism and educational attainment. All Hasidim, women included, were regarded as soldiers in Lubavitch's war on secular Judaism, with the *Hasidista* (Hasidic woman) positioning herself on the front line in this battle for the Jewish soul. Morris points out that although Lubavitch and the feminist movement are both concerned with the dignity and potential of women, Hasidim have rejected feminism for its perceived Eurocentric and Protestant bias and its attacks on traditional, patriarchal religion, which were construed as yet another instance of antisemitism. Lubavitcher women's activism, Morris concludes, is rooted in minority survival rather than in gender politics.

Koskoff's work is an inquiry into the performance of *nigunim* (melodies) among Lubavitcher Hasidim. She explores the role of music in Lubavitcher life—how it fosters a communal structure and the way in which it negotiates between traditional Lubavitcher values and the mores of mainstream secular society. Koskoff offers a hermeneutical analysis of the ways in which the Hasidim decode their own texts, in this case, the laws of *kol isha* (a woman's voice), and examines the rules of inference, association, and the logic of implication engendered in a musical performance. Although she treats the *nigun* as a bona fide case of Hasidic expressive behavior, Koskoff views it less as an instance of artistic virtuosity than as a cultural performance, an expression of social value. The joyful and enthusiastic performance of nigunim is above all a religious act that fosters repentance, self-knowledge, and a continuous dialogue between man and God.

The vitality of Hasidic community-life is a central theme in the articles by Kranzler and Belcove-Shalin. Both authors reflect on the widely successful attempts at community building by Hasidim, which run contrary to the ubiquitous skepticism among social thinkers on Hasidic survival in contemporary America. The articles cast new light on the waves of succession that doomed Jewish communities of the past, and offer alternative models of Jewish habitation innovated by Hasidim.

The economic revitalization of the old Hasidic community of Williamsburg is the subject of Kranzler's work. He demonstrates how the Hasidim of this neighborhood became ethnic activists in their pursuit of affluence and power. The Hasidic success in these areas is all the more remarkable in light of their reclusive ways and widespread poverty. Accentuating the infrastructural role of values, Kranzler shows how the religious mores of this community account for the success of Hasidic entrepreneurship and political influence.

Belcove-Shalin traces the "quest for home" that marks Hasidic life in Boro Park as residents symbolically transfigure the physical and spiritual landscapes of their neighborhood. In our postmodern age, home serves as a key symbol of presence that anchors the Hasidim to a physical and spiritual realm. By reclaiming dynasty, family, and neighborhood, the Hasid reinstates his relationship with the rebbe and, ultimately, with God. Moreover, the Hasid fulfills a cosmic agenda in his quest for home by restoring the divine to its original wholeness. In an analysis that explores the dialectical relationship between home and exile, text and territory, Boro Park is portrayed as the latest incarnation of home, built on the precepts of Torah.

Themes of renewal are also central to Shifra Epstein's account of the Bobover Hasidim's *piremshpiyl* (purim play). As a contribution to the field of the sociology of emotion, Epstein decodes the piremshpiyl as a ritual that allows the community to transcend the horrors of the Holocaust. Prior to World War II, European Jews viewed the piremshpiyl as a time for merrymaking and mayhem; the contemporary Bobover performance, by contrast, transforms the piremshpiyl into a ritual of survival—a collective grappling of *Klal Isroel* (the people of Israel) with the incomprehensible horrors of the Holocaust. This inversion transforms an event of near-total devastation into a life-affirming experience and serves as a culturally appropriate solution that better squares with the Hasidim's understanding of a merciful Almighty.

No volume on Hasidic life would be complete without an exposition on the Hasidic rebbe. The great scholar of Jewish mysticism, Gershom Scholem, writes that an innovation of the Hasidic movement was the creation of a new type of leader "whose heart has been touched and changed by God" (1941:334). A rebbe was not so much a legal authority, like the rabbi, but the embodiment of "an irrational quality, the *charisma*, the blessed gift of revival" (ibid.). Poll maintains that charisma is still a prime ingredient of the contemporary Hasidic rebbe to whom Hasidim attribute supernatural abilities, wisdom, and a profound spirituality. He examines a variety of Hasidic rebbes, each with his own politics and philosophy, and grounds his research in the teachings of Rabbi Elimelech of Lyzhansk, the theoretician of the Hasidic movement who developed the doctrine of the rebbe. Poll demonstrates that the charismatic qualities which Rabbi Elimelech described at the inception of the Hasidic movement still have salience in twentieth-century America.

In the three decades since Joshua Fishman lamented the paucity of research on Hasidim, Hasidic ethnography has transformed itself into a discipline that has attracted the attention of scholars and increasingly reflects the diverse theoretical and substantive perspectives of contemporary ethnography. Our volume attempts to take stock of these recent advances and identify new directions for research. As such, it is our hope that this undertaking will help to usher Hasidic ethnography into the mainstream of contemporary anthropological and sociological studies.

NOTES

1. On April 13, 1984, President Reagan signed legislation that declared the Lubavitcher Rebbe's birthday "Education Day—U.S.A." in honor of the Rebbe's role in "strengthening education and returning moral values to our society" (Jewish Press 1984b:8).
2. Rabbi Shmuel Butman, Director of the Lubavitch Youth Organization, opened the United States House of Representatives with prayer in honor of the ninetieth birthday of Rabbi Schneerson.
3. Rabbi Elimelech Naiman of Boro Park, Brooklyn, was asked to serve as a member of a distinguished panel of judges on President Bush's Award Program. Most recently, eight Lubavitcher rabbis from Brooklyn met with President Clinton on the occasion of his 100th day in office (Ifill 1993).
4. As communicated to me by Menachem Daum, Producer and Project co-Author of "A Life Apart: Hasidim in America," a documentary recently funded by the National Institute for the Humanities, for which I am a humanities advisor.

5. In the aftermath of the Israeli-PLO accords, Lubavitch has launched a multi-million dollar campaign, called "For the Peace of the People and the Nation," to warn against territorial concessions (Jewish Press 1993).

6. "Cagney and Lacey" and "The Days and Nights of Molly Dodd" were a T.V. movie and series episode, respectively, that spotlighted Hasidic Jews. Perhaps the most prominent Hollywood film that featured Hasidim until *A Stranger Among Us* was produced, was *The Chosen*. Most recently, Anna Deavere Smith's one-woman show, "Fires in the Mirror," a portrait of the relationship between the Black and Hasidic residents of Crown Heights in August of 1991, appeared on public television's "American Playhouse."

7. This term literally means "Master of Repentance."

8. The violence and bitterness between the Black and Hasidic communities of Crown Heights have a long and tragic history. According to Black community members, hard feelings between the two groups go back to 1976, when Crown Heights was partitioned into two community boards, one of which was dominated by Hasidim. Jewish residents, by contrast, trace the conflict to 1966, when Mayor John V. Lindsay established the Council Against Poverty. This council, they claim, was dominated by Blacks who systematically monopolized resources that might have gone to other metropolitan minority groups (Becker 1993).

The Gavin Cato tragedy was not the first, nor is it the last, violent confrontation between Blacks and Jews. Ironically, shortly before this book went into press, a Black driver of a van struck a Jewish child—nine year old Shulem Ber Vogel—who had just stepped off his school van. Shulem Ber Vogel fared better than Gavin Cato. The youngster was expected to have made a full recovery (Abraham 1993).

9. In the wake of the death of Gavin Cato and the slaying of rabbinical student Yankel Rosenbaum, a study was conducted by the State of New York. A two volume, 600-page report concluded that during the seventy-two hours of rioting, a vacuum of leadership existed in City Hall, and that there were "'systematic failures'" to contain the riot. It is believed that the impact of the report swayed many Jews, particularly Hasidim, to vote for Mayor Dinkins' Republican challenger, Rudolph Giuliani, who, in fact, won the 1993 mayoral election by a narrow margin (Goldberg 1993c).

10. The revitalization of Jewish society in the seventeenth and eighteenth centuries was paralleled in the Christian community. The Pietist Movement shares many characteristics in common with Hasidim: a reaction against the formalism and intellectualism of mainstream religion, an emphasis on personal piety, a valorization of the affective over the cognitive, a profound sense of God's presence in the world. Each found their roots in a mystical spirituality.

11. It should be noted that Hasidism was not the only religious movement within Judaism aimed at its revitalization. A number of false messiahs, notably Jacob Frank and Shabbatai Tzevi, claimed the mantle of leadership, promising their followers the world to come. These attempts at salvation were eventually thwarted at the expense of the disillusioned masses.

12. A number of historians have offered alternative explanations for the success of Hasidism. Some saw it as the popularization of mystical teachings (Scholem 1971; Buber 1960); others interpreted it as the outcome of class struggle that elevated secondary religious functionaries to key positions (Ben-Zion Dinur 1955; Weiss 1951); still others stressed the role of the rebbe as an embodiment of divine grace (Dresner 1983) and the antinomian elements in Hasidic teachings that appealed to the masses (Scholem 1941, 1971).

13. These persons now enjoyed a status unheard of in traditional society. This is the message one finds in a statement attributed to the Besht:

> Jews are like unto a vine, of which the grapes represent the scholars and the leaves the simple folk. The leaves of the vine have two important functions: they are essential to the growth of the vine and they have a task of protecting the grapes. Therefore they are of greater importance, since the power of the protector is greater than that of the protected. (Zborowski and Herzog 1952:183)

14. This was the ideal form of succession. In those instances where there was no son, a son-in-law, grandson, or other male family member could become rebbe.

15. The Misnagdim outlawed business to be conducted with Hasidim; they forbade appointments of Hasidim to public office; they prohibited marriages between their communities.

16. Actually, the Hasidic community of Hungary was quite small until the beginning of the twentieth century.

17. The Haskalah or Jewish Enlightenment was launched half a continent, but a whole world, away in Berlin by a contemporary of the Besht, Moses Mendelssohn (1729–1786). He and his disciples advanced the causes of secular knowledge, civic equality, and political emancipation for the Jews. This goal could best be achieved, they thought, by adapting Judaism to the modern world.

18. In January of 1991, Rabbi Shlomo Bentoulila and his wife Miriam arrived in Kinshasa, Zaire, a city with 200 Jewish families, in order to established a Lubavitcher presence. "The Chabad house," explains Rabbi Bentoulila, "is also a center for small Jewish communities across black Africa." This is where Jews can turn to for holiday provisions and kosher food, including meat (Lubavitch International 1992a:13).

19. See Even (1918) for further exposition.

20. See Robinson (1990:7–8) for further exposition.

21. Dr. Teresa Mular, acting director of obstetrics at Maimonides Hospital in Boro Park, Brooklyn, calculates that "The average is about 5 or 6 children [per family], but it is not unusual to have people coming in for their eighth or ninth, or 10th baby" (Henry 1982).

22. I should emphasize that these figures are highly suspect and most likely inflated by Hasidim for political purposes. Zalman Alpert estimates the U.S. Hasidic population to be closer to 100,000 (1992b:-475). There are a number of methodological problems involved in estimating Hasidic numbers. For one thing, before one can count Hasidim, one has to account for their identity: this is not always easy to do.

23. On the Upper West Side are the Sassover and Boyaner shtieblech (prayer houses); the synagogue of the Lisker Rebbe is located on the Upper West Side; a Boyaner shtiebl and a Belzer beyt medrash (house of study) can be found on the Lower East Side (Alpert 1980:241).

24. In this volume Shaffir refers to these vehicles as "tefillin mobiles" or "tefillin tanks." Mintz (1979) refers to them as "Torah tanks."

25. In 1990 there were over 250 Chabad Houses in the United States alone (Alpert 1992a).

26. For instances of their feuding, see Mintz (1979).

27. Lis Harris (1985) estimates the population to be about 35,000.

28. ROFEH denotes "doctor" in Hebrew, and is an acronym for Reaching Out—Furnishing Emergency Health care.

29. Although Rabbi Twersky is the heir apparent to the Hornistaypler Rebbe, my informants tell me that he has declined to take on the mantle of rebbe.

30. The Agudah is governed by a Council of Torah Sages comprised primarily of yeshivah deans (Alpert 1992b:475).

31. By contrast, there have been very few studies of Hasidic life in Israel. The recent work of Heilman on the Belzer and Reb Arelach Hasidim (1992), and El-Or on Ger (1993; 1990), are exceptions to an ethnographic trend that prefers to designate Hasidim and other "ultra-Orthodox" Jews as "Haredi" or "Haredim," and studies them as one monolothic community (in contrast to the chiloinim or secularists).

32. See Belcove-Shalin (1988) for instances when the comparative method was used.

REFERENCES

Abraham, I. 1993. Driver with suspended license hits 9-year-old. *Jewish Press*, Sept. 24, p. 20.

Alpert, Z. 1980. *A guide to the world of Hasidism*. In *The third Jewish catalog*, comp. and ed. Sharon and Michael Strassfeld, 233–244. Philadelphia: The Jewish Publication Society of America.

———. 1992a. Lubavitcher Rebbe: Menachem Mendel Schneerson. In *Jewish-American history and culture: An encyclopedia*, ed. Jack Fischel and Sanford Pinsker, 373–375. New York: Garland Publishing, Inc..

———. 1992b. Orthodoxy. *Jewish-American history and culture: An encyclopedia*, ed. Jack Fischel and Sanford Pinsker, 471–477. New York: Garland Publishing, Inc.

Asnin, M. 1992. Cover page photograph of Rabbi Menachem Schneerson. *The New York Times Magazine*, March 15.

Associated Press. 1993. Hasidic garb hits fashion industry. *Las Vegas Review-Journal*, Feb. 11, p. 6A.

Aviad, J. 1983. *Return to Judaism: Religious renewal in Israel*. Chicago: University of Chicago Press.

Barbanel, J. 1991. State assails hospital's care in Crown Heights stabbing. *New York Times,* Sept. 24, p. A1.

Barron, J. 1991. A child and a historian: Victims amid distrust in Brooklyn. *New York Times,* Aug. 21, p. A20.

Beck, M. 1991. Bonfire in Crown Heights: Blacks and Jews clash violently in Brooklyn. *Newsweek,* Sept. 9, p. 48.

Becker, J. M. 1993. In Crown Heights, inequalilty goes back to '66 (letter to the editor). *New York Times,* Jan. 19, p. A20.

Belcove-Shalin, J. S. 1988. The Hasidim of North America: A review of the literature. In *Persistence and flexibility: Anthropological perspectives on the American Jewish experience*, ed. Walter P. Zenner, 183–207. Albany: SUNY Press.

Buber, M. 1960. *The origin and meaning of Hasidism*. New York: Horizon Press.

Davidman, L. 1990. Accommodation and resistance: A comparison of two contemporary Orthodox Jewish groups. *Sociological Analysis* 51: 35–51.

———. 1991. *Tradition in a rootless world: Women turn to Orthodox Judaism*. Berkeley: University of California Press.

Davis, J. D. 1991. 100,000 Jews eagerly prepare for the coming of the messiah. *Las Vegas Review-Journal/Sun,* July 20, p. 5B.

Dinur, B.-Z. 1955. The beginning of Hassidism and its social and messianic foundations (Heb.). In *Bemifne Hadoroth.* 83–227. Jerusalem: Mosad Byalik.

Dresner, S. H. 1983. Hasidism through the eyes of three masters. *Judaism* 32:160–169.

Dubnow, S. 1971. *History of the Jews*. New Jersey: Thomas Yoseloff.

Dugger, C. W. 1992. As mother killed her son, protectors observed privacy. *New York Times,* Feb. 10, p. 1.

El-Or, T. 1993. "Are they like their grandmothers?": A paradox of literacy in the life of ultraorthodox Jewish women. *Anthropology and Education Quarterly.* 24:61–81.

———. 1990. Educated and ignorant—Women's literacy among the Hasidic sect of *Gur:* A link in a chain of paradoxes. Doctoral Dissertation. Bar-Ilan University.

Ettinger, S. 1969. The Hasidic movement—Reality and ideals. In *Jewish society through the ages,* eds. H. H. Ben Sasson and Solomon Ettinger, 251–265, New York: Schocken Books.

Even, I. 1918. Chassidism in the New World. *Jewish Communal Register of New York City,* 2nd ed., 341–346, ed. and pub. by the Kehillah (Jewish Community) of New York City: N.Y.

Finder, A. 1992. Jewish critics meet Dinkins in Brooklyn on complaints. *New York Times,* Dec. 17, p. B8.

Fishman, J. A. 1958–1959. American Jewry as a field of social science research. YIVO *Annual of Jewish Social Science* 12:70–102.

The Forward. 1992a. Satmar Chasidim turning up heat on Dinkins. *Forward,* Jan. 10, p. 1.

———. 1992b. Chasid booked in beating of Crown Heights derelict. *Forward,* Dec. 4, p. 1.

———. 1992c. Schneerson said to accept messianic role. *Forward,* Dec. 4, p. 14.

———. 1993a. 'Messiah' tag spurs rift. *Forward,* Jan. 29, p. 4.

———. 1993b. Jewish groups split over Kiryas Joel. *Forward,* July 23, p. 4.

Freilich, M. 1962. The modern *shtetl:* A study of cultural persistence. *Anthropos* 57:45–54.

Glaberson, W. 1991. Orthodox Jews battle neighbors in a zoning war. *New York Times,* June 3, p. B2.

Goldberg, J. 1992. N.Y. village rocked by Satmar violence. *Forward,* Aug. 7, p. 4.

1993a. Feds probe loan scam at yeshivahs. *Forward,* Aug. 13, p. 1.

1993b. As rebbe's health wanes, followers begin to feud. *Forward,* Nov. 19, p. 1.

1993c. Dinkins' woes to mount as Chasidic suit looms. *Forward,* July 23, p. 1.

Goldman, A. 1990. Schism in Hasidic sect erupts in violence. *New York Times,* April 21, p. 25.

Gonzalez, D. 1991. As storm rages in Brooklyn, Hasidic leader stays aloof . *New York Times,* Aug. 26, p. A12.

Greenhouse, L. 1993a. A school case goes to the heart of a great issue. *New York Times,* Dec. 5, p. 1 section 4.

———. 1993b. Justices will hear church-state case involving Hasidim. *New York Times,* Nov. 30, p. 1.

Haas, N. 1991. Hooked Hasidim: The long and secret road to recovery in Brooklyn's ultra-Orthodox communities. *New York,* Jan. 28, p. 32(6).

Harris, L. 1985. *Holy days: The world of a Hasidic family.* New York: Summit Books.

Hays, C. 1991. Hasidic couple is told to testify. *New York Times,* July 16, p. B5.

Heilman, S. C. 1976. *Synagogue life: A study in symbolic interaction.* Chicago: University of Chicago Press.

———. 1982. The sociology of American Jewry: The last ten years. *Annual Review of Sociology,* 8:135–60.

———. 1992. *Defenders of the faith: Inside ultra-Orthodox Jewry.* New York: Schocken Books.

Heilman, S. C., and S. M. Cohen. 1989. *Cosmopolitans and parochials: Modern Orthodox Jews in America.* University of Chicago Press.

Henry, J. 1982. Orthodox areas 'fertile' territory. *New York Daily News,* April 12, p. K17.

Herberg, W. 1955. *Protestant—Catholic—Jew: An essay in American religious society.* New York: Doubleday.

Hevesi, D. 1991. Rooted in slavery, pogrom and stereotypes, Crown Heights is no blend. *New York Times,* Aug. 21, p. B4.

Hoch, D. 1993. Chasidim flout separatist image. *Forward,* Jan. 8, p. 4.

Ifill, G. 1992a. The Lubavitcher Rebbe at 90. *Jewish Press,* April 10, p. 54.

———. 1992b. 90 mitzvah tanks parade honoring Lubavitcher Rebbe's 90th birthday. *Jewish Press,* April 10, p. 3.

———. 1993. Clinton's 100th: A good day for picture-taking. *New York Times,* April 30, p. A10.

Jewish Press. 1984a. Senior citizen housing to be built by Bobov. *Jewish Press,* Dec. 7, p. 22D.

———. 1984b. President and Congress honor rebbe for his "vision and leadership." *Jewish Press,* May 4, p. 8.

———. 1993. Israeli Chabad launches multi-million dollar campaign against trading land for peace. *Jewish Press,* Aug. 27, p. 2.

Kaufman, D. R. 1985. Women who return to Orthodox Judaism: A feminist analysis. *Journal of Marriage and Family* 47:543–55.

———. 1989. Patriarchal women: A case study of newly Orthodox Jewish women. *Symbolic Interaction* 12:299–314.

———. 1991. *Rachel's daughters: Newly Orthodox Jewish women.* Rutgers University Press.

Kifner, J. 1991a. Racial clashes in Brooklyn are persisting despite pleas. *New York Times,* Aug. 22, p. B10.

———. 1991b. Youth indited in racial slaying that followed automobile death. *New York Times,* Aug. 27, p. A1.

———. 1991c. Traffic death in Brooklyn fuels Black-Hasidic clash. *New York Times,* Aug. 21, p. A20.

Koltnow, B. 1992. Sidney Lumet says making 'A Stranger Among Us' was a longtime goal. *Las Vegas Review-Journal.* July 23, p. 12E.

Kranzler, G. 1961. *Williamsburg: A Jewish community in transition.* New York: Philipp Feldheim.

Las Vegas Israelite. 1992. Las Vegas mayor Jones declares 'Education & Sharing Day' to honor 90th birthday of Rabbi Schneerson. *Las Vegas Israelite,* April 19, p. 3.

Las Vegas Review-Journal. 1991. Brooklyn jury clears Jewish man. *Las Vegas Review-Journal,* Sept 6, p. 11A.

———. 1992. Israel debating Messiah claims: Is he Rabbi Schneerson? *Las Vegas Review-Journal,* March 6, p. 10a.

Lee, F. R. 1991. A bitter funeral for Crown Heights car victim, 7. *New York Times,* Aug. 27, p. A22.

Leventman, S. 1969. From shtetl to suburb. In *The ghetto and beyond,* ed. Peter I. Rose, 33–56. New York: Random House.

Lipschitz, M. 1967. *The faith of a Hasid.* New York: Jonathan David Publishers.

Logan, A. 1993. Never again. *The New Yorker,* Aug. 2, 31–35.

Lowenstein, S. 1988. Separatist Orthodoxy's attitudes toward community: the Breuer community in Germany and America. In *Persistence and flexibility: Anthropological perspective on the American Jewish experience,* ed. Walter P. Zenner, 208–222. Albany: SUNY Press.

Lubavitch International. 1992a. From Lubavitch to Lubumbashi. *Lubavitch International,* 11th of Nissan, p. 13.

———. 1992b. Lubavitch's northern exposure. *Lubavitch International,* 11th of Nissan, p. 12.

Malnic, E., and M. Chazanov. 1992. Rabbi, doctor arrested in elaborate fraud scheme. *Los Angeles Times,* Jan. 12, p. A1.

Mayer, E. 1973. Jewish Orthodoxy in America: Towards the sociology of a residual category. *Jewish Journal of Sociology* 15(2):151–165.

———. 1979. *From suburb to shtetl: The Jews of Boro Park.* Philadelphia: Temple University Press.

McFadden, R. D. 1990. Murder case in community of families: Jewish woman is held in the death of her son. *New York Times,* Nov. 13, p. B1.

Mintz, J. R. 1968. *Legends of the Hasidim.* Chicago: University of Chicago Press.

———. 1979. Ethnic activism: The Hasidic example. *Judaism* 28(4):-449–462.

———. 1992. *Hasidic people.* Cambridge: Harvard University Press.

Myers, S. L. 1993. Bail is set for rabbi held in religious kidnapping. *New York Times,* Feb. 15, p. A12.

Neuman, E. 1989. New Hasidic school district sparks constitutional debate. *Jewish Press,* Aug. 10, p. 1.

Newsweek. 1993. Where'd you get that yarmulke? *Newsweek,* Feb. 8, p. 59.

New York Times, 1991a. Blacks and Hasidim clashing in Brooklyn. *New York Times,* Aug. 21, p. 1.

Nordheimer, J. 1992. A college program ends up in a criminal inquiry. *New York Times,* Sept. 30, p. A13.

Poll, S. 1962. *The Hasidic community of Williamsburg.* New York: Free Press.

Robinson, I. 1990. The first Hasidic rabbis in North America. Paper presented at the Association for Jewish Studies Meeting.

Savage, D. 1993. Church-state debate gets another look. *Las Vegas Review-Journal,* Nov. 30, p. 1.

Schatz-Uffenheimer, R. 1971–72. "Hasidism." In *Encyclopaedia Judaica.* New York: McMillan Press.

Schick, M. 1979. Borough Park: A Jewish settlement. *Jewish Life Magazine,* Winter, pp. 23–35.

Scholem, G. G. 1941. Major trends in Jewish mysticism. New York: Schocken Books.

———. 1971. *The messianic idea in Judaism.* New York: Schocken Books.

Shaffir, W. 1974. *Life in a religious community: The Lubavitcher Chassidim in Montreal.* Toronto: Holt, Rinehart and Winston of Canada.

Sklare, M. 1972 [1955]. *Conservative Judaism.* New York: Schocken Books.

Steinberg, J. 1990. School feared Borough Park Boy was victim of abuse. *New York Times,* Nov. 14, p. B1.

Tabor, M. 1992a. Black is victim of beating by Hasidim in Crown Hts.; Arrest of a suspect ignites an angry protest. *New York Times,* Dec. 2, p. B3.

———. 1992b. Man in beating will sue the Hasidim, Sharpton says. *New York Times,* Dec. 13, p. 22.

Teller, H. 1990. *The Bostoner.* New York: Philipp Feldheim Inc.

Treadwell, D. 1991. Racial animosity is deep in troubled Brooklyn area; blacks see Jews as trying to push them out and are, in turn, seen as source of crime, social problems. *Los Angeles Times,* Aug. 23, p. A1.

Wallace, A. 1965. Revitalization movements. In *Reader in comparative religion,* eds. William A. Lessa and Evon Z. Vogt, 503–512. New York: Harper and Row.

Weinryb, B. D. 1972. *The Jews of Poland.* Philadelphia: The Jewish Publication Society of America.

Weiss, J. G. 1951. The dawn of Hassidism (Heb.). *Zion* 16:46–105.

Wertheim, A. 1992. *Law and custom in Hasidism,* trans. Shmuel Himelstein. Hoboken, New Jersey: Ktav Publishing House.

Wiesel, E. 1972. *Souls on fire.* New York: Random House.

Winerip, M. 1994. yeshivahs carry political punch far bigger than their sizes. *New York Times,* Feb. 4, p. A10.

Woodward, K., and H. Brown. 1991. Doth my redeemer live? *Newsweek,* April 27, p. 53.

Zborowski, M., and E. Herzog. 1952. *Life is with people: The culture of the shtetl.* New York: Schocken Books.

Zenner, W. P., and J. S. Belcove-Shalin. 1988. The cultural anthropology of American Jewry. In *Persistence and flexibility: Anthropological perspective on the American Jewish experience,* ed. Walter P. Zenner, 3–38. Albany: SUNY Press.

CHAPTER 1

Boundaries and Self-Presentation among the Hasidim: A Study in Identity Maintenance

William Shaffir

Just before I began my graduate studies in sociology at McGill University in September 1968, a conversation with a faculty member persuaded me that a study of the Hasidic community would make an interesting master's thesis. Although I had been raised as a Jew in Montreal—indeed, Yiddish was my mother tongue—I knew little about the Hasidim, and the thought of studying them had never crossed my mind. Nonetheless, I decided I would try. As a newly minted Bachelor of Arts who had taken no courses in sociological theory and methods, my ideas about such a study's theoretical guidelines and research methods were rudimentary. The professor with whom I had spoken had suggested it would be important to learn about how the Hasidic community was organized and how its members resisted assimilation, but he mentioned no theoretical perspective that could serve as an organizing framework. Data collection, I hoped, could come, at least initially, from hanging around places where the Hasidim gathered, and by meeting them.

As I began the McGill graduate program and became familiar with the faculty, I realized that I had chosen well. A number of my teachers had studied at the University of Chicago in the late 1940s and were sympathetic to the use of field research methods. As well, several of the junior faculty emphasized the credibility of ethnographic-based research. The work of the figures of the symbolic interactionist tradition—G. H. Mead, C. H. Cooley, and W. I. Thomas, along with that of Herbert Blumer, Tamotsu Shibutani, Erving Goffman, Anselm Strauss, and Howard Becker—became increasingly familiar through course-related readings and conversations with members of the faculty. Nevertheless, my adviser, Malcolm Spector, who taught the graduate seminar on field research methods and was undoubtedly the primary shaper of my development as a sociologist, did not insist or even strongly encourage that I adopt any particular sociological perspective or theory in my work. In retrospect, the questions I began to ask the Hasidim about their way of life were as much influenced by my experiences in the field as from reading some of the classic community studies.[1]

Several years and many vicissitudes later, I completed my thesis, which was eventually published (Shaffir 1974), and intermittently I have continued my professional interest in the Hasidim. The purpose of this chapter is both to share some of my findings and to consider how symbolic interaction has proved useful in my study.

My research on the Hasidic communities of Montreal has been shaped by the symbolic interactionist perspective, which, with its emphasis on interpretive social processes, has also provided some theoretical foundations for ethnographic inquiry. I wish to briefly consider some central tenets of the variation of symbolic interactionism that I have found most useful for my work, its methodological implications, and the credibility of this perspective for researching social life in general and Hasidic communities in particular.

Of several variants of the symbolic interactionist tradition, my work has drawn most heavily on Blumer's formulation of the interpretive tradition which he, so aptly, termed symbolic interaction (see Blumer 1966, 1969). Attributing his theoretical notions largely to George H. Mead, Blumer developed the theoretical and methodological significance of Mead's ideas for the social sciences. Symbolic interaction, according to Blumer, rests on three simple premises: (1) that human beings act toward things on the basis of the meanings they have for them; (2) that the meaning of such things is derived from or arises out of the social interaction that a person has with his or her fellows; and (3) that these meanings are handled in and modified through an interpretative process used by the person in dealing with the things he or she encounters (1969:2).

For Blumer, as for Mead, the essence of society and of group life is the study of the ongoing process of action. Social behavior, through which the society is constituted, is possible only because people, in the course of social interaction, develop selves and are able to make meaningful indications to themselves and others. It is in this respect that the term "symbolic interaction" is appropriate for designating the process of human interchange:

> Symbolic interaction involves *interpretation*, or ascertaining the meaning of the action or remarks of the other person, and *definition*, or conveying indications to another person as to how he is to act. Human association consists of the process of such interpretation and definition. Through this process the participants fit their own acts to the ongoing acts of one another and guide others in doing so. (Blumer 1966:537–38; emphasis in original)

This interactionist approach to the study of human behavior has two important implications for ethnographic research. First, any methodology used to study human group life generates some unique problems for researchers, for it involves the study of acting units—individuals and collectivities that interpret and interact. Second, researchers must achieve intimate familiarity with their subject matter. It was precisely with regard to conducting research that ethnographic inquiry was envisioned as the only way that one could achieve intimate familiarity with human group life as it is actually accomplished:

> No one can catch the process merely by inferring its nature from the overt action which is its product. To catch the process, the student must take the role of the acting unit whose behavior he is studying. . . . To try to catch the interpretive process by remaining aloof as a so-called "objective" observer . . . is to risk the worst kind of subjectivism—the objective observer is likely to fill in the process of interpretation with his own surmises in place of catching the process as it occurs in the experience of the acting unit which uses it. (Blumer 1969:86)

Although one can imagine methodological approaches other than field research being employed to study the Hasidim, it is doubtful whether they would yield a comparable measure of intimate familiarity with the organization of their distinctive lifestyle. In particular, any analysis of social change within the Hasidic community should not be attributed to societal factors such as "cultural prescriptions," "social roles," or "structural pressures." Rather, it is best understood within the context of the interpretive process in which lines of action are organized by the participants' ongoing interpretation of each other's activity and by their assessment of situations and events in the larger society.

The chapter is organized as follows: The rest of this introduction provides some background on the Hasidim of Montreal and on the city and province in which they live. The following section describes some of what I saw among the Hasidim during my earliest research; the anecdotes it relates point to the importance of the Hasidim's attempts to distinguish themselves from and insulate themselves against the surrounding culture. The next section explains the concept of boundary-maintaining mechanisms and details three used by the Hasidim, and is followed by a conclusion.

BACKGROUND

Although all Hasidim seem the same to uninitiated outsiders, they do not constitute a uniform group but are divided into a number of distinct sects. All are committed to the observance of Orthodox Jewish law, but the sects differ in details of attitudes, customs, and beliefs, as well as commitment to the teaching of their rebbe or charismatic religious leader (Gutwirth 1978). It is, therefore, only in a loose sense that the Hasidim constitute one community.

Montreal is, similarly, many communities, and relations among its groups can be tense. A basic distinction is linguistic. The majority of residents are French-speaking, but there is also a large English-speaking population, and much of the history of the province reflects the two groups' struggle for ascendancy.

What is less well known outside Quebec is that Montreal also contains many immigrant groups whose roots are neither anglophone nor francophone. One of them is the Jewish community, which is very large and institutionally complete. The result of a wave of immigration from Central Europe in the first quarter of the twentieth century, it has generally allied itself with anglophone Montreal (indeed, all Quebec school boards being confessional, Jewish children in public school fall under the Protestant School Board of Greater Montreal), but integration is by no means complete.

The Hasidim of Montreal

Today about 4,000 Hasidim live in Montreal, the only Canadian city with such a large Hasidic population. Although a few Hasidim lived there before World War II, the substantial influx began in the late 1940s and early 1950s. Immigrants were attracted to the city because of its proximity to New York—the center of Hasidic life in North America—because of the economic opportunities of Quebec, and eventually because of the established infrastructure of Hasidic institutions.

The city includes followers of ten Hasidic sects. The largest are Lubavitch, with about 225 families; Satmar and Belz, each with memberships of some 150 families; and Tash, which includes about 120 families. The three most recently arrived sects—Munkatch, Pupa, and Square—number approximately 30, 20, and 50 families respectively. The Bobover and Klausenburger Hasidim have remained relatively small, numbering approximately 20 and 15 families respectively, while the Vishnitzer, with some 20 families in the early 1970s, have tripled in size.

Despite their growing numbers, the Hasidim have not substantially altered their residential concentration within the city since their arrival. Except for members of Tash, who have relocated to the small municipality of Boisbriand to establish a colony, the majority reside in the area that held most of the Montreal Jewish community until the mid-1950s. That larger community then began to move outward to more westerly and suburban parts of the city. In the early 1960s, many Lubavitchers followed, settling in the Snowdon district.

DISCOVERING THE RESEARCH PROBLEM

Very early during my research, in November 1968, my friend and I stood outside the Satmar yeshivah talking in Yiddish[2] with some young boys who were curious about us.[3] Since we were in the Hasidic neighborhood, we wore yarmulkes (skull caps), which the boys noticed. One of them asked: "What's your name? Where do you live?" Suddenly, another, directing his gaze at my friend, yelled: "*Goy, goy, di bist a goy*" (Gentile, gentile, you're a gentile). A Satmar rabbi was drawn by the commotion. My friend explained in Yiddish that one of the boys had called him a goy.

Carefully examining my friend and then glancing at the boy, the rabbi stroked his beard and replied, "*A goy bisti nit, ober a yid bisti oikhet nit*" (A gentile you are not, but a Jew you are also not).

It was indeed the opinion of many members of the Hasidic sects that the Jewishness of secular Jews such as myself and my friend was suspect. This attitude was particularly clear when I applied to teach secular studies for the Tasher Hasidim. Late in 1968, after a brief visit to Tash during Hanukkah (the Festival of Lights), I concluded that my analysis of Hasidic life in Montreal would be incomplete if I omitted the Tasher. But how to gain entrance to the community? I believed that I had found a solution when I learned their school was looking for a part-time instructor for secular studies. The role of teacher, I surmised, would provide a range of opportunities for acquiring data about many aspects of the community. My hopes were raised when I drove to the interview with the two other candidates. Assessing their educational backgrounds, I realized that I seemed to be the best-qualified applicant. Following the interview, however, I was promptly rejected. Assuring me that I would be bored teaching students whose interest in secular studies was minimal, a Tasher rabbi explained:

> We believe that certain forms of dress are not in keeping with the teachings of the Torah. You don't have to have a beard and earlocks, but your long hair isn't suitable.

I quickly concluded that these statements were simply excuses, and I was not surprised to hear that the position was awarded to a young Orthodox Jew whose secular studies had formally ended with the completion of Grade 9. In fact, I subsequently learned that secular subjects are often taught by Gentiles, since the Hasidim generally prefer to employ non-Jews rather than nonobservant Jews, whom they consider likely to set a poor example for the pupils.

I had already encountered this apprehension of outsiders. Several months earlier, a summer job had put me near the Hasidic summer colony in the Laurentian mountains north of Montreal which mainly included families from Satmar but also from Klausenburg. On my first visit, my welcome was anything but warm. Replies to what seemed routine questions—for example, the time for prayer services—were curt and sharp. As I waited for services to begin, I could see and feel glances in my direction, but no one extended a greeting or offered to engage me in conversation. The indifference to my presence was feigned, however. In fact, I was closely observed,[4] by the younger boys, who, it appeared to me, deliberately positioned themselves close to where I stood so as to observe whether I donned my *tefillin* (phylacteries) correctly and recited the appropriate prayers. I felt anxious and entirely out of place. Extremely conscious of my outsider status, I could do little but endure the stares. In large measure, my anxiety also stemmed from my unfamiliarity with the sequencing of prayers or the correct way to put on tefillin. I quickly calculated the advantages of appearing competent even when uncertain. Despite such attention, it seemed to take the longest time for anyone to greet me in even the most perfunctory manner. When I finally was approached, the individual matter-of-factly inquired, "You're here to say *kaddish?*" (the traditional mourner's prayer)[5] I realized instantly that this conclusion was logical—he could not imagine any other reason for my presence in the Satmar yeshivah.

Over that summer, I continued my visits to the summer colony and I became somewhat friendly with some of the *bochurim* (older students) of the Klausenburg sect. Perhaps because we were close in age, they were interested in my background, and after prayers, several of them would almost insist on walking with me in the direction I was heading. I was struck by their curiosity about my lifestyle: What do I do at university? What kind of Jewish school did I attend if its curriculum did not focus around Orthodox Judaism? Although our conversations never exceeded fifteen or twenty minutes, these bochurim impressed me with their stereotyped impressions of Jews in the larger community, and for the first time I was introduced to their fears of secular influences. They did not watch television, they said, because they might see things that would be improper for an observant Jew. Reading English-language newspapers was forbidden to them because they might come across a story that might influence them negatively. They never went shopping in downtown Montreal; window shopping not only constituted a waste of precious time but, worse still, might expose them to sights improper for an Orthodox Jew to observe, such as women dressed immodestly.

One morning, the bochurim invited me to return in the afternoon. "Come at around two o'clock, and we can play some Ping-Pong," my acquaintance said. I happily obliged, and several students watched as he and I played. Suddenly one of the other bochurim ran toward us shouting, *"Dein tatte is doo"* (Your father is here). Almost before we had an opportunity to react, the father grabbed his son by the neck and began slapping him. *"Far daym is doo tzeit?"* (For this [activity] you have time?) he yelled. The group quickly dispersed, and I was left standing alone. I never saw this acquaintance again, and I was told he returned to Montreal for the remainder of the summer. I couldn't help but wonder whether his transgression consisted of wasting time by playing Ping-Pong or of spending time with an outsider.

Eventually I obtained a part-time position as a secretary with Tash. As I became familiar with these people, I was impressed by the degree to which they were removed from the mainstream, both physically and culturally. With time, I came to appreciate their deep regret about such matters as Jewish-Gentile intermarriage and the religious practices of Reform Jews. I was astounded, however, that most of them lacked basic information about events in the larger society, such as political happenings in the province of Quebec, cultural and national celebrations in Canada, and major news stories on the world scene. For the overwhelming majority of the students, even those born in Montreal, the city was foreign territory, and they were unfamiliar with its major landmarks. I suppose that I shouldn't have been too surprised at this state of affairs had I taken at face value one of the rabbi's remarks to me following our introduction:

> There are many things that you take for granted that the majority of people here [in Tash] have probably never heard about. Ask people about the space program and they'll look at you funny. Ask if they know what "grass" [marijuana] is, and they'll say, "It's what grows outside."

The community's bylaws banned English- and French-language newspapers, while those in Yiddish or Hebrew were frowned on; radio and television sets were forbidden. Yet the older students often appeared eager to learn about events in the wider society from which they were cut off. They would ask me about the latest news from Israel and the Middle East, as well as the use of drugs at the university. At such times, the rabbis, observing our encounters, would encourage the bochurim to move on, explaining that such conversations interrupted some of my important office duties; I, in turn, would be reminded that the students, committed to studying and prayer, were not expected to engage in idle conversation. Although my clerical skills were appreciated, my influence on the young people was suspect.

By contrast, the Lubavitcher Hasidim were welcoming. Before my first visit to their yeshivah, in September 1968, I had thought I might be informed that an outsider who had come to conduct research was undesirable. In fact, the Lubavitcher did not seem to find my visit peculiar. Nonobservant Jews frequently visited their yeshivah. I was to discover that the large banner in English over the yeshivah's entrance, "Join millions of Jews the world over who have begun to put on tefillin," reflected this sect's proselytizing efforts. The Lubavitchers' zeal in befriending all Jews made it relatively easy to engage them in conversation. The bochurim seemed especially delighted by my visits and were eager to tell me about their spiritual leader, the Lubavitcher Rebbe—about his role as a leader of world Jewry and particularly about the successful tefillin campaign he had initiated in 1967.[6] In short, although I discovered later that several individual members of the sect were deeply suspicious about my research, the Lubavitcher welcomed me warmly and always encouraged me to return.

Within the first week of my visit, I arranged to meet twice weekly with an older *bays medresh* (study hall) student to learn Hasidic philosophy, but we soon abandoned the topic in favor of reading and reviewing the Rebbe's discourses, which interested me more. I was especially pleased when this student accepted my suggestion that we set aside some time during each session for me to ask questions pertaining to my research. These meetings were very informal, and several other students often joined our sessions.

The Lubavitcher Hasidim proved familiar with worldly events. Indeed, it almost seemed that they deliberately set out to be intelligently informed. Whether the topic was Middle East politics, the benefits of a secular education, or the assimilation of North American Jewry, they voiced opinions which, I soon discovered, usually mirrored the views of their rebbe. Nonetheless, they knew about political and social events occurring around them. As well, the bochurim were familiar with the city and exchanged accounts of their forays on "tefillin routes." In contrast to the Tasher and Satmarer, who had never even heard of McGill University, Lubavitchers were familiar with the institution; several of the older students who offered to visit my class even knew the precise location of the building where I taught.

These anecdotes give the flavor of the field research adventure. They also share an underlying theme. Each points to individual and/or collective efforts to address a central organizing feature of any religious-based community: the cultivation of a distinctive identity, one whose preservation is ensured and secured through boundary-maintaining mechanisms separating insiders from outsiders.

BOUNDARIES AND THE PRESERVATION OF A DISTINCTIVE IDENTITY

Despite ideological and social differences among Montreal's various Hasidic groups, all attach great importance to preventing assimilation by insulating their members from the secular influences of the host culture—a theme commonly addressed in ethnographic studies of Hasidic sects (Gutwirth 1970; Mintz 1968; Poll 1962; Rubin 1974; Shaffir 1974).

An essential question is how the various sects are organized to ensure that their boundaries remain secure. As Kanter (1972) observes, boundaries not only define a group, setting it off from its environment but, in giving it a sharp focus, also facilitate commitment. In an early reference to boundary maintenance, Loomis and Beagle link the activity to identity retention.[7] Boundary maintenance, they assert, "is the process whereby the system retains its identity and interaction pattern; that is, retains its equilibrium involving both integration and solidity" (1957:18).

Frederik Barth's formulation of the concept of "ethnic group boundaries" has proved especially useful to me, as it has to many social scientists. "If a group maintains its identity when its members interact with others," he writes, "this entails criteria for determining membership and ways of signalling membership and exclusion" (1969:51). There may be social contact between persons of different cultures, such as Hasidim and outsiders; however, as long as all members of the group consider themselves to be members and frequently interact with other group members on a primary level, while keeping the rest of society at arm's length, the ethnic boundary is maintained.[8]

Barth's concept was innovative because it suggests that it may actually be boundaries, rather than the structures enclosed by them, that both primarily define ethnic groups and account for much of the dynamics of ethnic persistence (1969:9, 15, 32–33).

According to Barth (1969:38), a group boundary represents a criterion of membership that marks off a continuing unit. His discussion identifies two interacting sets of influences affecting boundaries: one facilitating integration of the group, and another differentiating the group from other groups. Ethnic boundaries persist despite the flow of personnel across them partly because they may be based on identities and ascribed characteristics that are often independent of contemporary or transient social situations and that are not characteristics individuals can readily discard.[9]

Applying Barth's formulation to a Hasidic community suggests that its viability as an identifiable entity is shaped by the presence of marked differences of behavior—cultural and social structural differences—distinguishing members from outsiders. Thus, the persistence of boundaries requires not only criteria and signals for identification but also a structuring of interaction that allows for the perpetuation of cultural differences. The strategy most commonly used by the Hasidim both to cultivate and to maintain a distinctive identity is insulating themselves from outsiders. Their exotic customs are a protective fence around the community. As Mintz observes:

> By distinguishing themselves from the gentiles and nonreligious Jews, the hasidim believe that they can best preserve their identity, keep their children from becoming acculturated, and prevent possible infractions of the religious law. . . . This need to maintain their insularity is a recurrent theme in hasidic tradition (1968:138)

In the rest of this section, I consider three components of the Hasidim's boundary maintenance: institutional control, specifically with regard to the organization of secular education; proselytization in the case of the Lubavitcher; and the negotiation of public controversies.[10] The three do not apply equally to each of the sects. The organization of institutions to channel and control members' activities is common to all, but the form of both the institutions and the channeling differs. Proselytizing, or the coordination of outreach activity within the larger Jewish community, is the hallmark of the Lubavitcher Hasidim; followers of the other Hasidic sects do not absolutely refrain from such activity, but it is initiated and conducted by individuals and not organized at the community level. Finally, the negotiation of public controversies does not necessarily involve all of the Hasidic sects; indeed, it usually pertains only to those involved in a particular incident or those singled out by the media for special attention. What typically occurs during such controversies, however, is that all of the Hasidim become tarred by the same brush, and in this sense, such controversies become the concern of all of the sects.

The Coordination of the Secular Curriculum

A feature common to all the Hasidic sects is their organization of various institutions so as to minimize the potentially harmful impact of the surrounding cultural influences. Chief among these organizations are the schools, which emphasize religious studies but, almost grudgingly, also include a secular curriculum. As a Tasher pamphlet (printed in English) says:

> The Tasher community is living proof that one need not have advanced degrees in secular studies in order to succeed. Although the yeshivah and girls' school do teach French, English, and mathematics and other secular subjects, the Rebbe does not place too much emphasis on these.

The way in which the Hasidic boys' schools[11] coordinate their secular offerings is a form of boundary maintenance. The secular principal of an Hasidic school attempted to explain the philosophy to me:

> One day, in a discussion with the Chief Rabbi, I told him, "Three hundred years and you haven't changed. You still wear the same clothes and everything. It boggles my mind. . . . " He told me, "Listen, if you have a nice piece of furniture that has been there three hundred years, you're not just going to sand it and make it into any old piece that you can buy in the store. . . . " See, you get his idea here. These are things we cherish, not suffer through. You have to be proud of your parents and grandparents and what they left you. You have to nourish it and keep it alive. So I understand this philosophy, build on it and try to teach these kids as much as possible without breaking down any of their values.

The Hasidim maintain that secular education threatens their traditional values. In order to shield their children against its potentially harmful influences, several of Montreal's Hasidic sects—Lubavitch, Satmar, Belz, Tash, and Square—run their own schools in which secular classes are closely supervised to ensure that the pupils will not see any conflict with the contents of their religious studies.[12] In each case, separate schools are maintained for boys and girls in accordance with the principle of separating the sexes.

Of the Hasidic schools, those of Lubavitch, Square, Satmar, and Belz are subsidized by the Quebec provincial government and meet its minimal standards.[13] The Satmarer and Tasher schools, however, have long refused any government subsidies; as a Satmar school official explained:

> Were it [the school] subsidized, then there'd be a minimum of three hours per day of secular studies. . . . They don't want to be obliged to be exposed to things they don't want their children exposed to.

The program, particularly for the boys, who end their secular studies at the Grade 6 level, is oriented around practicality. A school principal explained:

> All they want is to know how to read, how to write, mathematics, a bit of geography, a bit of French to communicate. . . . They want the basic language to communicate, to get along in society. . . . And they need it for business because most of them become businessmen.

The schools must look to the outside to staff their secular departments (their own graduates lack the qualifications to provide such instruction). Although school officials claim to be primarily interested in applicants' educational qualifications, less formal criteria may be important to the hiring decision. When the ideal secular teacher—a practicing Orthodox Jew with a teacher's certificate—is difficult to find, Gentiles may be hired in preference to nonreligious Jews, since some Hasidic authorities believe that the former is less likely to sway students, intentionally or otherwise, from their religious beliefs.[14]

To help ensure that students' religious beliefs are not challenged by secular materials, teachers are specifically instructed about the constraints within which they must conduct their work. Typically, they receive verbal instructions from the principal concerning proscribed topics. As one administrator remarked:

Teachers are told that we don't expect them to talk about boys and girls. Girls have their activities and boys have activities, but not together. You wouldn't talk about sex or anything that has to do with reproduction. Or boyfriends, girlfriends, birthdays. Then there's the great theories—evolution and the creation of the world millions of years ago. We don't get into these conflicts. A secular teacher does not talk about religion. It's out of his field. That's the way we lessen the friction.

A teacher in a secular program recalled:

He [the principal] told me a few things that I shouldn't be discussing with the kids. [Such as?] Things that would be conflicting with their religious beliefs. . . . Don't talk in terms of time, long periods of time, because they just won't believe you . . . because the earth has been in existence for a certain amount of time for them and if you talk in terms of millions of years, it won't make any sense.

Written instructions may be used to make matters more formal. The secular staff in the Tasher school receive the following directive:

1. All textbooks and literature to be used by the students in class or at home for extra-curricular activities, etc. must first be approved by the principal.

2. No stencil or photocopy of any other book may be used without the principal's approval.

3. Students are not permitted to go to the library nor is the teacher permitted to bring into the school, for the students, such books.

4. No newspaper or magazine may be read in school or hung up. Students are not permitted to read the above at home either.

5. No record or tape may be used in the classroom without the approval of the principal.

6. No extra subjects, books, magazine supplement or other information which is not on the required curriculum of the school may be taught.

7. For extra credit work or for class projects, etc., students should not be told to write away for such material. The

teacher should supply them with the material with the principal's approval.

8. No discussions on boyfriends.

9. No discussions on reproduction.

10. No discussions about radio, TV or movies.

11. No discussions about personal life.

12. No discussions on religion.

13. No discussions on women's lib.

Secular teachers in the Satmarer school are informed in writing:

1. Every book, workbook, reading book, which is used in the classroom by the teacher or the students has to be checked and approved by the religious committee appointed by the school; the teacher is not allowed to bring or advise the students to use any book which is not given by the school.

2. No stencil or photocopy of any book except school books which are stamped approved are allowed.

3. Sending students to libraries or reading to students from library books is strictly forbidden.

4. No reading of newspapers is allowed in class. The teacher should not encourage the students to read newspapers; only publications approved by the school are permitted in the classroom.

5. No tapes or recors [sic] are allowed in the classroom.

6. All books are strictly edited from harmful influences according to our religion. If you notice anything which might have been overlooked, please notify us promptly.

7. No subjects, books, magazines supplements, information which have not been given to you by the school are to be taught or brought to school.

8. When setting up school projects, all ordering of materials is to be done by our office staff.

9. Avoid discussing any subject involving Zionism or the State of Israel.

10. Do not speak Hebrew.

11. Do not talk about boyfriend-girlfriend-parties and so on.

12. Do not discuss adult subjects which are not for children.

13. Do not discuss radio, television, movies, theatres, which you might have heard or seen on these with the students.

14. Do not discuss your private life with the students.

15. Do not discuss any religious subject, including the Jewish faith.

16. No homework should be given before a Jewish holiday.

17. Any discussion or story regarding boy-girl relationship, romance, sexual problems; sexual organs; etc . . . is strictly forbidden.

18. Please behave in school in a way befitting for a religious school such as dressing and talking in a modest way.

19. Certain subjects should never be discussed when in the classroom: the theory of evolution; the creation of the world; . . .

These instructions demonstrate the stringent measures taken to ensure that children are not exposed to ways deviating from a strict Hasidic lifestyle. Complementing these limits are censorship applied both to the selection of books for classroom use and to the specific material that such books may include.

Textbooks go through a detailed screening. To paraphrase one of the school administrators, stories told the children must not include "ultramodern" views. As an example of what he considered harmful, he offered a tale about a Jewish boy who was a pupil in a non-Jewish school and was accepted for the baseball team. One Saturday, the group came to pick him up to play, but his father refused to let him go. The administrator commented:

> Now that's a game that we think a boy shouldn't have on his mind, that he could go and play baseball on Shabbess [the Sabbath] afternoon. . . . I'm not saying that that's the worst example of a story that might be passed [over]. But there are stories that have sex in them, and things like that which are totally out.

The process of book selection is typically initiated by the principal, who is charged with the responsibility of reviewing the appropriate material for a particular grade. For those schools accredited by the ministry of education, such a review includes examination of the multitude of books and material it recommends. If the program does not conform to the ministry's guidelines, the principal can look at any materials in making his selection. In either case, however, the principal simply recommends; the final decision rests with the sect's religious authorities. The process was described by one of the principals as follows:

> I don't order the books. I make recommendations. I say, for example, for the first grade I'd like this and this book. So I receive complimentary copies of the books from the publisher. . . . Now the books that are selected are evaluated by the rabbis. There's someone in the community specifically charged with this task, and he might conclude that a particular book is inappropriate because of the material. So the rabbis might say: "Page 84, you can't use the material on that page." Now if there are too many deletions, then I just don't order the book. And I take the texts they have selected and try to adapt them. So we don't use books per se. We make photostats. We create our own texts and we distribute the material to the students. Students receive the text that we have assembled.

Only the Lubavitcher and Belzer schools distribute actual textbooks to the students. The other schools provide photocopied materials, allowing the authorities to exercise even greater scrutiny over what their students see.

The techniques for censoring materials range from actually removing pages to substituting more appropriate words, phrases or sentences in a text. A principal offers an example of the latter:

> A teacher finds a story and I read it. I say: "Okay, remove this word." We try not to lose the idea, the context, but we change certain words. [Can you think of an example of a word that you'd change?] Television. "At night he went to the living room and watched television." You'd change that to "At night he went to the living room and read a book." So we take white ink, cover it and write on top of it.

Another technique is to excise with black marker any written or pictorial content deemed offensive. A principal comments: Sometimes they've [the rabbis] gone over parts of it [a story] in black with a marker. . . . Usually it happens in the geography book when they talk about fossils that are a million years old because it would come into contradiction with everything they're learning. . . . [Do you also censor pictures in books?] . . . You can't see a woman with her arms bare, you can't see a woman wearing pants. So usually you try to find drawings rather than real life pictures. But in a subject such as geography you have pictures of people, streets. . . . So usually with a marker you go over things you don't want them to see.

To some extent, censorship varies according to the predilections of the individual. For instance, one person was charged with screening blacked out photographs that showed women and even young girls dressed immodestly. By contrast, another Hasidic administrator considered it unnecessary to ink out a picture of a little girl not wearing socks, especially when it was clear from the context that the child was a Gentile. As he explained:

> Our kids are aware that the goyim [Gentiles] do not dress the way we dress. . . . I mean, if you're reading a story about goyim, then you know that goyim don't wear socks. As long as it's not a mini skirt or anything like that, it's O.K. It's no use blacking everything out.

Yet another technique—the one typically adopted by the Lubavitcher—is to refrain from excising but to simply substitute something suitable for the objectionable material. A former Lubavitcher principal illustrates this point:

> Let's say . . . the reader series [published by] Gage, they are oriented to . . . the Protestant School Board way of thinking.[15] So, therefore, sometimes, when they plan a book to be finished in Grade 1 or in Grade 2, right in the middle of the book . . . there'll be a story about Christmas and about Pere Noel. We just replace it by something else. [Do you replace the pages?] No, I don't replace the pages. I just tell the teacher: "Don't get into these stories, leave this story, take the other one." [So the children can still read it?] You cannot close the child. Anyway the child goes out in the street and he sees this Pere Noel. On the other hand, in the Hebrew department, the child gets this: this is not for me, this has nothing to do with me.

All the Hasidic schools except that of Lubavitch limit the secular educational experience to the classroom. Only occasionally are students expected to complete assignments at home, the time for which should not exceed fifteen minutes. Extracurricular activities offer too many temptations to secular involvement and are simply discouraged. As one principal explained:

No, we don't even talk about public libraries. We don't encourage students to go to public libraries because then they'd be exposed to all kinds of literature that's not censored. We don't even mention libraries, we don't mention newspapers. . . . You have to be careful about what you bring in. Newspapers are out, publications are out. No audio-visual equipment. We work like in a jungle—a few books here and there. We have a blackboard.

In the end, however, the Hasidim are aware of the impossibility of shielding their students completely. Teachers and parents alike view such potentially disruptive secular influences as the inevitable accompaniments of secular education, and both hope and expect that the school's religious studies program will offset them.[16] As an intentionally organized mechanism of social control, the coordination of secular studies helps the Hasidim to maintain the boundaries separating them from the surrounding culture.

The Proselytizing of Lubavitch

To any observer of the Hasidic scene, Lubavitcher are set apart and set themselves apart from the other Hasidic sects by their outreach to other Jews, encouraging Jewish observance. A self-proclaimed landmark of this sect, this proselytizing work is organized at the local level, as well as at world Lubavitch headquarters in Crown Heights, Brooklyn, and it has increased dramatically over the past few decades.

During the late 1960s, Lubavitch was mainly identified with a Tefillin Campaign initiated by its rebbe. Shortly before the outbreak of the Six Day War in the Middle East in 1967, the Rebbe urged his followers throughout the world to ensure that as many Jews as possible observed this precept. Doing so, claimed the Rebbe, would inevitably aid the Jews in Israel, especially those in the army, in their war with the enemy. In Montreal, pamphlets and newspaper advertisements in the English and Yiddish press extended invitations to perform this commandment at the Lubavitcher yeshivah or at other synagogues. To reach as many Jews as possible, the Lubavitcher also carefully coordinated a witnessing drive. They approached Jews at cultural gatherings, established tefillin booths at locations, such as shopping malls and plazas, known to attract a mainly Jewish clientele, and drove trucks (aptly called "tefillin mobiles" or "tefillin tanks.") decorated with slogans urging Jews to don tefillin.

The community's growth in size has resulted in a proliferation of other outreach activities and the creation of new institutions to facilitate such "witnessing." Those organized in Montreal include seven *Chabad* houses[17] (drop-in centers for Jewish youth and adults located in various parts of Montreal); eight telephone numbers for "Torah-On-The-Line," in which a caller receives a message about a particular Torah portion; educational classes on specific facets of Orthodox Judaism organized for men and women of various age groups; an encounter weekend geared to college and university students; an institute to inform soon-to-be-marrieds about the Jewish laws regulating marriage and the family; two summer camps and two day schools (one of each for boys and for girls); and a public celebration of Hanukkah with a motorcade and the lighting of huge candelabras strategically located throughout the city.

Although the practice of proselytizing is not officially delegated to a specific age group, many of the organized activities involve the participation of the bochurim. For example, these fifteen- to nineteen-year-olds were mainly responsible for visiting college campuses to contact Jewish youth for the Tefillin Campaign. They also regularly devote periods of time to making the acquaintance of and even befriending Jews whose observance of Jewish law is minimal.

These outreach activities are puzzling at first thought. The other Hasidic sects discourage outsiders from mingling in their institutions. The young in particular are protected from interaction with outsiders that could easily expose them to situations inimical to Orthodox Judaism (consider, for example, the way the Satmarer leaders have institutionalized separation of the bochurim from unobservant Jews and indeed all outsiders).

Avoidance of institutionalized proselytizing or witnessing is much used in boundary maintenance. It is commonly believed that witnessing, especially among those who challenge a group member's set of beliefs, is a threat to the group's identity. Confronted by skeptics, the disinterested, and nonbelievers, individuals may come to question and eventually doubt the set of principles around which they have organized identity. It is for this very reason that many groups trying to maintain a distinctive identity intentionally segregate themselves from the larger society.

Nevertheless, a less obvious effect of witnessing—one that seems to explain its use by the Lubavitcher—is that it strengthens the distinctive identity at both the individual and community levels (Shaffir 1978). As Mol observes, "Every act of witnessing anchors the belief system deeply in the motions of the believer, since faith has to be proclaimed against the non-believer. The boundaries around the belief system are thus firmly drawn" (1976:238).

Thus it can be argued that Lubavitchers' contacts with nonreligious Jews serve, in fact, to reinforce the sect's distinctive identity and fortify members' self-identification. Although an analysis of the manifest consequences may show the proselytizing itself to be largely ineffective—few newcomers are actually added to the group, and the number of Jews appreciably influenced by the Lubavitcher is small—its latent consequences contribute to the group's persistence.

Festinger et al., in their study of a religious cult, the Seekers, suggest that if others either question or do not believe the group's central beliefs, proselytizing is an effective means of reaffirming the member's identity with that group. As the writers state, "If more and more people can be persuaded that the system of belief is correct, then it clearly must, after all, be correct" (1956:28). An important point here is what the group members *think* they are achieving. Although the Lubavitcher might privately concede that an overwhelming proportion of Jews neither practice Orthodox Judaism nor share their convictions about their rebbe, whom they regard as the central figure in Jewish life today, they would nonetheless claim that they are making extraordinarily swift progress in these directions.[18] Stories abound of prominent and ordinary men and women who have, for the first time, donned phylacteries, lit Sabbath candles, or made their homes kosher in accordance with Jewish dietary laws. For the Lubavitcher, these activities symbolize an important beginning to what, they hope, will result in an ever-increasing identification with and commitment to Orthodox Judaism. Inroads and successes created by their proselytizing are always current topics of conversation and are featured in local and national Lubavitcher publications. So are the names of politicians and entertainment personalities who seek to meet and be photographed with their rebbe and who publicly endorse the Lubavitcher's spiritual contribution to the quality of Jewish life. Coca Cola and Lubavitch, claim these Hasidim, are two commodities that can be found everywhere in the world—a testimony to the success and zeal of their proselytizing work.

An important motivating force for Lubavitch's missionary zeal is its teaching that no Jew is ever lost to God. Within every Jew, so the teaching goes, there is a point of authentic Jewish faith, *dos pintelle Yeed*. Weiner, recounting a conversation with one of Lubavitch's chief administrative officials, observes, "One has to remember that 'the soul itself was so much deeper than what appeared to the eye,' and hence surface appearances ought never to discourage one from attempting to tap a man's inner capacity for faith in and love for Judaism" (1969:145). When Weiner asked this official the number of Lubavitcher followers in the world, the rabbi replied, "How many Jews are there in the world?"

The Thomas dictum, "If men define situations as real, they are real in their consequences" (1928:572), can be modified to state that if a community collectively defines a situation to be real, its members will organize their behavior accordingly. Defining all Jews as readily susceptible to the tenets of Orthodox Judaism and encouraged by continuous streams of reports of Jews' intensified determination to practicing halakhic principles, the Lubavitcher become increasingly committed to participating in the multitude of witnessing activities coordinated by their community. At this point, any objective evidence indicating that relatively few Jews are influenced by the Lubavitcher outreach work hardly affects these Hasidims' definition of the situation. Although their definition of the situation may be false, several mechanisms are set into motion leading to behavior that makes the prediction come true; in short, their behavior is characterized by a self-fulfilling prophecy.

We can now understand better how witnessing consolidates the Lubavitcher's identity. The act of witnessing in the larger Jewish community reinforces the members' beliefs and enables the community to retain its specific boundaries. When individual Lubavitchers attempt to influence and convince a nonobservant Jew of Orthodox Judaism's relevance, they are, in fact, influencing and convincing themselves. This is so because, as Mead (1934) observes, people can act socially toward themselves just as they act toward others and can thus become the object of their own actions. By discussing and arguing with others about their rebbe's accomplishments or the lasting significance of Torah observance, the Lubavitcher must think about the facts and arguments themselves and thereby reinforce their identity.

The involvement of the Lubavitcher bochurim in witnessing is now understandable. These young men are the very members of the group whose beliefs require strengthening. Their commitment to the Lubavitcher way of life is less intense than that of the adults who have raised families and organized their lives around the Hasidic community. Involving these students in witnessing is no doubt an important way of building their belief systems. By teaching and becoming witness to their beliefs and by urging them on others, they learn to think of themselves as Lubavitcher Hasidim.

Proselytizing activities have an additional aspect related to boundary maintenance. Accounts of the relationship between witnessing and maintaining an identity indicate that those engaged in such activity are expected to control the contexts within which the interaction with outsiders unfolds (Glick 1958; Stevenson 1967; Lottes 1972).[19] Such encounters are bounded by the specific expectation that they assume a religious base, making religion an explicit focus of attention. Indeed, the kind of contact situations that may threaten both the individual and the group are those in which the distinctive differences separating group members from outsiders are *not* the focus of concern—that is, where the context does not impose the differences as the reasons for contact. Thus, although a Lubavitcher may enter a conversation that is initially about a sporting event or any general issue pertaining to everyday life, the objective is to eventually relate the topic to Judaism, specifically focusing on the issue of religious observance.

We see then that Lubavitchers' proselytizing activity can be related to identity and boundary maintenance. At the same time, it must be recalled that such organized activity is unique to the Lubavitcher sect of the Hasidim.

Negotiating Public Controversies

Boundary maintenance can also be secured through external constraints—intentional or unintentional conflict with outsiders. Two recent situations unexpectedly focused attention on the Hasidim in Montreal and drew an unfavorable response from their immediate neighbors as well as the print media. Although one involved the followers of several sects while the other was unique to Tash, each situation drew the Hasidim together in search of solutions to a common problem.

A Zoning Request—and an Anti-Hasidic Outcry in Outre-mont What became identified as "l'affaire Outremont" suddenly transformed the Hasidim into leading characters of a drama in which they would have preferred no role at all. As events unfolded, their lifestyle, including their customs and religious practices, became the focus of attention in the city's print and television media.

Outremont, one of several separate municipalities enclosed by Montreal, abuts the Old Jewish section of the city, and some of the Hasidim live in or near its boundaries. Increasingly, its residents are upper-middle-class francophones.

The incident began in spring 1988 with a request by the Vish-nitzer Hasidic sect to rezone a vacant lot, from residential to com-mercial-institutional, for purposes of constructing a synagogue in the eastern extremity of the municipality. On June 6, the Outrem-ont City Council, in a vote of 6 to 3, denied the request.

The principal opponents of the zoning change were new fran-cophone residents, mainly professionals. The champion of their cause, Gerard Pelletier, remarked to *The Gazette*, Montreal's English-language daily newspaper, "There's no question of giving a synagogue for every 75 families." The requested change, accord-ing to Pelletier, would only compound the area's parking prob-lems. Immediately, *Le Journal d'Outremont*, a local monthly paper, voiced its criticisms against the Hasidim. According to Bauer:

> In its July 1988 issue, it [*Le Journal d'Outremont*] had no less than three articles referring to the problem, including an appeal for somebody to demand "the closing of an illegal syna-gogue . . . in order to defend the quality of life in Outremont" (p.8), antisemitic letters (p.27) and a cartoon showing the Mayor in discussion with a Hassid about small houses; the shadow of the Hassid is a capitalist, a cigar between his lips and a huge building in his hands. (p.3)

One letter, for instance, described the Hasidim as "disturbing, encroaching, bothersome and, what's more, they don't even look like us. . . . Very soon, Outremont won't belong to us anymore," it continued. "It's the children of these Jews who will buy your houses within a few years. It's those Jews who have money."

On September 13, 1988, the first day of Rosh Hashanah, *La Presse*, an important French-language daily, published a front-page article headlined "Outremont se decouvre un 'probleme juif'" (Outremont discovers its "Jewish problem"), evoking for many Jews the language of Nazi Germany. The article described the Hasidim as a "bizarre minority, with the men in black looking like bogeymen and the women and children dressed like onions." It also referred to Hasidic families' high birth rate, noting that "Outremont is discovering its minority has children . . . and with their families of often ten or more—they really make babies, these people—they'll keep taking up more space." According to the article, Jews already represented 11 percent of the area's population of about 23,000.

La Presse columnist Gerard Leblanc's articles on the subject then added fuel to the tensions. In one column, he blamed the massive integration of Jews into the city's anglophone minority for tensions between francophones and Jews (excluding the French-speaking Sephardic Jews). In another he wrote, "Jews are often found in the higher reaches of anglophone organizations like Alliance Quebec [an English-language-rights-protection association] and certain English media which did everything to make it difficult for francophones to ensure the survival and promotion of French society in North America." He also suggested that Outremont's Hasidim never spoke French when dealing with francophones and concluded that the Hasidim were a problem in the area. He wrote, "I don't like [the way] that these Hasidim . . . park in the middle of the street and refuse to advance, under the pretext that their religion forbids them from seeing me."

On Wednesday, September 21, which was Yom Kippur, *La Presse* ran an editorial apologizing for the article describing a "Jewish problem" in Outremont. Jews who had protested the article were criticized, however, for not understanding the French language and culture; the reference to "dressing like onions" was defended as a colloquialism from a particular region of Quebec. The editorial, signed by Alain Dubuc, concluded that "what some Jews have a tendency to see as manifestations of anti-Semitism are nothing more than a facet of tensions between the francophone majority and groups who chose English as their language." The two-page editorial spread also included a cartoon, titled "Le Probleme Franco-Quebecois," (The French Quebecois Problem) implying that the small minority of Hasidic Jews in Outremont expected the francophone majority to adapt to their ways. In addition, several letters to the editor appeared on the subject of the Outremont article. Most of them defended the Hasidic Jews and criticized *La Presse*'s treatment of them. One letter, however, was a collection of classic antisemitic smears, and it blamed the Jews for their own persecution because of their "self-imposed" isolation: "Is there a single country in the world where the majority of the native population really likes the Jews?" Eventually, Lysiane Gagnon, columnist and prominent journalist for *La Presse*, wrote a devastating attack against the anti-Hasidim campaign. A number of other prominent Quebecers also rose to defend the Hasidim.

Characteristically, when the Hasidim were catapulted into the limelight, unprepared and astonished by the controversy surrounding their presence in the area, they hoped that the troubling situation would quickly vanish from the media. Eventually, following a series of negotiations between the various interested parties, including officials from two Jewish interest groups—the B'nai Brith and the Canadian Jewish Congress—who sought to mediate the controversy, the Hasidim disappeared from the front pages.

Although the incident did not alter the particular lifestyle of the Hasidim, it unquestionably disturbed their much-sought-after isolation. The hostile reaction they encountered drew the area's Hasidic sects closer together. Realizing how swiftly public opinion could be marshalled against them, they tested and even strengthened communal boundaries. "L'affaire Outremont" demonstrated that ideological and religious disputes internal to the Hasidic community are of no interest to outsiders, who stereotypically perceive all Hasidim to be alike. Above all, the episode emphasized the importance of increasing the community's political sophistication and public relations skills to enable it to impress both politicians and neighbors with the requirements of its distinctive lifestyle.

An Application for Municipal Status While "l'affaire Outremont" focused generally on all the Hasidim in and around the area, the Tasher's unique bid for autonomy singled them out from their Hasidic counterparts. In 1951, following the Tasher Rebbe's arrival in Montreal from Hungary, the followers of this group lived in the Fairmount–St. Viateur area of the city along with most of the other Hasidim. But in 1963, to escape what they saw as the deteriorating moral climate of the city and to locate in a secluded setting that would be highly conducive to a lifestyle based on the teachings of the Torah, the Rebbe and a number of his followers moved to Boisbriand, a small municipality about eighteen miles north of Montreal. Eighteen families initially moved to the new settlement; today it includes some 120 households and 70 yeshivah students housed in a dormitory.

In 1979, in what Maclean's magazine headlined "A Strange Bid for Autonomy," the Tasher submitted an application to the government of Quebec for full municipal status, including the power to turn their religious rules into bylaws. At first it seemed that they were unlikely to encounter serious opposition. Indeed, their achievement of separate municipal status would apparently have served the interests of several parties. The Hasidim would have obtained not only religious autonomy but also an industrial tax base and the right to issue municipal bonds. The wider municipality of Boisbriand would have settled a tax dispute.[20] And the provincial government, burdened with a reputation for antisemitism, saw in the plan a way to demonstrate its ready tolerance of Jews.

The Quebec government agreed to grant the request provided the plan was approved by the Boisbriand municipality. Meanwhile, the Hasidim had obtained the support of the mayor and most of the municipal councillors. It was proposed that the residents of Boisbriand express their views through a referendum, the cost of which would be borne by the Tasher. The latter appeared confident that they would be granted a municipal charter within a matter of months.

At that stage, however, newspapers catering to both anglophone and francophone readers intervened. *The Gazette*, Montreal's English-language daily, claimed in an editorial on July 27, 1979, that the Hasidim's problems were rooted in matters of taxation. It added a further difficulty: that under the Charter of Rights and Freedoms, it was not possible to make residence conditional upon religion.

Two months later, on September 29, 1979, Montreal's French daily, *La Presse*, published a lengthy article titled, "Quebec veut-il legaliser la creation d'une ville-ghetto?" (Does Quebec Want To Legalize the Creation of a City-Ghetto?) The Tasher were described as "the most intransigent" of the Hasidic sects residing in Quebec and the provincial government, in its wish to be tolerant of cultural minorities in general and of the Jewish community in particular, "could risk committing a grave historical error." Shortly following the publication of that article, the mayor of Boisbriand withdrew his support of the Tasher's application.

The failure to secure a municipal charter does not seem to have been a severe blow for the Tasher. In the end, they managed to reach a settlement on the taxation dispute and even acquired additional acreage adjacent to their settlement. Most important, they succeeded in obtaining rezoning from the Boisbriand Town Council so they could erect new dwellings on land previously designated for agriculture.

A significant outcome of the unsuccessful bid was that it compelled the sect's religious and administrative leaders to enter a series of negotiations with outsiders, including people from various levels of government and the media, which helped them acquire a more knowledgeable approach to advancing the community's agenda. The process of becoming better skilled at negotiating with outsiders served the Tasher simultaneously to protect and to preserve their distinctive identity.

CONCLUSION

Although the Hasidic community is perceived as relatively static and largely unresponsive to major societal changes over the past decades, a more precise appraisal is that it is constantly adapting to environmental, political, and social circumstances and at the same time acting on opportunities which their particular configuration offers (Peter 1987). "In the modern marketplace of ideas and social movements," writes Heilman, "even the hasidim were touched. . . . Change masqueraded as continuity" (1992:185).

The Hasidic community is best investigated in terms of the dynamic interplay between institutional organization and the continuous evaluation of the perceived threat of foreign influences—in short, what may be conceptualized as boundary-maintaining activity. Such activity requires an assessment of one's current practices and their continued suitability; it can be initiated either at the individual level or by collectivities within the community charged with the responsibility of preserving a distinctive identity.

The symbolic interactionist perspective, with its emphasis on the interpretive process, is particularly suited to analyzing any such unfolding processes of negotiation. A few examples can illustrate this claim. First, an observer of the Hasidim in Montreal cannot help but be impressed by their increase in numbers over the past two decades. When young couples married in the past, they usually selected identified Hasidic enclaves in New York state for settlement; now Montreal has emerged as an attractive city for pursuing a Hasidic lifestyle. The reasons for this change involve a combination of social, economic, and political considerations, but it is clear that the determination of any future course of action— in this case, where to live—requires the individual, in consultation with others, to define and assess situations and events.

Second, as noted earlier in the paper, a number of Hasidic educators report that the role of secular education in the Hasidic schools is being reappraised. In response to a changing economic and political climate, Hasidic parents appear increasingly concerned that their children achieve a basic foundation of secular knowledge, at least in reading, writing, and mathematics, in order to be able to respond to the exigencies of daily life in a secular society. Such reassessments entail a collective evaluation of the relevance of secular studies and are based on the elementary building blocks of social behavior—participants' coordinating their respective lines of conduct by constant interpretation of one another's ongoing activities.

Third, the process by which public controversies become defined within the Hasidic community and negotiated toward an acceptable resolution involves an ongoing series of interpretive activities enabling members to calculate and evaluate appropriate lines of activity. Attention to such ongoing activities helps to explain some seemingly puzzling behavior. When the Tasher's bid for autonomy was denied, it might have been expected that they would continue marshalling support for independent municipal status. Instead, such activities suddenly ceased. "We thought about it quite a lot," remarked an administrator, "and we decided that this is not the time to push." "Anyway," he continued, "we have received approval for our request to rezone some land for houses, and that solves our problem for now."

Whereas the controversy surrounding the Tasher was largely confined to the members of this Hasidic sect, "l'affaire Outremont" cast aspersions on all the Hasidim in that neighborhood and, because charges of antisemitism were raised, involved the participation of various interest groups from the Jewish community as well as a cast of non-Jewish characters. Before they could embark on a course of action that would settle matters, even if only temporarily, the Hasidic community's leaders had to evaluate the various claims-making rhetoric offered by parties to the controversy.

One outcome of the situation was a decision to become more active in informing non-Jews in the area about approaching Jewish holidays and Hasidic customs and traditions. Notices were even posted around the neighborhood announcing the impending visit of a Hasidic rebbe that would result in a celebration that might tie up local traffic (one of the charges leveled at the Hasidim by several non-Jewish neighbors). More significant, perhaps, is a recently released documentary by a Montreal film maker describing the mores and beliefs of the city's Hasidim. It focuses on the Hasidic-francophone confrontation in Outremont and includes interviews with a number of Hasidic spokespeople, who, I surmise, believed that cooperating with the making of the documentary would help ease tensions and create a rapprochement between the two communities. Such decision-making processes are an outcome of an ongoing interpretive interactive enterprise.

In this paper, I have only begun to detail some of the dynamics relating to boundary-maintaining devices among the Hasidim, mainly focusing on such devices as they pertain to outsiders. Further research employing the boundary metaphor could investigate whether certain Hasidic communities rely more heavily on certain boundary-maintaining devices than on others, as well as on inter-Hasidic devices enabling the respective sects to preserve a measure of distinctiveness. Such analyses should help to capture the processes by which the Montreal Hasidic community is increasing in numbers, experiences few defections, and is skillfully transmitting its values and traditions to successive generations.

This paper has also addressed the viability of the symbolic interactionist perspective, with its emphasis on ethnographic research, as the most credible theoretical and methodological approach for capturing the meaning and organization of the Hasidic lifestyle. In essence, it requires the researcher to focus on the interpretive and interactive processes of social interaction and to strive for an intimate familiarity with the subjects of the research. In the case of the Hasidim, as in most field research, there are few, if any, precise rules concerning the process by which access is gained, rapport established, and relations maintained—elements that are critical to achieving intimate familiarity. In reflecting on my various approaches to securing access and conducting my research among the various Hasidic sects, I can conclude that my initial acceptance or rejection was closely tied to the group's energies in boundary work—that is, in securing measures of control over undesirable foreign influences. Where such efforts were perceived as critical for the group's cohesion and continuity and resulted in detailed attention to curtailing interaction with outsiders, my presence was greeted by suspicion and concern. By contrast, where attention to boundary work was differently defined, so that the distinction between insiders and outsiders was seemingly less critical, my presence was met with expressions of warmth and even friendship. Committed as they are to welcoming newcomers, my experiences among the Lubavitcher Hasidim were far less problematic than those among the other sects.[21]

Overall, however, I have found that the achievement of inti-mate familiarity is most critically shaped by two features. The first is spending an inordinate amount of time observing and partici-pating in as many aspects of community life as feasible, so that the researcher's presence eventually becomes, as much as possible, a routine feature of the setting. Such intensive involvement not only heightens the researcher's visibility but, more significantly, leads to the cultivation of social relationships with members of the group and the ability to appreciate situations and events from the latter's perspectives. The second, I believe, is the presentation of self. As I have discovered repeatedly, my personal credentials have consistently outweighed academic ones in gaining entry to the research setting, and my ability to engage in sociable behavior has consistently been more important than any scientific canons in gaining the cooperation from my subjects that has enabled me to conduct my studies. It has been shaped primarily by their percep-tion of me as an ordinary human being who respects them, is gen-uinely interested in and kindly disposed toward them, and is will-ing to conform to their code of behavior when I am with them.

NOTES

1. Including those of H. Gans (1962), E. C. Hughes (1943), E. Lie-bow (1967), R. Redfield (1941), W. L. Warner and P. S. Hunt (1941), and W. F. Whyte (1943).

2. My knowledge of Yiddish proved invaluable for studying the Hasidim. Although almost all have enough English to make themselves understood and may even speak it fluently, their usual language of com-munication is Yiddish. For the most part, for instance, notices posted in the synagogue or at corner stores are in Yiddish, and even spoken English is peppered with Yiddish and Hebrew words and expressions. To be

unable to communicate in Yiddish would place the researcher at a serious disadvantage.

3. As routinely observed in the literature on field research (see, for example, Wax 1971; Gurney 1991), the researcher's status, such as sex, may engender a type of observational limitation. Among the Hasidim, where the sexes are separated, the researcher's sex severely influences and affects the data-collection process. It is thus important for the reader to note that the bulk of the data in this paper are about men and boys. Boundary-maintaining work is not the exclusive domain of Hasidic males, however. For instance, the proselytizing work of the Lubavitcher is enacted by the married and unmarried females, but the organization of their activities differs from the men's. Similarly, the boundary-maintaining device of controlling secular education is executed in different ways for males and females. Though not my purpose in this chapter, it should be possible to delineate those aspects of boundary work that are common to the sexes and those pertaining to one or the other. Along this line, one could consider additional relevant categories, such as age and social class.

4. My experience seems to have been much like what Geertz (1973) recalls at the beginning of his Bali research.

5. Kaddish, the traditional mourner's prayer for the dead, is usually recited in a synagogue in the presence of a quorum. Although any synagogue will do (the kaddish is recited at every service), it is customary for an individual to select a particular synagogue for the purpose. Occasionally, however, circumstance may lead a person to select a synagogue convenient for the moment.

6. All Jewish males who have reached the age of thirteen are commanded to wear tefillin, two small leather cubes, each containing a piece of parchment inscribed with specific Biblical verses. They are strapped, one to the left arm and the other to the forehead, during the morning religious services on days other than the Sabbath and holy days. To popularize the observance of tefillin, Lubavitch organized a campaign that became their most successful proselytizing activity in the late 1960s.

7. The idea of boundary maintenance is pivotal to the functionalist view of deviance and was first introduced in the writing of Emile Durkheim, who claimed that crime is a necessary component of any social system as it indicated and designates its moral boundaries. K. T. Erikson, continuing Durkheim's theoretical direction, claimed, "Deviance makes people more alert to the interests they share in common and draws attention to those values which constitute the *collective conscience* of the community. . . . Boundary-maintaining devices . . . demonstrate to whatever audience is concerned where the line is drawn between behavior that belongs with the special universe of the group and behavior that does not" (1966:1). Since Durkheim's original essays on the func-

tionality of deviance, numerous scholars have used the notion of boundary maintenance as a mechanism of social control (for instance, see Ben-Yehuda 1985).

8. Breton addresses much the same phenomenon, calling it "enclosure," by which is meant "the existence of social boundaries between groups and to the mechanisms for the maintenance of the boundaries" and "a particular pattern in the contours of such boundaries" (1978:149).

9. This concepts of ethnic group boundaries has served as a central analyzing theme in many studies of ethnic group assimilation and persistence, with emphasis on matters of collective identity (Juteau 1979; Schultz 1979; Depres 1975). In particular, researchers have sought to identity specific boundary-maintaining mechanisms enhancing and/or detracting from a group's distinctive identity (Buck 1978; Driedger 1979, 1980; Heilman 1992; Mol 1976; Molohan et al. 1979; Tinker 1973; Whyte 1986; Woon 1895).

10. One could, of course, cite other institutions within the Hasidic community that feature prominently in boundary work, including, for instance, the family, the bays medresh, the yeshivah, and the *mikveh* (ritual bath). Most significant is the role of the rebbe, who serves as a sect's charismatic leader as he directs affairs, and who in his relationship to his followers "functions in the uncertain areas of life rather than in the clearly defined domain of the law" (Mintz 1968:89). In this regard, the rebbe serves as a central agent of social control whose outlook and philosophy shape the contours of a particular Hasidic sect's social, economic, and political boundaries. For an interesting analysis of the Lubavitcher Rebbe's role and the institutionalization of this charismatic leadership, see Levy (1973).

11. The coordination of secular studies differs for males and females, and my discussion focuses on the former. As a general rule, the girls' secular program is more extensive than the boys'; females receive secular instruction for more hours per day, complete a higher grade level, and cover a broader range of subjects. As in the boys' schools, however, the contents are screened and the secular teachers are closely supervised.

12. The Hasidic sects that do not maintain their own schools send their children to other sects' schools. The choice of the particular school is based largely on the Hasidic sect's religious philosophy, which determines the organization of its religious and secular curricula and the school's reputation. In Montreal, many families from the smaller sects send their children to the Squarer schools.

13. Like many Canadian provinces, Quebec provides sizable subsidies to any school, secular or religious, that educates children. To receive a per-pupil subsidy in Quebec, a school must have its secular studies curriculum approved by the provincial ministry of education and provide a

specified number of hours of instruction in French each week (anglophone cynics claim that the latter qualification is more important that the former).

14. As matters currently stand, almost all of the staff in the boys' secular studies programs are Jewish, either Orthodox or traditional in their religious identification.

15. As already noted, all Quebec schools are at least nominally confessional. The Protestant School Board of Greater Montreal proved what many North Americans would consider "public schooling.

16. In recent years, the religious authorities have given the secular program somewhat greater support. This shift is probably attributable to the complexity of economic life and the necessity to be familiar with changing expectations. As one of the secular principals explained:

> Look, they realize that it's not like before where if you opened a business then you could hire one bookkeeper. You better know how to manage your business instead of relying totally on someone else. But also in terms of simple matters: the street signs are all in French and you won't know where to park your car if you can't read them. The extent of this change must, however, be kept in proper perspective. Another principal cautioned against exaggerating its magnitude: "There was a kind of evolution in the last few years, but nothing revolutionary. Just a slight movement, barely noticeable."

17. Chabad is an acronym for *Chochmah* (wisdom), *Binah* (understanding), and *Daat* (knowledge)—the three basic principles elucidated by the first Lubavitcher Rebbe in his interpretation of Judaism as a way to God. "Chabad" and "Lubavitch" are used as synonyms, referring to the same Hasidic sect.

18. I would strongly suggest that Lubavitch's campaign proclaiming the Messiah's imminent arrival may be understood from this perspective. The *Moshiach* (Messiah) Campaign serves as the most recent example of this sect's witnessing activities, and testifies to its use of the most modern and sophisticated techniques to achieve its objectives. As of this writing (May 1992), that campaign appears to have lost at least some of its momentum and spark due to the Lubavitcher Rebbe's illness and recuperation. The social history of the Moshiach Campaign, the controversies surrounding it, and its impact on the Lubavitcher Hasidim constitute the main focus of this writer's recently initiated research project.

19. For an interesting analysis along this line, see Buck's discussion of the tourist enterprise among the Old Order Amish. While seemingly obstructing the preservation of a distinctive identity by facilitating interaction between outsiders and the Amish, the organization of the enterprise in fact promotes a necessary measure of insulation:

> The theater-like atmosphere created by tourist entrepreneurs appears to structure contact between "viewers and the viewed" in ways that mini-

mize tourist–Amish interaction. . . . Tourist enterprise, in its apparent success in containing tourists, and thus reducing autonomous roaming, produces a situation where Old Order Amish desire for separation continues to be met to a remarkable degree. (1978:225)

20. When the Tasher settled in the Boisbriand area in 1963, they sought to have their community declared tax exempt as a religious institution. The municipality agreed to do so in respect to some of their buildings but claimed that part of the open land was being retained for speculative purposes and therefore taxed it. This dispute over the real estate status of part of the community's lands eventually reached the Supreme Court of Canada in 1965. For a brief account of the tax dispute, see Shaffir 1987.

21. Although my observations on the relationship between preoccupation with boundary maintenance and access accorded the researcher are based on my experiences with the Hasidim, they could, I suspect, be generalized to other conventional and deviant groups that are studied by social scientists. However, as the literature on field research methods indicates (Kornblum and Smith 1989; Taylor and Bogdan 1984), the dynamics of the field research adventure are both ambiguous and complex; skillful researchers can sometimes penetrate even the most seemingly intractable groups, while less seasoned practitioners of the craft may encounter numerous obstacles, which may even jeopardize the completion of the research, that someone else could handily overcome.

REFERENCES

Barth, F. 1969. *Ethnic groups and boundaries*. Boston: Little, Brown and Company.

Bauer, J. 1988. Racism in Canada: A symposium. *Viewpoints* 16:1.

Ben-Yehuda, N. 1985. *Deviance and moral boundaries*. Chicago: University of Chicago Press.

Blumer, H. 1966. Sociological implications of the thought of G. H. Mead. *American Journal of Sociology* 71:535–548.

———. 1969. *Symbolic interactionism: Perspective and method*. Englewood Cliffs, NJ: Prentice-Hall.

Breton, R. 1978. Stratification and conflict between ethnolinguistic communities with different social structures. *Canadian Review of Sociology and Anthropology* 15:148–157.

Buck, R. 1978. Boundary maintenance revisited: Tourist experience in an Old Order Amish community. *Rural Sociology* 43:221–234.

Despres, L. 1975. Towards a theory of ethnic phenomena. In *Ethnicity and resource competition in a plural society*, ed. L. Despres, 187–207. The Hague: Mouton Publishers.

Driedger, L. 1979. Maintenance of urban ethnic boundaries: The French in St. Boniface. *Sociological Quarterly* 20:89–108.

———. 1980. Jewish identity: The maintenance of urban religious and ethnic boundaries." *Ethnic and Racial Studies* 3:67–88.

Erikson, K. T. 1966. *Wayward Puritans: A study in the sociology of deviance.* New York: John Wiley & Sons, Inc.

Festinger, L., H. W. Riecken, and S. Schachter. 1956. *When prophecy fails.* New York: Harper and Row.

Gans, H. 1962. *The urban villagers.* New York: The Free Press.

Geertz, C. 1973. Deep play: Notes on the Balinese cockfight. In *The interpretation of cultures: Selected essays,* ed. C. Geertz, 412–453. New York: Basic Books.

Glick, I. 1958. The Hebrew Christians: A marginal religious group. In *The Jews: Social patterns of an American group,* ed. M. Sklare, 415–431. New York: The Free Press.

Gurney, J. 1991. Female researchers in male-dominated settings: Implications for short-term versus long-term research. In *Experiencing fieldwork: An inside view of qualitative research,* ed. W. Shaffir and R. Stebbins, 53–61. Newbury Park, CA: Sage.

Gutwirth, J. 1970. *Vie Juive traditionnelle: Ethnologie d'une communaute Hassidique.* Paris: Les Editions De Minuit.

———. 1978. Fieldwork method and the sociology of Jews: Case studies of Hasidic communities. *The Jewish Journal of Sociology* 20:49–58.

Heilman, S. 1992. *Defenders of the faith: Inside ultra-Orthodox Jewry.* New York: Schocken.

Hughes, E. C. 1943. *French Canada in transition.* Chicago: University of Chicago Press.

Juteau, D. 1979. *Emerging ethnic boundaries.* Ottawa: University of Ottawa Press.

Kanter, R. 1972. *Commitment and community: Communes and utopias in sociological perspective.* Cambridge: Harvard University Press.

Kornblum, W., and C. Smith. 1989. *In the field: Readings on the field research experience.* New York: Praeger.

Levy, S. 1973. *Ethnic boundedness and the institutionalization of charisma: A study of the Lubavitcher Hassidim.* Ann Arbor, MI: University Microfilms.

Liebow, E. 1967. *Tally's corner.* Boston: Little, Brown.

Loomis, C., and J. Beagle. 1957. *Rural sociology: The strategy of change.* Englewood Cliffs, NJ: Prentice-Hall.

Lottes, K. 1972. *Jehovah's Witnesses: A contemporary sectarian community.* Master's thesis, McMaster University.

Mead, G. H. 1934. *Mind, self and society.* Chicago: University of Chicago Press.

Mintz, J. 1968. *Legends of the Hasidim.* Chicago: University of Chicago Press.

Mol, H. 1976. *Identity and the sacred: A sketch for a new social-scientific theory of religion.* Agincourt: The Book Society of Canada Ltd.

Molohon, K., R. Paton, and M. Lambert. 1979. An extension of Barth's concept of ethnic boundaries to include both other groups and developmental stage of ethnic groups. *Human Relations* 32:1–17.

Peter, K. 1987. *The dynamics of Hutterite society.* Edmonton: The University of Alberta Press.

Poll, S. 1962. *The Hasidic community of Williamsburg.* New York: The Free Press.

Redfield, R. 1941. *The folk culture of Yucatan.* Chicago: University of Chicago Press.

Rubin, I. 1974. *Satmar: An island in the city.* Chicago: Quadrangle Books.

Schultz, S. 1979. Marriage preferences and ethnic boundaries: The Greek-American case. *International Journal of Sociology of the Family* 9: 197–208.

Shaffir, W. 1974. *Life in a religious community: The Lubavitcher Chassidim in Montreal.* Toronto: Holt, Rinehart and Winston of Canada.

———. 1978. Witnessing as identity consolidation: The case of the Lubavitcher Chassidim. In *Identity and religion: International, cross cultural approaches,* ed. H. Mol, 39–57. London: Sage.

———. 1987. Separation from the mainstream in Canada: The Hasidic community of Tash. *The Jewish Journal of Sociology* 29: 19–35.

Stevenson, E. 1967. *The inside story of Jehovah's Witnesses.* New York: Hart Publishing Company Inc.

Taylor, S., and R. Bogdan. 1984. *Introduction to qualitative research methods: The search for meanings.* New York: John Wiley and Sons.

Thomas, W. I. and D. S. Thomas. 1928. *The child in America.* New York: Alfred A. Knopf.

Tinker, J. 1973. Intermarriage and ethnic boundaries: The Japanese American case. *Journal of Social Issues* 29: 49–66.

Warner, W. L., and P. S. Hunt. 1941. *The social life of a modern community.* New Haven, CT: Yale University Press.

Wax, R. 1971. *Doing fieldwork: Warnings and advice.* Chicago: University of Chicago Press.

Weiner, H. 1969. *9 1/2 mystics: The Kabbala today.* New York: Holt, Rinehart and Winston.

Whyte, J. 1986. How is the boundary maintained between the two communities in Northern Ireland? *Ethnic and Racial Studies* 9:219–234.

Whyte, W. F. 1943. *Street corner society.* Chicago: University of Chicago Press.

Woon, Y. F. 1985. Ethnic identity and ethnic boundaries: The Sino-Vietnamese in Victoria, British Columbia. *Canadian Review of Sociology and Anthropology* 22:534–558.

CHAPTER 2

HaBaD & Habban: "770's" Impact on a Yemenite Jewish Community in Israel

Laurence D. Loeb

One can only imagine how strange it must have been as the first of these mostly olive-skinned young men straggled into the *shul* (synagogue) on Eastern Parkway in Brooklyn. It was the early 1960s, and despite having gone to school for some years at Kfar HaBaD in Israel, the English and Yiddish speech was largely unintelligible to these young men. To the local HaBaDniks (Lubavitcher Hasidim), the fluent Israeli Hebrew with occasional Arabic nuances was likewise unusual, and a Kulturkampf between these quaint and rather naive oriental Jews and the Brooklyn Hasidim must have seemed to be inevitable. What were Yemenite Jews doing among the Lubavitchers? Where is this relationship a generation later? What do rural Israeli Jews originating in the remoteness of the East Aden Protectorate share with the followers of a Sorbonne-trained engineer holding court as a charismatic religious leader in urban Brooklyn?

In a 1978 paper presented to the Israel Anthropological Society, *Habban and Habad: The Impact of Lubavitch Hasidism on the Structures and Processes of a Yemenite Community*, I regis-

Fieldwork in Israel was supported by grants from the Social Science Research Council, Memorial Foundation for Jewish Culture, and Fullbright Hays.

tered serious concern about the apparent stifling of indigenous Habbanite culture and values in favor of Lubavitcher ones. At that time, a schism had opened between community HaBaDniks and resisters, young and old, who wished to preserve the traditions evolved in the Yemen. By 1990, open resistance to HaBaD had totally crumbled. Nevertheless Habbanite values and customs were flourishing, and young HaBaDniks were praising the merits of the older generations, their piety and wisdom.

This chapter examines the relationship of Habban and HaBaD, exploring the thesis that the visitation with the Rebbe in Brooklyn concretely expresses the transformation of a traditional religious community into an acceptable participant in the ongoing creation of the Jewish State in Israel. This symbolic integration also represents a successful effort in directed change applied by HaBaD to a non-Ashkenazic ethnicity, with implications for understanding non-state sponsored planned change projects.

INTRODUCTION

Lubavitcher Hasidism, HaBaD, differs markedly from other Hasidim in its effort to reach outside its group to win new adherents. Its efforts to seek out the unaffiliated and nontraditional Jews to effect *teshuvah*, a return to observance and spirituality, is well known (Shaffir 1974; Levy 1973; Harris 1985; Danziger 1989). But HaBaD has also long sought to maintain and intensify Judaism for Orthodox Jews unacquainted with the genius and charisma of their rebbe. Kfar HaBaD, established in 1948, not far from Lod Airport in Central Israel, became an important resource institution in this effort, which quickly centered on new immigrants, most particularly traditionalists from the Middle East and North Africa. The implications of acculturating non-Ashkenazic Jews to Hasidism by integrating residence and schooling could not have been anticipated at that time, and the difficulties HaBaD would incur in this effort have yet to be fully resolved.

Anthropologists have long been interested in the problems of acculturation; thus, Israel became a fertile field for research into this process in the 1950s and 1960s. In fact, the literature clearly demonstrates that what occurred there was not the result of the chance mixing of immigrants and indigenous populations, but resulted instead from certain ideological assumptions of the Israeli

Government and the absorption policies of the Jewish Agency. Thus, results of this effort should then be studied under the rubric of "directed" change—in this case, with guidelines provided by the state (Kushner 1973; Shapiro 1971; Weintraub 1971).

HaBaD was also acting to direct change among these populations. But where the state was concerned with economic and social integration into Israel with an emphasis on secular values, HaBaD wanted to make sure that these immigrants did not abandon religious observance for secularist behavior. It accomplished this chiefly by making inexpensive yeshivah education available for young men and special vocational and/or teacher training for young women. Many religious high schools in Israel are boarding schools and those at Kfar HaBaD, only about twenty minutes from the main Habbani settlement, are likewise residential. In the course of a day, children are exposed to Lubavitcher living and values, integrating what does not clash violently with their previous upbringing and calling into question everything else. HaBaD competed with many religious schools and yeshivot, Yemenite, Oriental, and Ashkenazic,[1] but overall its program, its proximity, and the influence of its emissaries won increasing numbers of participants.

The literature on HaBaD and other Hasidic groups often views them as sectarians, resisting the pressures and vicissitudes of modern living, or as revitalization movements led by charismatic figures. HaBaD, under the leadership of the late rebbe, Menachem Schneerson, might be said to have returned to its original Hasidic roots by emphasizing a strong outreach program marked by the open recruitment and proselytizing of other Jews. These Jews typically come from weakly defined traditions, and after much schooling in the fundamentals of Judaism, embrace the Lubavitcher lifestyle in its entirety. By contrast, in its encounter with Habbanite Jews, HaBaD's efforts were directed towards a highly committed, homogeneous, strongly identified community of pious Yemenite Jews. In the time since the Yemenites were targeted at their *aliyah* in 1950, HaBaD influence over the Habbanites has proven to be profound, even if achieved with some difficulty and clouded by misunderstanding. What native configurations, one must ask, have favored HaBaD hegemony and how is HaBaD success to be measured?

HABBAN

The Habbani came from a remote area in the East Aden Protectorate, hundreds of kilometers and many days distance to the east
of their nearest Jewish neighbors. Centered in an important trade
town astride the old incense route, they had formed a positive
long-enduring relationship with the Muslim populations of the
region. Little of the excesses described for Zayidi Shi'ite Yemen
apply to the Sha'afis of South Yemen. Jews were free to develop
economically and culturally, restrained primarily by tradition and
the hardships of survival in an agriculturally marginal environment.

For at least 250 years, Habbani subsistence depended on a single occupation—silversmithing—requiring most men to wander
among the towns and villages of the region for extended periods
of time. In their absence, women maintained appropriate ritual
observance and made sure that the young boys strictly observed
the law and attended their studies with the *Mori* (teacher), an elderly man, or a volunteer who stayed behind to accept responsibility for teaching the young and to provide freshly slaughtered meat
for the remnant community.

In Habban, it was not uncommon to be fired with religious
fervor. Piety, manifested through meticulous ritual observance,
gave satisfying meaning to the recurrent patterns of the day, the
week, and the festive year. It provided significance for the otherwise meaningless wanderings of Habbani men through the coun-
tryside searching for work and the incredible boredom for the
women and children usually left behind. The men in their sojourn,
carried their tools and a sack of books including a *Tiklal* (prayer
book), *Torah* (five books of Moses), *Dinim* (laws), *Zohar* (mysticism), and others. When not working, men would sit and study,
and if accompanied by a young apprentice, would listen to the rec-
itations of the apprentice while attending to their silversmithing.
Among the Habbani, the more ignorant men were fairly competent readers of Torah and capable *shaliach tsibur* (precentors),
while the more learned were well versed in *halakhah* (law), *mish-
nah* (the first portion of the Talmud) and *midrash* (biblical exige-
sis). Nearly one-thrid of the men were ordained *shochtim,* (ritual
slaughterers). The community had two synagogues, two ritual
baths, and an active *Bet Din* (court). While few Habbani were
accomplished legal scholars—Mussa bin Rom Shamakh, in the

late seventeenth century, was the only one of significance—Habbani men were creative religious poets and many of their best works have been preserved. Habbani women, too, developed poetry and, in the absence of menfolk, special traditions for the observance of Hanukkah and Purim. Remote from the "cultured" environs of Sana'a or Aden, the Habbani were nevertheless highly respected for their piety.

Habbani folklore is replete with tales of culture-heros. One Suliman al-Hakim, a reputedly blind sage, provided the advice which enabled the Sultan to overcome an extended siege of the city. Another, Mussa bin Rom Shamakh, a contemporary of Shalom Shabazzi [1619–79?], was a poet and sage in his own right, and the last to have had sufficient learning and prestige to singlehandedly make binding legal decisions. The qualities admired in Habbani men included piety, scholarship, generosity, individuality, perseverance, and integrity. Charisma was also much admired as it was among North African Jews (cf. Shokeid 1979; Weingrod 1990), though it was hard to ascertain just what constituted "charisma."

Prior to their mass immigration to Israel in 1950, their Muslim neighbors pleaded with them to remain and plied them with rumors they had heard about the secularism of Israeli Jews and the immodest behavior of Jewish women. Nonetheless, Jews left Habban after considerable deliberation, determined to return to Zion and fearful of remaining as the last Jews in the Yemen.

HaBaD

Hasidism's rapid acceptance by large numbers of Jews in southern Poland and Russia in the late eighteenth century filled a spiritual vacuum created a century earlier when the Cossack invasion devastated Jewish communities and destroyed a large portion of its rabbinic leadership.

Part of the special appeal of Hasidism came through the message of the Baal Shem Tov. It proclaimed the potential spiritual equality of all Jews, whether learned or ignorant. Sincerity, commitment and emotional involvement were the hallmarks of spirituality, not mere knowledge of Talmud. The allure of this teaching lay in reopening the portals of participation to Jewish masses long bereft of learning and scholarship. What made this message even more palatable was the obvious charisma of Hasidic leadership, especially of the master, the rebbe, who was designated a *zaddiq* (righteous man). In most groups, it became dogma that the rebbe was not a mere human, but endowed with superior knowledge, piety, and access to the Divine; thus his statements, opinions, interpretations and answers were to be acted upon accordingly (Scholem 1941:344; Zborowski and Herzog 1952:180).

HaBaD (Chochmah, Binah, Daat: "wisdom, understanding, and knowledge") arose in the late-eighteenth-century Poland in response to the ministrations of Schneur Zalman of Liadi, a disciple of Dov Baer of Mezritch. A true mystic, Schneur Zalman taught meditative practices to enable the individual to achieve communion with God.[2] He nevertheless called for a piety which would blend study and scholarship, previously the exclusive domain of the opposing *Misnagdim,* with the mystical, emotional, and ritual elements already well ingrained in Hasidism.

Dov Baer, his son, moved to Lubavitch in 1813, and for the next hundred years this town became the center of the HaBaD world. Leadership was passed down agnatically, occasionally through sons-in-law when no appropriate son could assume the mantel of leadership. HaBaD opposed emigration to the United States in the 1880s (Hoffman 1991:23), actively resisting anti-semitism in Russia. During World War I, the center was moved from Lubavitch, and finally the sixth Lubavitcher Rebbe, Yosef Yitzchak, left the Soviet Union altogether, taking HaBaD to Riga, Latvia, and thence to Warsaw, Poland, and finally to the United States. Following Yosef Yitzchak's flight from Nazi-occupied Poland in the early 1940s, Crown Heights, Brooklyn, became HaBaD's spiritual center. Menachem Mendel Schneerson, son-in-law of his predecessor, was chosen leader of Lubavitch in 1950 and lived, until his recent death, at 770 Eastern Parkway, Lubavitcher headquarters. The Lubavitch movement has established infrastructures throughout the world, including settlements in Israel.[3]

I have not found any meaningful demographic information on Hasidim, but given the propensity to proselytize, it is likely that the ubiquitous HaBaD is today both the fastest growing and largest in number.[4] In the 1950s, when HaBaD first attempted to attract new immigrants to Israel from Arab and other Eastern communities, they and other Hasidic communities were markedly homogeneous and solidly Ashkenazic. There is evidence that ultra-Orthodox Jews and Hasidim in particular were deeply concerned about the survival of these traditional, observant communities, but most of their efforts seemed to have been concentrated in the issuance of diatribes against Zionists and Zionism (Schonfeld 1980). HaBaD however, reached out, establishing residential secondary schools for girls and boys at a very reasonable cost. Eventually they even established institutions in Morocco and Tunisia (unfortunately, long after the vast multitudes had already emigrated), though for some reason never succeeded in establishing themselves in Iran.

The Habbani were approached by HaBaD as early as 1951, while still residing in a heterogeneous *Ma'abara* immigrant camp in Zarnuqa, outside of Rehovot. At that time, only a year into settlement in Israel, there was little assimilation or acculturation, but Habbani leaders were already disgusted with the secularism and immorality they observed among their neighbors. Furthermore, Habbani were appalled by the secularism and assimilation of a small contingent of Habbani who had settled in the Tel Aviv suburb of Salameh some six years earlier. HaBaD emissaries apparently impressed them with their piety, sincerity, and loving reverence for their "rebbe." Several Habbani teenaged boys were permitted to attend school at Kfar HaBaD and returned home revitalized and more knowledgeable. The Habbani soon moved away to an abandoned Moshav (agricultural cooperative) in the low hills east of Lod airport and there proceeded to create a reasonably insular homogeneous community able to assert traditional values and reinstate traditional practices.

The Moshav, intended for farming, was not an economic success for many reasons, and internal relations proved explosive. The old patrilineages reestablished their hegemony over political, economic, and social decision-making, ultimately reasserting themselves in ritual matters as well. The attempt to maintain a central synagogue soon fragmented, partially along lineage lines, so that six well-attended synagogues coexisted by the 1960s. By the late 1950s the Moshav population had grown from less than 400 to more than 560, and the 80+ households residing on the Moshav were subsisting primarily from male farm and nonfarm wage labor off the Moshav and women's highly compensated household cleaning in the nearby suburbs of Tel Aviv. Primary schooling was within the Moshav, but more frequent interacting with secular outsiders in educational and work environments was worrisome to many Habbani.

In the meantime, the fruits of HaBaD education were being reaped on the Moshav in the 1960s. There was considerable pride in the piety of HaBaD-educated young people, but many were shocked and then angered that their children refused to eat Moshav-slaughtered animals. The sanctity of Habbani ritual-slaughter had been questioned and many community members were deeply offended. In fact, no objection to Habbani practice could have struck so deep a chord of anguish, because the Habbani had prided themselves for generations on their thorough training and meticulous adherence to the *shichitah* (butchering) law. They boasted that they had refused the slaughter of other Yemenites at the Hashid refugee camp in Aden in 1950 because they had observed in them a lack of zeal in their fidelity to ritual requirements.

By the 1960s all but the aged had long abandoned traditional Habbani dress, so there was no difficulty in coping with the strangely formal dress of the young HaBaDniks. Young Habbani, even HaBaDniks, continued to marry endogamously, so HaBaD was not engendering great cultural tension through family heterogeneity. Besides, these young people were proud observant Jews, unconcerned about appearing different, with men sporting long *peyot* (side locks) and women dressing in modest clothing and covered heads. However, many of the older generation still failed to understand why immigrants to the holy land needed to expend outrageous sums to visit a rabbi half way around the world in *galut* (exile) in Brooklyn, in America. There continued to be considerable ambivalence about the interaction with HaBaD, but the strong emphasis on secondary religious education sat so well with the traditional Habbani worldview, that parents nevertheless sent their children to HaBaD.

By the early 1970s, some Habbani had become alarmed about HaBaD. Young adult HaBaDniks were exhibiting increasingly less respect for traditional Habbani practices and values. Some responded to the threat by sending their sons to non-HaBaD yeshivot, but there seemed to have been no adequate reasonably priced educational substitute for religious girls. Much to their shock, Habbani found that outside HaBaD, they were subject to discrimination by Ashkenazim. In one highly publicized case, a Habbani teenager was refused admission to the prestigious

Nehalim Yeshivah despite outstanding grades and superb recommendations. Public pressure forced the Yeshivah to reverse this decision and offer admission, but by that point he had decided to enter a largely Sfardic yeshivah.

The 1970s was a time of renaissance for Yemenite Jewry. Social and cultural associations were established, journals like *Afikim* were published, and many books on history, culture, and religious thought and behavior were authored. Yemenite yeshivot were established and attracted a significant student body. The Habbani partook of this pan-Yemenite revitalization, which continues to some degree in the present, both culturally and religiously, but most of them did not enthusiastically embrace the educational umbrella provided by pan-Yemenism.

More young people were embracing HaBaD, choosing their spouses from HaBaD sympathizers,[5] and as residential areas disappeared on the Moshav, many settled in HaBaD neighborhoods and settlements, especially in nearby Lod.[6] By the mid-1980s Habbani sentiments were strongly HaBaD and a HaBaD synagogue was created by remodeling a building on the edge of the old school complex in the center of the Moshav. The publication of *Alon Bareqqet*, a journal prepared by the Moshav HaBaD Youth Society and dedicated to the synthesis of HaBaD teachings with traditional Habbani values and wisdom which many had come to venerate, may have been the final step needed to reconcile the disaffected partisans of both groups. By 1990, I detected no animosity nor reluctance to eat meat slaughtered by Habbani slaughterers. Even the least supportive households had at least a large photograph of the Rebbe and probably a volume of *Tanya*.

FIT OR MISFIT

If there had ever been a "cultural symbiosis" between Arab and Jew in Yemen,[7] there was little evidence of it in ninetieth- or twentieth-century Habban. While socializing certainly occurred and some mutual partaking of folk arts, poetry, and music was possible, the implications of religious cleavage were such that little of real importance could be generally shared. Habbani were comfortable with the overall milieu of Yemen: conducive to piety and not overly demanding of time.

The clash of cultures between Habban and HaBaD observed in the 1970s, and the attempt by some to seek alternatives such as pan-Yemenism, ultimately reinforced the Habbani sense of estrangement and anomie in Israel. Twenty years earlier the clash had been with the lifestyle of North African neighbors. Thereafter ensued the continual struggle with Israeli secularism. The ultimate acceptance of HaBaD by the Habbani was, in effect, a surrender to an alien life style that at least expressed an ideology and a fierce pious adherence to ritual which paralleled the self-image the elder generation retained of their life in Yemen.

As explained above, the older generations had difficulty with HaBaD's rejection of their ritual slaughter. With the increasing influence of HaBaD came the imposition of Yiddish culture, Ashkenazic dress style, stricter prohibition on cross-gender physical contact, Euro-American-centrism, and cliquishness, e.g., whereby HaBaDniks preferred to worship among themselves rather than with the rest of the community—even choosing the HaBaD liturgy over the customary Yemenite. For many, these conditions imposed great difficulties in the way of HaBaD–Habban integration.

Since I did not conduct research on HaBaD itself, I am not certain why, when, or how HaBaD altered its own thinking and practice with regard to the integration of Jews from non-Hasidic Orthodox traditions, but during the 1980s adjustment became easier. The younger generation no longer believed that the only wisdom was to be found in Brooklyn—that the pan-Yemenite tradition and Habbani values in particular were to be likewise prized. In lieu of this new respect for Habbani traditions and values, resistance (born of ethnic pride) collapsed. I can only assume that HaBaD, too, recognized that by reaching out to a culture milieu as authentic and as old as its own, commitment to the movement and the Rebbe were far more important than homogeneity obtained by restricting ritual variation. Besides, HaBaD's overall strategy has come to assume that essential homogeneity can be achieved over time without the imposition of cultural constraints.

In return for acceptance of HaBaD, the majority of young Habbani are now more comfortable with traditional ritual, while secularism has receded as an significant threat. Traditional poetry in Arabic and Hebrew has become of greater interest to the generations born in Israel. Traditional music and dance remains appreciated and is, to some extent, actively participated in by all. As of the late 1980s there was little evidence of Ashkenazic dance infiltrating Habbani celebrations, though Ashkenazic as well as other non-Habbani *zmirot* (table songs) for Sabbath and holidays have come to dominate that aspect of semi-sacred ritual.

PILGRIMAGE TO BROOKLYN

In the late 1970s a number of Habbani asked whether I had visited the Rebbe in Crown Heights. When I replied that I had done so many years earlier they responded that I ought to go again. In most Habbani extended families at that time, at least one person had been to the Rebbe for the High Holy Days and Sukkot and was informally considered the household's emissary. The cost for such a journey was prohibitive and, given the generally low wages of most Habbani, a tremendous financial drain. Perhaps over the years some Habbani had prospered or the attraction and prestige of visiting the Rebbe outweighed other financial considerations. In either case, by the 1980s, increasing numbers of Habbani traveled to Crown Heights, many of them for up to a year. Numerous adult men and an unusually large proportion of middle-aged men went along with the growing numbers of young men. A few adult women and many more younger ones have also been to Brooklyn. Moreover, some people had returned to Brooklyn for a second and third visitation. They revel in displaying their use of Yiddish expressions and bask in their acceptance by the Ashkenazim.[8]

The spiritual experience of visitation to the Rebbe is a strange one for Habbani. This most important event is inevitably conducted in Yiddish: The Rebbe's followers crowd together, hanging on his every word as he explicates Torah and teaches the meaning of law and custom. Oriental Jews are far outnumbered by Ashkenazim. They do not, for the most part, understand much as they attend a *farbrengen* (a gathering) with the Rebbe. Arguably it is "the feeling of comradery that pervades the room" and "the charismatic relationship that exists between the Rebbe and his followers" (Levy 1973:100) that nevertheless validates the experience for all attendees. Participating in a drink from the "Rebbe's bottle" is a concrete means of sharing in the Rebbe's personal holiness (Levy 1973:104). Intragroup activities among Lubavitchers may be guided by principles of stratification, but at a farbrengen everyone is equal (Levy 1973:109). The farbrengen is an important liminal experience for all the Rebbe's followers, but for the "pilgrim" it represents the highest achievement of oneness with HaBaD.[9] The Rebbe's meeting with his Habbani visitor (*Yichidus*) is the most memorable experience for the Habbani. In that brief encounter, the Rebbe's special charismatic qualities and insight come to the fore and any blessing offered on the pilgrim's behalf is imbued with special meaning. The feeling of personal closeness to the Rebbe is very important to the Habbani community, which had always been small enough for everyone to be personally close to one another.

It would be misleading, I believe, to overemphasize the social advantages accrued as significant factors, even implicit ones, in motivating the Habbani in their trips to Brooklyn. There is much anthropological cynicism and skepticism when it comes to religious behavior, perhaps because the researchers themselves are often secular. The Habbani, though, are truly *Homo Religiosus* in the sense conveyed by Joseph Soloveitchik in *Halakhic Man* (1983) or by Horton in the *Ritual Man* (1964). The *Ritual Man*, Horton writes, "has a sense of dependence on pure existence of pure-act-of-being, and as one who, in all ages and places, is passionately engaged in trying to overcome the inherent difficulty of expressing this sense of dependence." The thread that ties the lives of contemporary Habbani, whether HaBaDnik or not, to their now soon-to-become-"mythic"-past is the striving to be, to remain *halachic* (Soloveitchik 1983), i.e., to continue along the guided path ordained by Jewish tradition. As indicated elsewhere (Loeb 1985), the Habbani past sometimes seemed more vibrant and authentic than the present. Nevertheless, Habbani concede that despite recent attempts to recapture some of the glories of their pious antecedents in Yemen, in Israel they are, in effect, cut off from the *religious* past. It is the quest for that kind of tie that I believe underlies and motivates their pilgrimage to Brooklyn.

It is unclear from the folklore just how important charismatic leadership was to the Habbani in Yemen. But given to strong emotion and the expression of it, it is likely that piety, influence, and charisma went together. However, miracle working was not attributed to even the most pious Habbani. Contemporary religious leadership in the older generation in Israel certainly possessed charisma, but this was not as important as has been suggested for Tunisian and Moroccan Jews (Weingrod 1990; Shokeid 1971, 1979; Deshen and Shokeid 1974). The Rebbe embodies the ideal religious charisma Habbani attribute to their forbearers. But, the Lubavitcher Rebbe, both man and symbol, is bigger than life. His charisma reaches far beyond anything attributed to any Habbani: He symbolizes the triumph of fervent religious living in a secular state. Most of all, he is *alive* and the Habbani see him as the embodiment of righteousness and piety achievable by humankind.

The Brooklyn experience is overwhelming. The flight, America, the megalopolis of New York, but most of all, the farbrengen and audience with the Rebbe—even as part of a group—restores the religious "thrill" which Habbani feel had been part of their lives while in Yemen. The younger generation can then better identify with their elders and appreciate the continuity of this powerful experience with what had been a part of the past heritage of their community.

So a new generation, the third, draws closer to the traditional values of the community. Instead of a cultural imperialism, in which HaBaD replaces Habban, a revitalized religio-ethnic experience, better able to survive in contemporary Israel under the protection of a well-recognized ally, emerges and triumphs over the whole community. That the Habbani are valued by HaBaD Ashkenazim cannot but increase their self esteem.

In sum, the pilgrimage to Brooklyn represents a confirmation of Habbani success in making the transformation from oriental religious diaspora to a dynamic invigorated religious community in Israel. I doubt whether more than a handful of rural Yemenite Jewish communities or other communities in Israel generally have achieved this level of "realization" so in keeping with the aspiration of the leaders of the immigrant generation.

IMPLICATIONS

Aliyah to Israel was more than a change of scenery for the Habbani. Their religious life in Yemen had been totally integrated with their subsistence, social interaction with Muslims, and the environment itself. The sudden severance of those physical links, the ensuing total loss of control over their lives, their inability to adequately communicate in their new environs in Israel, the loss of much of their material possessions (including sacred items stolen from their lifts while stored by the Jewish Agency), the incomprehensibility of pervasive secularism, the inability to adequately provide a livelihood—these were shattering to this self-reliant, proud community.

In Israel, the Habbani struggled mightily to retain their ties to the past. They sought to resist the dangers of secularism by establishing a local homogeneous primary school, securing strong family ties and local endogamy, and stressing ethnic pride and ritual observance. While HaBaD missionizing had, in fact, reinforced a commitment to Habbani ritual observance, it inadvertently undermined the validity of Habbani values and tradition. This, in turn, engendered intense Habbani hostility directed against apparent HaBaD "cultural imperialism." The younger generation of HaBaD-educated Habbani, venerating their family ties and community values, sought an appropriate path leading to syncretism. As a result of these efforts, HaBaD eventually came to accept Habbani culture and practices, particularly its strong nostalgia and its emphasis on community and extended family. Reverence for the wisdom and role modeling of past Habbani generations are examples of HaBaD attitudes which served to reinforce elements of indigenous Habbani culture. However, other aspects of Habbani culture, such as the open manifestation of cross-gender affection and the conflict with HaBaD norms will probably be eliminated in the next generation.

In addition to studying the interesting religious interactions between Habban and HaBaD—the importance of a new charisma, strong ideology, and parallel ritual piety that allowed Habbani to successfully integrate into Israeli society—the implications for understanding directed change ought to be briefly explored. Habban/HaBaD interaction is a not uncommon example of acculturation (Redfield, Linton, and Herskovitz 1936). Its uniqueness lies in HaBaD's motivation and goal. They were set in motion to resist the efforts of Israel's absorption policies that were meant to integrate and assimilate immigrants in syncretizing a new Israeli culture with a basically secular value system. HaBaD did not seek to affect the Habbani immigrants' learning and use of modern technology nor their participation in the nation's civic, political, and social processes. Rather, its influence appears to have been directed to the preservation and enhancement of Jewish religious values and behavior. Unlike the agents of state-supported change, HaBaDniks employed no obvious financial incentives or sanctions. Nor did HaBaD demand strict adherence to its platform and agenda. While this is not the place to present a careful analysis of these conflicting efforts for the hearts and minds of Habbani Jews, it would seem that HaBaD was more effective than the state. While the Habbani are fully and unabashedly Zionist and protective of Israel, they look to Brooklyn for inspiration and leadership. In the struggle between a work ethic contributing to national growth and their own prosperity on the one hand, and a life of piety, study, and missionizing on the other, the younger generation is increasingly choosing the latter path. Thus, economic "progress" and social acceptance are increasingly giving way to ideological commitment and pietist community norms.

The anthropological literature is all but mute about social agencies essentially uninterested in material change, and in fact, most agencies ultimately foster technological and/or economic change.[10] This chapter nevertheless raises the possibility that there is much to be learned by examining directed change unencumbered by primarily economic consideration.

NOTES

1. In the 1970s, Habbani quickly pointed out that really bright young men were *rarely* sent to HaBaD, instead attending the more intellectually prestigious yeshivot such as Nehalim, Kfar Haro'eh, etc.

2. These teachings are imbedded in his writings entitled the *Tanya*.

3. Arguably, many of HaBaD's important operations are now organized at Kfar HaBaD in central Israel. A detailed reconstruction of 770 Eastern Parkway, the Rebbe's residence, stands at the northern end of Kfar HaBaD—presently empty—awaiting the arrival of the Rebbe. Since it could not have been built without the Rebbe's expressed permission and because the Rebbe has never suggested immigrating to Israel, it must be seen as a symbolic statement of the Rebbe's expectation of the imminent arrival of the *Mashiah*, the Messiah who will whisk him to his new residence in Zion, restored under the rulership of the Divine.

4. Levy (1973:31) correctly points out that while HaBaD never achieved the numbers attained by some other groups in the past, they also never suffered the losses to secularism which devastated other Hasidic groups in the first part of this century. Recruitment from the outside Jewish community resulted in ever increasing numbers and enabled HaBaD to overcome the ravages of the Holocaust.

5. Marriages were not always arranged with the Rebbe's permission, apparently. The pattern remained highly endogamous with respect to the community.

6. Habbani have had no difficulty with the incipient class system well described in Levy (1973:41–56). Habbani largely prefer to marry among themselves, and ethnic "integration" is not a highly esteemed goal. Levy (1973:53) reports that 90 percent of her sample married in their own "category" or were hypergamous (i.e., women could marry up).

7. Cf. Goitein (1955), who refers to a rather sophisticated culture unlike the reality of the normative cultural interaction of Arab and Jew.

8. Many had also used the occasion to return with electronic and other items prohibitively priced in Israel.

9. This feeling is echoed in studies of the Islamic *Hadj* to Mecca and in other pilgrimages, cf. Turner (1964), Turner and Turner (1978).

10. Charles Brooks (1989) examines in detail the motivations, methods, and success of an agent with somewhat similar objectives, the Hare Krishnas, but he does not approach the subject from the viewpoint of directed change.

REFERENCES

Brooks, C. R. 1989. *The Hare Krishnas in India.* Princeton: Princeton University Press.

Danziger, M. H. 1989. *Returning to tradition: The contemporary revival of Orthodox Judaism.* New Haven: Yale University Press.

Deshen, S., and M. Shokeid. 1974. *Predicament of homecoming: Cultural and social life of North African immigrants in Israel.* Ithaca: Cornell University Press.

Gotein, S. D. 1955. *Jews and Arabs: Their contact through the ages.* New York: Schocken Books.

Harris, L. 1985. *Holy days: The world of a Hasidic family.* New York: Summit Books.

Hoffman, E. 1991. *Against all odds: The story of Lubavitch.* New York: Simon & Schuster.

Horton, R. 1964. Ritual man in Africa. *Africa* 34:85–104.

Kushner, G. 1973. *Immigrants from India in Israel: Planned change in an administered community.* Tucson: University of Arizona Press.

Levy, S. 1973. *Ethnic boundedness and the institutionalization of charisma: A study of Lubavitcher Hasidism.* Dissertation, City University of New York. University Microfilms.

Loeb, L. D. 1985. Folk models of Habbani ethnic identity. In *Studies in Israeli ethnicity,* ed. Alex Weingrod, 201–216. NY, London: Gordon & Breach.

Redfield, R., R. Linton, and M. J. Herkovits. 1936. Memorandum for the study of acculturation. *American Anthropologist* 38:149–152.

Scholem, G. 1941. *Major trends in Jewish mysticism.* Jerusalem: Schocken Books.

Schonfeld, M. 1980. *Genocide in the Holy Land.* Brooklyn: Bnei Yeshivos.

Shaffir, W. 1974. *Life in a religious community: The Lubavitcher Chassidim in Montreal.* Toronto: Holt, Reinhart, and Winston of Canada.

Shapiro, O., ed. 1971. *Rural settlements of new immigrants in Israel.* Rehovot: Settlement Study Centre.

Shokeid, M. 1971. *The dual heritage.* Manchester: Manchester University Press.

———. 1979. "The decline of personal endowment of Atlas Mountains religious leaders in Israel. *Anthropological Quarterly* 52:186–197.

Soloveitchik, J. B. 1983. *Halakhic man.* Philadelphia: Jewish Publications Society of America.

Turner, V. 1964. Betwixt and between: The liminal period in *rites de passage.* In *The proceedings of the American ethnological society, symposium on new approaches to the study of religion,* 4–20. Seattle: University of Washington Press.

Turner, V., and E. Turner. 1978. *Image and pilgrimage in Christian culture: Anthropological perspectives.* New York: Columbia University Press.

Weingrod, A. 1990. *The saint of Beersheva.* Albany: SUNY Press.

Weintraub, D, et al. 1971. *Immigration and social change: Agricultural settlements of new immigrants in Israel.* Jerusalem: Israel Universities Press.

Zborowski, M., and E. Herzog. 1952. *Life is with people.* New York: Schocken Books.

CHAPTER 3

The Language of the Heart: Music in Lubavitcher Life

Ellen Koskoff

As a small child growing up in Pittsburgh, Pennsylvania, in the late 1940s, I was often drawn to the sounds I heard when, on my way to school each day, I passed the Lubavitcher yeshivah at my corner. I was struck by the spirit and intensity both of the singing and of the radiant faces of the men and boys I could see through the window on Hobart Street. I would often stop to listen, attracted by the sense of purpose that the singing seemed to have, and by the sometimes joyful, sometimes yearning, quality of the music. Coming from a "secular" Jewish family where I was expected to become a classical musician, I could not fully understand the relationship these people had to Judaism nor to their music. Later, as an ethnomusicologist—a trained outside observer—I came not only to better understand this relationship, but also to develop a high regard for the musicianship and musical creativity of the men and women with whom I worked.

This chapter examines the traditional music of Lubavitcher Hasidim (*nigun*), its meaning and use in Lubavitcher life, and its role in the ongoing negotiation between traditional Lubavitcher values and those of the U.S. urban mainstream. I regard nigun as a musical expression of essential Lubavitcher religious and philosophical beliefs, and its performance as an articulation of these beliefs within the realm of social and musical action. "Making a nigun" is not simply a joyous activity for Lubavitchers, it is a reli-

---

Musical transcriptions in this article were made by the author from field recordings and from recordings made within the Lubavitcher community.

gious act, carrying with it the same awesome responsibility as prayer.

THE CONTEMPORARY SETTING

The contemporary Lubavitcher court, led by the late Rabbi Menachem Mendel Schneerson (1902–1994), is the largest of the modern Hasidic courts, its members numbering around 250,000 worldwide. The Brooklyn community of Crown Heights (approximately 100,000), according to Lis Harris, encompasses an area "whose borders are loosely defined by their synagogue [770 Eastern Parkway], schools, kosher shops, and the last Hasidic family on a block" (Harris 1985:13).

Contemporary Lubavitchers in Brooklyn live in many ways much as their Eastern-European counterparts did in the eighteenth and nineteenth centuries. Strictly adhering to the laws of Orthodox Judaism, wearing specific garments of piety that mark their identity, and joyously, often loudly, participating in frequent gatherings (*farbrengens*) with their rebbe, Lubavitchers seem anachronistic to their New York neighbors. Moreover, their activities are often a point of curiosity, sometimes ridicule, for fellow, less observant Jews from Manhattan and elsewhere.

Although they may resemble their Eastern-European ancestors, contemporary Lubavitchers do recognize considerable differences in class and economic opportunity here in America that would have been impossible in Europe. For example, some hold jobs outside the community; many live quite comfortably on the tree-lined streets of residential Brooklyn, and even some women continue to work, most often within the community as teachers, after children begin to arrive. Lubavitchers feel that this increase in social and economic access is primarily the result of an unprecedented tolerance of Jews in today's America. Such tolerance, though, also represents a potential threat—the lure of the secular, with its life of spiritual impoverishment. For women, especially, the threat of the secular presents a special challenge. As one woman states:

> Years ago, the role of the woman was to sit at home and to learn within her home all that she needed to know to prepare her for a later life as a wife and mother. . . . But, in this day and age, when we are such a part of our society, there is no such thing as living

in your own home anymore. By way of the media, the neighborhood, where you walk, where you move, what you hear, what
you read, you are by your very nature so affected by the world
you live in. . . . The Jewish woman must, if anything, prepare herself even more so, by going out. It has become *the* thing to work,
for economical or emotional reasons. . . . I would say that the
trend is so strong now, I hardly know any of my contemporaries
who just stay at home—very few. (Rosenblum 1975)

In spite of the ever-present dangers of "contamination" and
assimilation, one of the most interesting features of contemporary
Lubavitcher society is its willingness (and its administrative ability)
to forge links with the surrounding modern, urban, non-Hasidic
society. For example, Lubavitchers run an extensive outreach program that reaches local, often non-Jewish communities and educational institutions, where Lubavitcher "mitzvah-mobiles"—
large vans, often wired with loudspeakers blaring music—seek out
less-observant Jews and invite them to learn more about their *Yiddishkeit.* Men are encouraged to don *yarmulkes* (skullcaps) and
tefillin (phylacteries), and women to light Sabbath candles.

Over the past twenty years or so, these activities have resulted
in a heavy influx of new, predominantly American-born, non-
Orthodox Jews who wished to return to Orthodoxy, the baalei
teshuvah (newly Orthodox, returnees). The contemporary community now counts more baalei teshuvah among its members than
those who have been observant from birth.[1] Baalei teshuvah often
describe themselves as being on a perpetual journey toward spirituality. This journey takes years of study and contemplation, and
parallels, if on a different plane, the spiritual journey of Lubavitchers who have been Orthodox from birth. Many baalei teshuvah, however, are regarded as slightly suspect by their lifetime
counterparts, as their roots are in the mundane world of contemporary U.S. culture. It is usually with marriage (often to another
baal teshuvah) and the birth of children that they are truly
accepted.[2]

THE SPIRITUAL HERITAGE

Like all modern Hasidim, Lubavitchers trace their spiritual lineage to the great seventeenth-century Zaddiq, Israel ben Eliezer,
the Baal Shem Tov (d. 1760), and like other groups, their philos-

ophy borrows heavily from the Lurianic kabbalist tradition, the *Zohar*, and other mystical and halachic works. Unlike other Hasidim, though, Lubavitchers adhere to a philosophy developed by their founder, Rabbi Schneur Zalman (1745–1813) of Liadi, a philosophy known as *Habad*, an acronym based on three Hebrew words: *Chochmah* (conceptualization, where an idea is first conceived); *Binah* (the cognitive faculty, where an idea is analyzed); and *Daat* (the final state in which an idea attains comprehension) (Mindel 1969:33).

Schneur Zalman codified his essential philosophy in the *Tanya*, a four-volume collection of writings and commentaries upon Talmudic and mystical texts. At the core of Habad is the concept of the *benoni*, or the "intermediate" man—a category of Jew who stands between two opposing souls, expressed metaphorically as the animal and divine souls. The benoni status is within the grasp of any person who succeeds in living his or her life without intentionally committing an evil act. This can be accomplished if the Hasid strives continuously to achieve *devekut*, or adhesion to God (i.e. "oneness," or unity with the Divine). Devekut is brought about by adhering to the laws of Orthodox Judaism and by living all aspects of one's life with the proper intention (*kavannah*). Kavannah is often activated by the expression of two essential emotional states: *simhah* (joy), and *hitlahavut* (enthusiasm).

The process of achieving devekut is described as moving from the animal to the divine soul, so that when the divine soul is reached, the animal "falls away." The animal, or mundane soul, is conceptualized as neutral, yet potentially out-of-control, often needing restricting laws or codes, whereas the divine soul is seen as being ordered, or, having the capability of ordering. One's spiritual quest for devekut, then, is regarded as a movement away from disorder toward order. Lubavitchers thus speak at once of the binary polarizations of animal and divine souls, of the ongoing process of moving from animal to divine, and of the difficulties of accomplishing this process in everyday life.

Achieving devekut is not conceived, though, as a one-time goal, but rather as an ongoing process, one that is repeated daily throughout one's life. The divine and earthly realms, often referred to metaphorically as the head (associated directionally with the right) and the heel (associated with the left), are to be in constant communication through the heart (central and inward), which is the seat of emotion. It is precisely the energetic repetition of religious precepts and rituals—that is, the endless, intensely felt reenforcement of the bond between God, who is always pure, and human, who is daily tainted by impure influences—that promotes devekut. Thus, Lubavitchers conceive their religious philosophy somewhat as a three-dimensional, "fluid" model, endlessly moving in both an upward/downward and an inward/outward movement through a centralized node of "emotion."

THE ROLE OF MUSIC IN LUBAVITCHER LIFE

Lubavitchers often refer to their music as the language of the heart. Words, they say, are from the brain—they express the mundanities of life; they are connected to the material, everyday, "on-the-surface" aspects of existence. But music, especially a nigun, is able to go far beyond that—it expresses the essence of the Godly soul that lies in the heart of every Jew. Music, unlike words, can carry one to the highest spiritual levels, can bring forth the spirit of a longed-for ancestor, or can directly communicate with the Divine.

Lubavitchers regard their melodies, or *nigunim*, as essential vehicles for expressing simhah and hitlahavut, as nigunim are believed to hold traces of these properties, or "sparks," that are "freed" through active performance. Music is thus a primary link to the divine realm and the performance of nigunim is regarded as an essential activity of Lubavitcher life. Further, Lubavitchers make a distinction between texts, even those taken from Biblical sources or prayers, and pure music. Musical sound itself exists at a higher and deeper spiritual level from words; it can communicate more directly and more powerfully with one's own Godly soul and with the Divine. Thus, many Lubavitcher nigunim are performed using vocables, or syllables without referents in spoken language.

Musically, nigunim resemble other Jewish and non-Jewish Eastern-European folk songs, marches, or dance tunes. Although Lubavitchers themselves categorize nigunim into many different groupings according to their use (e.g., Sabbath nigunim, High Holiday nigunim, dance tunes, etc.), I will broadly define two categories based on musical style: nigunim simhah (happy tunes) and nigunim devekut (yearning songs). Generally, nigunim simhah are

Figure 3.1 Nigun Rikud
Performed by Habad Choir on NICHOACH, 1969.
Transcribed by Ellen Koskoff

Yam ya di di di yam bam ya di di di yam bam bam bam ya di di di ya di di di

yam ya di di di yam bam ya di di di yam bam bam bam bam

Oh --------- di di yam ba------m ya di di di da da da yam ba-----m

Oh --------- di di ai a yai ya ya a yam bam

Ai ye ye yai ye ye yai ye ye yam bam ai ye ye yai ye ye yai ye ye yam bam

a a ya ya a ------ a ------ a ------ a------ ai yai yai yai ya.

those tunes with a regularly recurring duple meter (often highly
emphasized in performance), without extensive ornamentation,
occasionally in the major mode, and are most often performed by
large groups, especially in the context of a rebbe's farbrengen, a
gathering of the entire community where the Rebbe speaks and
there is much singing throughout the night.

Figure 3.1, "Nigun Rikud," is a dance tune performed frequently at farbrengens and other gatherings. Lately the Rebbe has
come to favor simhah over nigunim devekut, as he wishes to

Figure 3.2 Nigun Shalosh Tenuot
Performed by R. Ephriam Rosenblum, April 1976.
Transcribed by Ellen Koskoff

infuse the souls of his following with enthusiasm, not to bring them down into despair in the face of their difficult task of Jewish redemption in the modern world. It is an excellent example of a nigun simhah, and is often performed with much stamping, clapping, and increase of tempo. Its scale employs a lowered second and raised sixth degree, giving it the quality of a Southern-European, or Middle-Eastern mode.

Figure 3.2 is a nigun devekut, "Nigun Shalosh Tenuot," ("Nigun of the Three Parts"), part 1 of which is attributed to the Baal Shem Tov; part 2, to the Maggid of Mezeritch, his disciple; and part 3, to Rabbi Schneur Zalman, the Maggid's disciple and founder of Habad. This particular nigun is greatly revered among Lubavitchers, as its three composers, linked together, form a musical chain of holiness.

LUBAVITCHER SOCIAL STRUCTURE AND MUSIC PERFORMANCE

We have seen how nigun acts to communicate with the divine realm. But the performance of nigunim also acts to delineate internal social divisions within Lubavitcher society itself.

The Hierarchy of Spiritual Lineage

Observing the seating pattern at the late Rebbe's farbrengen underscores beautifully the social and musical hierarchy that exists within Lubavitcher society. The men and women are, of course, separated, with the women above in their own gallery and the men below near the Torah scrolls and the Rebbe. Seated at the Rebbe's table are his closest associates—his secretary, perhaps a visiting dignitary, and others who will assist him during the course of the hours-long event. Radiating outward from the Rebbe in row after row of bleacher-style seats are the rest of the men, arranged in almost perfect correspondence to their relationship to the Rebbe and to Lubavitch. The most recent baalei teshuvah are found, most often, in the last, highest bleacher row, at the same level as the plexiglass screen shielding the women from view.

Close to the Rebbe, in addition to his associates, are various men who act as the Rebbe's "musical assistants," starting specific nigunim or urging their fellows during a performance. In a sense they are extensions of the Rebbe and they carry the responsibility of choosing the appropriate nigun—one that corresponds to the basic theme of the *sicha* (the Rebbe's talk)—and of making sure that its performance is spirited, energetic, and effective. The musical assistants sit close to the Rebbe, either at his table with the others, or in the front rows of the large synagogue at 770 Eastern Parkway.

These men are also responsible for another important musical task—choosing an appropriate nigun for the Rebbe's birthday. Each year, as the Rebbe's birthday approaches, various Lubavitcher composers begin setting the words to the Psalm that corresponds to the Rebbe's new year. A committee, made up of the same musical assistants that help the Rebbe at a farbrengen, chooses the best song. The winning song is introduced at the farbrengen held closest to the Rebbe's birthday and is immediately learned by the entire community, spreading quickly throughout Crown Heights.

Who are these men? How have they been "chosen" to carry out these musical responsibilities? At first, I assumed that they were chosen on the basis of their musical ability—yet not all of them were musically active nor had what we might consider "beautiful" voices. Perhaps they had been selected on the basis of age—yet not all were elderly. Later, I came to realize that the main criterion was one of spiritual lineage; all of the Rebbe's close associates were Lubavitchers from birth, who learned the nigun repertoire from their fathers and, most importantly, who could trace their lineage back through many, if not all, of the seven generations from the present Rebbe to Schneur Zalman, the founder of Lubavitch. Thus, it was their connection to the holy men and holy music of the past, ultimately validating their own spirituality, that accounted for their special musical status.

Gender

Various Orthodox Jewish laws prohibit men and women from praying, singing, or otherwise engaging in social activities together where there is a danger of unacceptable sexual behavior between them, or where unwarranted sexual stimulation (*ervah*) might occur between people who are, for various reasons, prohibited from marrying. Eschewing the values of contemporary feminists and the exhortations of other Orthodox Jewish women who

have begun to fight for more equality—especially in areas of public ritual observance—Lubavitcher women adhere strictly to such
laws even though they clearly separate them from the domain of
men, stating:

> The *Torah*'s restrictions are the Jewish woman's safeguard. For
> where the *Torah* restricts, it does not demean—it protects and
> sanctifies. . . . Any hint of inferior status [is] not a result of
> *Torah* law, but a reflection of the times and culture. (Lubavitch
> Foundation 1970:219)[3]

The voice of a woman (*kol isha*) has long been seen as a source
of male sexual stimulation, and various prohibitions have developed limiting men's interactions with singing, and at times, speaking women.[4] Briefly, the question of kol isha centers on the many
interpretations of a small passage in the Bible from *The Song of
Songs* (2:14), "Let me see thy countenance, let me hear thy voice,
for sweet is thy voice and thy countenance is comely." The first to
comment on this passage was the sixth-century Talmudic scholar
Samuel, whose interpretation first linked women's voices to prohibited sexuality. Samuel proclaimed, *"kol b'ishah ervah"* (the
voice of a woman is a sexual incitement) (Cherney 1985).

Later, the great philosopher, Moses ben Maimon (Maimonides,
1135–1204) added a refinement. He saw the word *ervah* as referring to the woman and to the performance context, not specifically
to the woman's voice. He preceded the word *ervah* by the definite
article, *ha*, or "the." The original commentary by Samuel now read,
"kol b'ishah ha-ervah," or, "the voice of an illicit woman is prohibited."[5] Maimonides, in effect, shifted the emphasis from the
inherent sexuality of women and their voices to the context of a
potential illicit relationship between a man and a prohibited
woman. Sexual stimulation, in itself, was not prohibited; rather,
it was the potential to create a context of sexual stimulation
between a Jewish male and a forbidden partner, especially a "public
woman" (i.e., a non-Jewish courtesan, or prostitute, who sang and
danced in the context of clubs or other public meeting places) that
was restricted.

Although kol isha prohibits men from hearing women sing, it
does not prevent women from singing. Thus, women, when not in
the presence of males, freely engage in many of the same musical
activities as their male counterparts. It is not uncommon, for example, to hear women singing nigunim in the home while lighting Sab-

Figure 3.3   Dvorah Leah's Song
Performed by Leah Namdar, Dec.1990.
Transcribed by Ellen Koskoff

Words: Miriam Bela Nadoff

Music: "Har Ha-Gilboa"

The song we sing be - gins with tears, but tears are not al-----ways sad.   Some

times we give   and   then   we find we've gained more than all ------ we   had.   D -

vor-- ah Le ---ah's   song ------.   The   song on-- ly   wo-men can sing.   Who

know the pain   that   part-ing   brings   but   still in   Ha-Shem they   trust.   Who

know the joy   that   lov-ing   brings,   but   still they do   what they   must.

2. My father called me in one day
And told me about a tree.
"You have to guard it thirty years
And tend to it carefully.
And then the tree stands firm
It's branches spread out to the sun.
And all the people far and near
Can gather its fruit so sweet.
And all the people far and near
Can gather its fruit to eat."

3. "Hasides is just like a tree
Growing up strong and true.
Until the time Meshiach comes
We need it for every Jew.
The Ba'al Shem Tov sowed the seeds
It grew to a tall tree of life.
Now thirty years have passed," he said.
"With my life I'll guard that tree."
"Now thirty years have passed," he said.
"There's fruit here for all to see."

4. My father's eyes filled up with pain,
Told more than he meant to say.
Our precious tree might come to harm,
Wither and die away.
I saw as he could see.
How evil had gathered around.
There was danger to his very life
From someone we hardly know.
There was danger to his very life
From someone we hardly know.

5. "My father, we can't risk your life.
We need you to lead us on.
You know the way through dark and gray
Until a new day must dawn.
I know what must be done
The tree I will guard with my life.
Only take my little boy
And keep him so close to you.
Only take my little boy
And teach him to be a Jew."

bath candles. One particular event, the *forshpil*—a party given for a young woman on the Sabbath before her wedding—rivals the musical and spiritual intensity of the predominantly male farbrengen.

More recently, women have begun to form their own choirs, and to hold their own farbrengen complete with story-telling, personal reminiscences, and much spirited singing. In addition to traditional nigunim, one particular song, "Dvorah Leah's Song" (Figure 3.3), is frequently sung at women's farbrengen. Based on a contemporary Israeli tune, "Har Ha-Gilboa," the text, composed by Miriam Bela Nadoff,[6] tells the story of Dvorah Leah, the daughter of Schneur Zalman, who, fearing that her father's imprisonment on charges of treason, and his resulting depression, would kill him, sacrifices her life so that his teachings can continue. She leaves behind her small son, whom she gives to her father to raise. That virtually every woman I interviewed knew this song attests not only to its popularity but to its salient and idealized message of women's sacrificial love.

TRADITIONAL USES OF NIGUN

Central to the expression of Lubavitcher philosophical and religious beliefs, nigun holds a special status within Lubavitcher life, acting in many ways to articulate these values. First, nigun is a supreme vehicle of communication. In performance, the individual comes to "know himself," to transcend himself, and, ultimately, to enter the realm where divine communication is possible. Thus, nigun provides the Lubavitcher with a key to self and divine knowledge. Second, the performance of nigun validates and reenforces Hasidic beliefs and thus acts not only to ease divine communication but also to bind people together in this effort. Finally, nigun acts as a group signifier, defining the boundaries of the Lubavitcher worldview, and is thus used as a primary means of communicating Lubavitcher values to other Hasidim and of negotiating Hasidic values with other, non-Hasidic groups.

Many stories attest to the power of music in performance, especially as a vehicle for self knowledge. For example, a story is told of Menachem Mendel (the Zemach Zeddik), who came questioning his grandfather, Schneur Zalman, as to the essence of the Jew:

When the Zemach Zeddik was still a child, he asked his grandfather, "What is a Jew?" His grandfather answered that a Jew is
a person who can reveal the root of his soul. A Hasid must know
himself and do something good for himself. But he may study
Torah and the ideas of Hasidism and still not be complete. It is
the responsibility of the Hasid to know himself—and he can
only do this with a *nigun*. A *nigun* shows him who he is, where
he has to be, and where he can be. A *nigun* is a gate through
which he must pass in order to know what he is to be. A *nigun*
is not only a melody—it is a melody of *yourself*. (Zalmanoff
1948:41)

Another story shows the power of nigun to achieve a spiritual
union with holy men of previous generations, who are said to live
at a higher spiritual level, closer to the divine "head." Here, nigun
becomes the agent through which the singer and those present
achieve devekut and are thus bound to each other and united with
earlier, more holy, Zaddiqim:

> Everyone stood up and joined the singing. When they got to the
> place, where the words are "Happy are they who will not forget
> Thee," everyone became ecstatic—so much so that their faces
> became inflamed and on their cheeks tears began to flow. You
> could see that these people were reliving [a] holy moment. There
> was no shadow of a doubt that everyone there knew and felt that
> he [Menachem Mendel, the Zemach Zeddik] was standing near
> the Rebbe and was seeing and hearing how the Rebbe prayed.
> (Zalmanoff 1950:25)

Another important use of music is expressed in this story of
Schneur Zalman and an old man who had come to him to study
Torah. Here, a nigun communicated where words failed:

> The Ladier [Schneur Zalman] noticed an old man among his
> listeners who obviously did not understand the meaning of his
> discourse. He summoned him to his side and said: "I perceive
> that my sermon is unclear to you. Listen to this melody, and it
> will teach you how to cleave unto the Lord." The Ladier began
> to sing a song without words. It was a song of Torah, of trust in
> God, of longing for the Lord, and of love for Him. "I under-
> stand now what you wish to teach,' exclaimed the old man. I
> feel an intense longing to be united with the Lord." (Newman
> 1944:283)

Although Lubavitchers compose some of their own music, the majority of nigunim are either older melodies that have been re-texted (or have had their texts removed and vocables added), tunes whose texts have been reinterpreted, or those that have been borrowed from other, often secular sources, such as Russian drinking songs or, today, musical comedies or TV commercials. Indeed, according to the Zohar, the sparks of Godliness resulting from the breaking of the *kelipot* or holy vessels at the time of Creation are deeply hidden, often in the most mundane places, and only a person with the proper holiness and intention can free the sparks from their bondage. The following story of the organ grinder clearly illustrates this spiritual need to rescue the holy sparks perceived as trapped in a simple peasant tune:

> Rabbi Schneur Zalman once heard an organ grinder sing a song which he thought was beautiful, and he asked him to sing the song again. He paid him a couple of coins and he asked him to sing it again until he learned it. And after the Alter Rebbe [Schneur Zalman] learned it, he asked the organ grinder to play it again, but he wasn't able to. He had forgotten it completely. It seems that there are profound songs which are somewhere else, too . . . like one can speak of a lost soul, one can also speak of a lost piece of music. So, the Hasidim have adapted and adopted it because they feel there's something in it. (Ephriam Rosenblum 1975)

This story also illustrates a traditional strategy used by Lubavitchers to negotiate with the non-Hasidic environment. In redeeming the holy spark within the (originally, non-Hasidic) tune, it was transformed into a nigun. The (non-Hasidic) organ grinder was also transformed—he forgot the tune, that is, he no longer had the power to use the tune toward an unholy end (i.e., as mere entertainment). Thus, the borrowing and transformation of the tune effectively neutralized both the power of the mundane, earthly music and of its user, the organ grinder.

MUSIC AS EMISSARY

Over the past two decades, as various music technologies, such as digital recordings, synthesizers, and computers, have become more and more sophisticated in mainstream society, so, too, have the means by which Lubavitchers have preserved and disseminated their music. When I first began visiting the Crown Heights community in 1973, for example, one of the local stores, Drimmers, carried a few LP recordings produced by the Nichoach Society, a music publishing house established in the 1940s by the previous Lubavitcher Rebbe, Joseph Isaac Schneersohn (1880–1950). Now a visit to Drimmers includes sampling a variety of audio and video cassettes, CDs, and movies aimed at both adults and children for home use. The Rebbe has recently stated that the new technology is not, in itself, harmful to an observant life—if it transmits a Divine message. Thus, today's Lubavitcher home may include a radio, VCR, and an occasional synthesizer, in addition to the more standard piano or accordion.

Because of its importance as a vehicle for self-knowledge and spiritual attainment Lubavitchers have begun to use a variety of musics as "emissaries" to attract new adherents to the group and as pedagogical tools to introduce Habadic concepts to those just entering the community. Performed frequently at Lubavitcher-run schools, camps, small home gatherings, and other meeting places, both in and outside the Crown Heights community, these tunes not only enliven and inspire a gathering, but, in the Lubavitcher view, reach the heart of even the most stubbornly nonobservant Jew. The popular Jewish song, "Ufaratzto" (see Figure 3.4), has become, in recent years, somewhat of a rallying cry for Lubavitchers in that it's text, taken from Genesis 28:14, enthusiastically urges one to "go forth" and spread *Hasidut* to the west, east, north, and south. It is frequently sung at camps, school, and other gatherings for baalei teshuvah.

Although Lubavitchers who have been Orthodox from birth, especially the younger, unmarried ones, often participate in musical activities, it is the baalei teshuvah who excel as teachers of new members. Older Lubavitchers say that the baalei teshuvah still have the drive and energy to accomplish the difficult task of translating Habadic concepts to those unfamiliar with such ideas, and that they are especially well suited to the task because their own transformation is still occurring. After all, a baal teshuvah understands, perhaps better than a lifetime Lubavitcher, how much of the mundane, modern world one must give up to lead a truly observant life. That is why, in fact, they have been given the honorific title baal teshuvah—every Jew does teshuvah, but only one who has given up everything to do so is truly a master (Schneerson 1990).

Figure 3.4 Ufaratzto
Performed by Habad Choir on NICHOACH, 1969.
Transcribed by Ellen Koskoff

Many baalei teshuvah who have recently entered the community have had considerable experience with music. As is true for most of the American, white, middle class, many baalei teshuvah have had piano or other instrumental lessons, either privately or in public school. Some, such as Chaim Burston or Moshe Antelis, were professional rock musicians in their youth, and now perform both standard nigunim and newer songs, based on rock models, for a variety of audiences. Another baalat teshuvah, Ruth Dvorah Shatkin, a conservatory-trained classical musician, uses her talents as a composer and arranger of nigunim for various women's gatherings.

Thus, a new repertoire of music, never officially sanctioned by the Rebbe but used as a means of reaching a contemporary Jewish audience, has developed, often bearing a striking resemblance to rock, heavy metal, classical, and other forms of contemporary music. Two examples will suffice to illustrate how new concepts and uses of music, combined with new musical forms and technologies, have produced music that is at once accessible to a wide range of Jewish audiences, and still adheres to basic tenets of Jewish life.

The first example is Yisroel Lamm's "Philharmonic Experience," typical of a growing number of recordings of Hasidic medleys performed by classical symphony orchestras. The accompanying cassette literature states:

> The emanations of the symphony orchestra effect the heart and the mind. From euphoria to melancholia. From ecstasy to misery. The intrinsic value of music is profound. . . . Music is understanding. Music is unity. (Lamm 1988)

The tape includes various arrangements of Hasidic nigunim, including a "Carlebach Medley," arranged by Lamm from nigunim composed by Rabbi Shlomo Carlebach, a man considered by some Lubavitchers to have "fallen away" from Hasidic beliefs, and by others to have followed in the footsteps of the great Baal Shem Tov by creating a new Hasidic court in California. The music is performed by members of the Jerusalem Symphony and has the quality of any superbly produced classical music tape.

The second example is a recording known as "Radical Rappin' Rebbes," arranged by Moshe Antelis from raps composed and performed by three skilled Lubavitcher rock musicians, Solomon Bitton, Michael Herman, and Yosef Kilimick. Some of the selections include, "Aleph Beis," "Funky Dreidle," "Being Jewish," "Radical Rappin' Rebbe Rap," and an arrangement of Sam Kinnison's extraordinarily erotic "Wild Thing," called, "Shabbat Thing," performed with undulating synthesized guitar and bass. Below is the text of the opening verse:

"Shabbat Thing"

Let's do it!
Shabbat thing—I like to do the Shabbat thing.
Shabbat thing—I like to do the Shabbat thing.
Shabbat thing—I like to do the Shabbat thing.
(Words unclear) Workin' all week six days for my dough
So when Shabbes comes, I can go take it slow.
I can't do no work, because it's the day of rest.
We take a shower, all dress up, and try to look our best.
Do it every Friday night, when the sun don't shine.
The ladies do the candles and the guys do the wine.
After we pray to God, we come home, eat and sing—
And welcome the Shabbat Queen (if you know what I mean),
And we call it the Shabbat thing.
Shabbat thing—let me do the Shabbat thing (Anteles 1990).

Although most of the older, lifetime Lubavitchers regard this sort of thing as highly suspect, they do recognize its effectiveness in attracting otherwise unapproachable Jews to Hasidic life. Indeed, it was in the house of the renowned Lubavitcher musician, Rabbi and Cantor Eli Lipsker, that I first heard about "Radical Rappin' Rebbes." His son, who was watching the interview, confessed that he had recently purchased the tape, more or less as a joke. His father shrugged this off with some embarrassment, reassuring me that this was *not* Lubavitcher music—although, if it reached a Jewish soul it would have accomplished its purpose (Lipsker 1990).

CONCLUSION

Music, especially nigun, functions in Lubavitcher society as a "sound" expression of essential beliefs and values. Its use as a vehicle for self and Divine knowledge, as a channel connecting the heel of the foot with the divine head, and as a tool for spreading and teaching Hasidic values to others cannot be underestimated, for it is precisely the performance of *nigun* that ensures, like prayer, that the constant dialogue between God and man will continue. And, although local communities change, incorporating new members and adjusting to new social environments, the basic tenets and values of Lubavitcher life do not.

To Lubavitchers of past generations, the performance of music has always been regarded as a profoundly effective means of connecting the inherent Godly soul of every Jew with its Divine source. In today's America, with its many lures, both attractive and dangerous, music still functions not only as an essential expression of Hasidic beliefs, but also as a statement of positive social values. The captive, holy sparks of both the "secular," nonobservant Jew and the mundane ditty can still be freed to perform their Divine service through the performance of a heartfelt nigun, and its beauty and spirituality can bring even the most unlikely people together. As Rabbi Lipsker remarked to me—with considerable ironic amusement—"What *else* would have ever brought *us* together, but a nigun?"

NOTES

1. Lubavitchers do not keep accurate statistics on their total population, nor on the relative size of these two groups. Informally, however, most Lubavitchers agree that with the unprecedented influx of baalei teshuvah since the late 1960s, this group now outnumbers those who have been Orthodox from birth.

2. For a fuller description of this movement see Lis Harris, *Holy Days* (Summit Books 1985) and Adin Steinsaltz, *Teshuvah: A Guide for the Newly Observant Jew* (The Free Press 1982).

3. Two recent books present different sides of this controversy: Lynn Davidman's *Tradition in A Rootless World* (1991) and Debra Kaufmann's *Rachel's Daughters* (1991).

4. For a fuller explanation of kol isha in relation to musical performance, see Cherney 1985 and Koskoff 1976.

5. The word *ervah* in Maimonides's interpretation referred only to a woman of the "forbidden unions," that is, one who was not likely to become a marriage partner, one with whom a man might establish an illicit relationship. Thus, men may listen to their wives and premenstrual daughters sing. In addition, men may listen to an unmarried women, with whom a marital relationship could be possible, as well as one's wife

while she is a *niddah* (a menstruant)—because sexual intercourse would soon be possible.

6. Mrs. Nadoff resides in Pittsburgh. She has for many years taught in the Lubavitch school there, although she is not herself a Lubavitcher.

REFERENCES

Antelis, M. 1990. *Radical rappin' rebbes*. Mantelis Records Studio: R^3 Productions, 3242.

Cherney, Rabbi B. 1985. Kol isha. *The Journal of Halacha and Contemporary Society* 10, (Fall):57–75.

Davidman, L. 1991. *Tradition in a rootless world: Women turn to Orthodox Judaism*. Chicago: University of Chicago Press.

Harris, L. 1985. *Holy days: The world of a Hasidic family*. New York: Summit Books.

Kaufman, D. 1991. *Rachel's daughters*. New Brunswick: Rutgers University Press.

Koskoff, E. 1976. *The concept of nigun among Lubavitcher Hasidim in the United States*. Ann Arbor: University Microfilms.

———. 1993. Miriam sings her song: The self and other in anthropological discourse. In *Musicology and difference: Gender and sexuality in music scholarship*, ed. Ruth Solie, 149–164. Berkeley: University of California Press.

Lamm, Y. 1988. *Yisroel Lamm and the philharmonic experience*. Holyland Records and Tapes: Jerusalem.

Lipsker, E. 1990. Interview.

Lubavitch Foundation of Great Britain. 1970. *Challenge: An encounter with Lubavitch-Chabad*. London: Lubavitch Foundation.

Mindel, N. 1969. *Rabbi Schneur Zalman*. Vol. 1–3. New York: Kehot Publication Society.

Newman, L, I. 1944. *The Hasidic anthology: Tales and teachings of the Hasidim*. New York: Block Publishing Co.

Rosenblum, E. 1975. Interview.

Rosenblum, M. 1975. Interview.

Schneerson, M. M. 1990. Interview.

Steinsaltz, A. 1982. *Teshuvah: A guide for the newly observant Jew*. New York: The Free Press.

Zalmanoff, R. S., ed. 1948. *Sefer ha-nigunim*. Vol. 1. New York: Nichoach.

———. 1950. *Sefer ha-nigunim*. Vol. 2. New York: Nichoach.

CHAPTER 4

Varieties of Fundamentalist Experience: Lubavitch Hasidic and Fundamentalist Christian Approaches to Contemporary Family Life

Lynn Davidman and Janet Stocks

A major aspect of Lubavitcher Hasidism's appeal to modern secular Jews is their emphasis upon and support for the creation of "traditional" family life (Davidman 1991; Danzger 1989; Kaufman 1991; Shaffir 1983). Recent studies have found that the contested nature of gender and family in contemporary society makes Orthodox Judaism appealing to young adults who are seeking clear guidelines for establishing family lives of their own. The Orthodox community in general and the Lubavitcher community in particular (since they are highly sectarian and have more opportunity for social control) offer clear definitions of gender roles and normative guidelines for married life. The rabbis in these communities tell the recruits that the Jewish tradition offers a model of precisely the kind of family that is needed to establish stable households in the current social climate.

Although the rabbis tout their lifestyle as uniquely Jewish, students of Jewish life would do well to ask whether the rabbis' claims are simply self-congratulatory or whether the model of family they are promoting is, in fact, a distinctly Jewish vision. Most studies of Jews do not compare Jewish beliefs, ideology, and practices with those of other contemporaneous religious groups. Instead, Jews generally think of themselves as unique and do not see themselves as part of general trends in the society (Goldscheider and Zuckerman 1984). As Calvin Goldscheider and Alan Zuckerman wrote in the introduction to their comparative and contextual analysis of the impact of modernization on Jews, "efforts to explain a particular event almost always have begun with Jewish values and beliefs. . . . Generally the Jewish community has been studied with little regard for the social, ethnic, and political contexts in which Jews have lived" (Goldscheider and Zuckerman 1984:4).

Similarly, studies of the Jewish family rarely examine this construct under the lenses of social scientific analysis. Rather, "both Jews and Gentiles alike have constructed and perpetuated a romantically idealized image of the Jewish family as warm, supportive, and ever-nurturing" (Hyman and Cohen 1986:3). Stereotypes of the Jewish family abound; what is missing is an actual analysis of the images and realities of Jewish families as they compare to other families in the larger society. Jewish families can be accurately understood only when we question our assumptions about what is unique to Jewish culture and analyze the ways in which Jewish life is shaped by the larger social contexts in which Jews live.

In order to explore these questions, this chapter develops a comparative analysis of the teachings on family life in a particular religious community—the Lubavitcher Hasidim—with those comparable teachings in another sectarian religious group—fundamentalist Christians. Unlike the Lubavitchers, fundamentalist Christians are comprised of a wide range of denominations and communities. Since all congregations are independent, there are variations in faith and practice among them. Nevertheless, despite their independence, scholars claim that "Fundamentalist Churches exhibit a remarkable uniformity" (Ammerman 1987:19), especially in their teachings concerning gender and the family. By comparing and contrasting the way that two sectarian groups from different religious traditions—Jewish and Christian—approach the dilemmas of family life in contemporary society, we attempt to tease out what is distinctively Jewish from what is a more common response to broader social forces. In analyzing Hasidic and fundamentalist models of family life, our analysis focuses upon their teachings on courtship, family life, sexuality, and gender—in short, those issues that are highly contested in contemporary society.

Issues of personal life have been a central theme in the teachings and writings of conservative religious leaders. Their guidelines in this area are fundamental elements of their religious ways of life. Members' and recruits' accounts of their attraction to these groups emphasize the appeal of the conventional nuclear family and clearly defined gender roles that they find in the group (Ammerman 1987; Danzger 1989; Davidman 1991; Kaufman 1991; Nietz 1987; Warner 1988). Thus, the subject of marriage and family provides a fruitful arena for exploring similarities and differences across religious traditions. Our analysis seeks to delineate how the similarities between Lubavitcher Hasidim and Fundamentalists are a result of the groups' needs to respond to similar issues in the larger society and how their differences reflect their distinct traditions and heritage.

In their discussions of courtship, marriage, gender, and sexuality, the representatives of both groups claim that their guidelines are compelling because they represent a tried-and-true way of life, dating back to the origin of the tradition. However, studies of contemporary fundamentalist, charismatic, and evangelical Christians (Lechner 1985; Nietz 1987; Warner 1988; Ammerman 1987), as well as Orthodox Jews (Davidman 1991, Heilman 1978), emphasize that these groups, which claim to be "fundamental," are actually modern products developed in an attempt to resist the secularizing forces of modern society. As Nancy Ammerman wrote in her study of fundamentalist Christians, "Fundamentalism could not exist without modernity" (Ammerman 1987:3). Fundamentalism arose as a movement only when the old Orthodoxy encountered the challenges of modern pluralism and critical scholarship. It is most prevalent in those social locations "where tradition is meeting modernity, rather than where modernity is most remote" (ibid. 8). Thus, although fundamentalists and Orthodox Jews claim that their way of life represents an ancient and unbroken tradition, in fact their current religious organizations and ideas are actually constructed anew—in response to modernity—and then legitimated in "traditional" theological terms.

The use of the adjective "traditional" requires further discussion. Modern society is fraught with ambivalence and confusion about the meaning and abiding value of tradition. While politicians, advertising agencies, the mass media, and fundamentalist religious groups appeal to the nostalgic value of tradition, others reject the authority of established patterns and celebrate the increased freedoms available in a modern society. Nevertheless, it is not clear what people are referring to when they speak of traditional ways of life: for example, some scholars have recently pointed out that what individuals now refer to as the "traditional" family is in fact a product of nineteenth-century Victorian culture. As the anthropologist James Clifford emphasizes, in the twentieth century there are no continuous cultures and traditions: "Everywhere individuals and groups improvise local performances from recollected pasts, drawing on foreign media, symbols, and languages" (Clifford 1988:14).

None of these improvised performances, however, are constructed anew out of whole cloth. Each builds upon an inherited culture with its own distinct perspectives and traditions. By sorting out the characteristics that vary and are similar across religious traditions, we can analyze the ways in which tradition and modernity intermingle and stay separate. These Christian and Jewish groups have not been compared systematically in this way before. Such a comparison provides a useful case study for analyzing which aspects of a culture are more open to integrating modern ideals and behavior patterns, and which are not.

Christian and Jewish teachings are shaped not only by their distinct religious traditions, but by their social location in contemporary American society. Fundamentalist Christians are a much larger group than are the Lubavitchers, and they share more of the values of the wider culture. Hasidic Jews are a very small minority—numerically and cognitively—in the larger American society. Therefore, although both Hasidim and Fundamentalists, as sectarian groups, seek to establish boundaries between themselves and the wider society, for the Hasidim, the maintenance of strong boundaries is more essential to the group's survival. Thus, Lubavitcher Hasidim have many boundary-creating devices that reinforce the borders of the community from other Jewish groups as well as from the larger society. They have a distinct style of dress that sets them apart, they do not observe national holidays, and they avoid participation in popular culture. A great deal of the Lubavitcher Hasidic teachings, those heard by L. Davidman at Bais Chana, and those that appear in their publications, such as Rabbi Manis Friedman's *Doesn't Anybody Blush Anymore?* (1990), are instructions for reinstituting boundaries in our intimate lives.

THE POSTMODERN FAMILY CRISIS

In the late 1950s, sociologist C. Wright Mills wrote that "[w]e are at the ending of what is called The Modern Age" and it "is being succeeded by a post-modern period" (Mills 1959:165–166). Just as the original sociological project involved an attempt to discover the nature of "modern" society and what made it distinct from other forms, so many contemporary social scientists, philosophers, and cultural critics have been attempting to delimit the parameters and characteristics of this new, "postmodern" period in history. This phase is characterized by an overarching sense of "ephemerality, fragmentation, discontinuity," and chaos (Harvey 1989:44), the sense that there are no longer any overarching metanarratives that make sense of the lives of individuals within a larger society and that depict where this society is heading (Lyotard as quoted in Clifford and Marcus 1986:249). Instead, as Jameson writes, postmodernity is a pastiche, a hodgepodge drawn from many elements, with no sense of an overarching normative mooring; it sees "the jumbling of elements as all there is" (ibid.). Postmodernity is, in the words of Clive Dilnot, "an uncertainty, an insecurity, a doubt" (as quoted in Stacey 1990:16–17).

This normative confusion—the lack of a perceived overarching moral vision and pattern for life—has been felt at the most intimate level over the past three decades. The "modern family," that social form that originated with the industrial era and consisted of a nuclear family with a breadwinning husband, a full-time homemaker wife, and their children, has been eroding. Several social forces combine to aid this process of erosion, such as the switch from an industrial to a service economy that depends more and more on women's cheap labor, the rising divorce rates which highlight the contradictions in a marriage based on romantic love, and the emergence of alternative family forms—single-parent families, individuals living alone, cohabitation, and gay and lesbian units. Judith Stacey and others have termed "the fruits of these diverse efforts to remake contemporary life 'the postmodern family.' . . . Post words imply . . . the radical transformation of a familiar pattern of activity and the emergence of new fields of cultural activity whose contours are still unclear" (Stacey 1990:17). Postmodern family arrangements, like postmodern culture in general, are characterized by diversity, fluidity, and continuous reconstitution. Contemporary gender and kinship arrangements are contested, ambivalent, and undecided.

This characteristic confusion in a basic arena of private life is enormously troubling to many individuals who feel uncertain about how to constitute satisfactory gender and family arrangements. Some contemporary conservative religious groups—ultra-Orthodox Jews, evangelical and fundamentalist Christians, charismatic Catholics, and others—appeal to these individuals by offering a very clearly defined, authoritative model of gender roles and family life. They tap into and build upon a nostalgia for simpler times when "girls were girls and men were men" by offering clearly delimited gender roles and a model of a nuclear family that they claim is the "traditional" one. In fact, the family images they promote resemble the modern family, born in the 19th century, and now on its way out. Religious leaders imbue this particular historical variant of the "ideal" family form with stronger authority and roots, by claiming that this model was spelled out in the original religious texts such as the Bible.

METHODS

In order to obtain information on the religious teachings concerning courtship, marriage, sexuality, and gender in these two communities, we have relied on the following sources of data: The information on Lubavitcher Hasidism was obtained by fieldwork conducted by L. Davidman at Bais Chana, a Lubavitcher residential program for resocializing secular Jewish women to Orthodoxy. There, she attended classes for 10–12 hours a day with the new recruits and took extensive notes on all the teachings, many of which centered on the issues of gender, marriage, and sexuality (this research is described in detail in Davidman 1990a, 1990b, and 1991). She interviewed several rabbis there as well. In addition, the authors read Lubavitcher publications on these topics (Friedman 1990, Lubavitch Women's Organization 1981).

For sources on fundamentalists and their teachings on gender, marriage, and family, we relied both on primary and secondary data. Primary data was obtained from the numerous Christian publications on these topics, such as the books of Tim and Beverly LaHaye, James Dobson, Anthony Evans, Jerry Fallwell, and other ministers and Christian counselors. We selected our sources in the following ways: we asked well-known researchers in this area to suggest the most popular and respected authors in the field, we went into a Christian bookstore and asked the manager to show us the books in this area that sell most widely, and J. Stocks spent time in two Pittsburgh-area evangelical church libraries, collecting readings from their shelves relevant to this study. In addition, we relied on other researchers' accounts of fundamentalist communities (e.g. Ammerman 1987; Marsden 1984; Lawless 1988). Since both scholars and practitioners agree that evangelical Christian groups—from the most moderate to the most conservative—share similar teachings about gender and personal life, and that the lines on the Christian right are not so readily and neatly drawn, we drew upon the teachings of those most widely cited by other fundamentalists. The LaHayes' writings are a fair representation of Christian fundamentalism, since every author we have read—including conservatives James Dobson and Jerry Fallwell—refer their readers and audiences to the LaHayes, attesting to their acceptance among the wide spectrum of evangelicals, including those at the far right. Since Lubavitcher Hasidim are socially conservative, engage in "outreach" work that makes them widely known, and have numerous publications available in Jewish bookstores, we thought that their teachings could fruitfully be compared with the most widely accepted writings of Christian fundamentalists.

RELIGIOUS RECONSTRUCTIONS OF THE TRADITIONAL FAMILY

A dominant theme in contemporary fundamentalist religious groups (both Hasidic and Christian) is the centrality of the "traditional" family in religious life, and beyond that, for the survival of society. A shared interpretation of the current situation is that families, and consequently society, are coming apart and that a return to the traditional teachings of Orthodoxy or fundamentalism is needed.

In both Lubavitcher Hasidic and fundamentalist Christian communities, the breakdown of the family and society is attributed to the loss of borders that characterizes postmodern culture. Both communities use the term "borders" quite frequently in their literature. Without clear and secure boundaries, the foundational institution of society—the family—is threatened. As Rabbi Friedman, the primary teacher at the Lubavitcher institute Bais Chana wrote,

> The loss of borders even threatens to destroy families. Family life used to be a very strong border. A person's family was like a little world unto itself. There was a border that set the family territory apart from the non-family, what was private from what was public. Family was family; home was home. (1990:xviii)

These borders of the family were based on "loyalty, respect, and trust." As a result of the weakening of these borders, "family life is suffering" (ibid.). As a corrective to these pervasive troubles in the private realm, Rabbi Friedman offers a solution: "if our lives are not quite right today, if our relationships need fixing, if we want to know how to solve the problems of society, the solution is to strengthen our borders, and by that we mean morality" (ibid.:xxi).

Fundamentalist Christians, too, urge the strengthening of the boundaries of society and the family. Jerry Fallwell wrote,

> It used to be that the borders of the world were very clear. Day was day, night was night, good was good and bad was bad. Today the whole world is suffering from a pervasive loss of borders. . . . When the borders of the world fall, when the walls of morality fall, everything falls. To have no borders at all is to live with insecurity. (1981:101)

When family borders are strengthened, people's lives will be much more satisfactory. As Ammerman wrote about the fundamentalist Christians she studied,

> believers point to evidence that Fundamentalist homes are much more successful than others. . . . The fact that their marriages are surviving when divorce is so pervasive reassures them that using God's plan for husbands and wives is indeed the only right way to structure a marriage. (Ammerman 1987:134)

These religious groups believe that if we as a society would only return to the "traditional" family form, many other societal ills would be cured. "Once wanderers came 'home' and the poor acquired the sense of responsibility found in strong Christian familiality, poverty would cease in the world today" (Marsden 1980:37, as cited in Yuval-Davis 1991:13). In order to teach their members how to construct the type of family that would save our society, religious leaders in both communities spend a considerable amount of time and energy providing guidelines for establishing these goals.

Forming the Marital Bond

The first issue to be considered in the formation of families is the role of singles in the community. In Judaism, there is no place for singles. The Lubavitcher Hasidim make this very clear to their newcomers by such remarks as this one made by the Dean of Women at Bais Chana, "a single person is only a half of a person; people are incomplete unless they are married." Rabbi Friedman made the same point in his class at Bais Chana one day,

> Each of us needs to experience the pain of halfness in order to get married. Without feeling our own halfness, we aren't able to let someone else into our lives. We need to feel that we really are half and not whole; and that by remaining alone we'll never be whole.

In contrast, many fundamentalists do allow some room for singles in their community, and quote 1 Corinthians 7:8 to that effect: "To the unmarried and the widows, I say that it is well for them to remain single as I do. But if they say they cannot exercise self-control, they should marry for it is better to marry than to be aflame with passion." Practically speaking, however, single adults often experience a hard time finding a place in a fundamentalist Christian community. In Nancy Ammerman's study, she described a woman in her late thirties who

> finally left the Church when she could find no place for a person like herself. Another single woman, in her twenties, said, "If I had a family of my own, I'd probably go to the Church and I'd probably want my children to have that background. But for myself to go. . . . ' Being different means not fully being integrated into the life of the Church. (Ammerman 1987:112)

Just as Lubavitcher Hasidim have institutionalized mechanisms for ensuring that its members get married (they have *shadchanim* [matchmakers] and arranged marriages), some fundamentalist Christian communities are recognizing the needs of their singles and creating support and fellowship to keep these people in the church. However, in contrast to the Hasidim, the fundamentalists claim that their singles ministry "is not meant to promote singleness, nor is it meant to promote marriage. It is meant to lovingly meet the needs and interests of a major part of our population" (Campbell 1986:12).

The greater emphasis upon the necessity of marriage in the Hasidic community reflects differences between the religious customs of Judaism and Christianity: Judaism has no tradition of celibacy as a desirable state, whereas Christianity does. In addition, Jews may emphasize marriage more in order to promote high birth rates. Their minority status, coupled with the losses of millions in the Holocaust, motivates some contemporary Jewish leaders to push for high birth rates among Jews.

Courtship

The importance of courtship to fundamentalist religious groups that emphasize the family is obvious, since the initial selection of a partner will significantly shape the nature of the religious household that is established. All groups under examination encourage their members to carefully select a marriage partner who shares their religious faith. In comparison with Christians, however, Hasidim establish much stronger boundaries around their members' courtship behavior.

Within the Lubavitcher community, as well as in other ultra-Orthodox Jewish groups, dating is highly regulated. Young adults are allowed to date only when they are ready to get married. As Pearl Lebovic, a *shadchan* (matchmaker) in the Lubavitcher community, told the women at Bais Chana during a guest lecture,

> We start to date when we're old enough and serious enough to think about being married. When we do go out, it's with someone who has the same values we do. Usually, we come from families who know each other, or we have a mutual friend who thinks we're compatible and introduces us.

For the newly Orthodox Lubavitchers, dates are arranged by a third party and the couple is encouraged to go out only a few times and decide upon the person's suitability as a marriage partner. Among those who are brought up in the Lubavitcher community, parents are responsible for arranging for offsprings' mates. This tradition of arranged marriages has been attributed to Jews' history as a minority community in the larger culture (Lamm 1980:4–6). In Eastern Europe, Jews had matchmakers who trav-

elled between the small communities to assist Jews in finding partners. Given that Hasidim are a small minority group in the wider
American society, it makes sense that they would need to meet
through a matchmaker, too. Although in Crown Heights the
Lubavitchers are not a minority, Lubavitchers from birth are
sometimes introduced to mates from other cities and countries. In
addition, the arrangement of marriages allows the community to
shelter its youth and maintain control over the patterns of family
formations.

The fundamentalists, too, are concerned that members court
only other members. Timothy LaHaye, a fundamentalist author
who writes extensively on intimate relationships advises: "date
only Christians for dating is the prelude to marriage" (LaHaye
1976:262). Christians are warned of the difficulties that could
ensue if "unequally yoked" with a nonbeliever. "Be ye not
unequally yoked together with unbelievers: for what fellowship
hath righteousness with unrighteousness: and what communion
hath light with darkness?" (2 Cor. 6:14).

But although the fundamentalists encourage individuals to
date only members of their own group, they do not have such
elaborately devised mechanisms for assuring that its members get
married to the right person. Singles fellowships, while not explicitly devised to encourage marriage, do provide single adults within
the community with a way to meet other single adults who share
their faith. Because Christians are a majority in the population,
they have less basis for concern about adherents finding partners
outside the faith. In addition, the procedures for the "conversion"
of a partner from outside the faith are much more cumbersome in
the Jewish tradition. It is not surprising, then, to find these differences in teachings concerning courtship.

Guidelines for a Happy Marriage

Hasidim and fundamentalist Christians are so opposed to divorce
that their leaders liberally proffer advice on how to achieve a successful marriage. In the Lubavitcher community studied by Davidman, a large percentage of Rabbi Friedman's classes were devoted
to teaching the young women how to have a happy marriage
within the norms of the community. Friedman's recently published book, *Doesn't Anybody Blush Anymore?* (1990), deals
with the same topic, as does the Lubavitcher publication *The*

Modern Jewish Woman (Lubavitch Women's Organization 1981) and other advice manuals written by and for the ultra-Orthodox community.

Underlying many of Rabbi Friedman's guidelines for private life is the conviction that establishing a variety of strong borders will strengthen the family. For example, one major theme in his talks and writings is the need for individual privacy in the context of an intimate relationship. He writes,

> [W]hy do we think that getting close to someone means we have to know their every private thought? We're insulted when those we love won't tell us everything. We accuse them of "hiding" from us, and we're hurt. But if you try to peek behind the curtains of someone else's privacy, you won't get any closer to that person. Quite the opposite: you'll become estranged. In marriage, our most intimate relationship, respect for privacy is fundamental. (Friedman 1990:1)

His idea is that maintaining privacy between partners will encourage wives and husbands to protect the relationship by not being judgmental of each others' faults. His instructions for marital success emphasize that individuals need to accept their spouses, shortcomings and all, and not try to change them. Above all, maintaining friendship and intimacy requires respect for the other persons's weaknesses.

> The fact that your spouse isn't perfect shouldn't be your problem. If your husband or wife were perfect, then you wouldn't need any talent or wisdom. The idea is that this person isn't perfect, and it doesn't bother you. It's not your problem because you accept your spouse unconditionally. (Friedman 1990:6)

The idea of accepting one's partner unconditionally requires selflessness and devotion. These characteristics, too, are required for a healthy, stable marriage:

> in the context of your relationship with your spouse, you are not allowed to forget for a moment to whom you are married, to whom you are devoted. If you really want to make things better, you need to stop thinking about yourself. Stop thinking in terms of being a husband or wife; stop thinking about what you are. (Friedman 1990:14)

The selflessness required to achieve stable and harmonious marriages is Godly. As he writes, "marriage is the arena in which all we discover on the way to becoming 'like God' is put into practice" (Friedman 1990:23). When one is devoted to a relationship, one puts her/his partners' needs first. In doing so, two people merge into one. Achievement of these feelings will be accomplished through right action: individuals must act in a way that is respectful, loving, kind, and sensitive, and the feelings will follow.

In this community, the importance of romantic love, the ideal for forming relationships in contemporary culture, is largely deemphasized. Relationships should not be based upon feelings, which are fleeting. Rather, individuals should commit themselves to the roles they will play—wives, husbands, mothers, fathers— and the feelings will follow.

Among fundamentalists, the strictures against divorce are also taken very seriously. As Ammerman wrote in her book on a fundamentalist community, "The Bible decrees that husbands and wives stay together until death and that they relate to each other as Christ to the church" (Ammerman 1987:136). Leaders of this community, too, counsel right action, selflessness, devotion, and protection of one's partners' feelings as the path to stable and happy marriages. As Tim LaHaye, one of the most prolific and widely read fundamentalist ministers who writes on marriage and gender relationships states (LaHaye 1991:189), "the more you love a person the more you desire his praise. Conversely, criticism of the person with whom you share your life is devastating. For that reason, all couples should learn the art of praise rather than blame."

In another volume, he proffers advice similar to Rabbi Friedman's, encouraging his adherents to achieve stable marriages by overlooking the other person's faults and being devoted to her/ him despite them. "Ask God, the giver of love, to fill you with love for Him and for your partner so that you can genuinely love him in spite of his weaknesses. Look at his strengths and thank God for them" (LaHaye 1968:22).

In these practical guidelines for how to achieve a happy marriage, there are no distinct differences between the two communities. Rather, the advice by leaders in both groups seems to be largely shaped by the kind of psychological advice available in the wider society.

Reestablishing Gender Boundaries

Leaders of both communities are convinced that instituting traditional gender roles will reestablish order in the family and in society. At a time when these definitions are blurred and the boundaries and hierarchies are unclear, these religious communities share the goal of reinstating clear boundaries between the two sexes.

Their definition of the proper gender roles reinforces the centrality of marriage and childrearing in a woman's life. As the Dean of Women at Bais Chana told the group in a special class on women's roles,

> A woman must have children. . . . It fulfills her femininity to stay with her children. That is what femininity is. I feel it is a privilege to change my child's diaper. The radical women's movement is an aberration. They have lost the maternal instincts, the feminist instincts that are truly feminine. And this to me is truly feminine and feminism and what they have become is anti-male and I think that I have tremendous problems with that.

Lubavitcher philosophy posits that women's and men's biological differences are reflected in their distinct natures. Rabbi Friedman claimed that women love more easily than men and that they are more devotional. As Rabbi Friedman told his class one morning,

> It is more feminine to be devotional than to be narcissistic. It is masculine to be narcissistic. Biologically, a man does not really give of himself in any real sense to have children. A woman does. That's why there is a difference in teaching men and teaching women. When you teach a woman about devotion and marriage and selflessness and altruism, what you're really telling her is be yourself. The biological function is consistent with the rest of her so that the way her body behaves is also the way the rest of her mind behaves and it's also the way her soul behaves.

The idea that women are naturally devotional and selfless reinforces the community's traditional definitions of women's roles in the family. Lubavitcher women are told that they should not pursue their own selfish gains; rather, their own inner biological and spiritual natures demand that they devote themselves to their husbands, children, and the larger Jewish community. By presenting the communities' role choices as rooted in biology, Rabbi Friedman imbues them with an aura of necessity.

These ultra-Orthodox Jews are opposed to feminism because feminism emphasizes the egalitarian division of roles and the need for women to fulfill themselves. As Rabbi Friedman told the women at Bais Chana,

> The flavor that feminism carries is a very narcissistic one and the flavor that Yiddishkeit carries is a very selfless one. I don't think narcissism is necessarily feminine. That is why, for many women to relearn devotion, to replace the narcissism with devotion, is really a very natural thing because it's more feminine to be devotional than to be narcissistic.

In addition, they are opposed to feminism because they see it as a recent innovation that could not possibly stand against such a long-standing tradition as Judaism. Feminism is seen as antifamily and therefore as opposed to basic Jewish beliefs and practices.

Christian fundamentalists, too, see feminism as antifamily. In fact, in Christianity, the hierarchical division of roles in the family is made quite explicit. Leaders rely on the quotation from Paul stating that wives must submit to their husbands just as all must submit to Christ, the head of the Church:

> Wives be subject to your husbands as to the Lord. For the husband is the head of the wife as Christ is the head of the church, his body, and is himself its Savior. As the church is subject to Christ, so let wives also be subject in everything to their husbands. (Ephesians 5:22–24)

In many ways, fundamentalist Christian ministers attempt to discourage women's independence. As Tim LaHaye wrote,

> If the wife works and keeps her money separate from her husband's, it breeds a feeling of independence and self-sufficiency which God did not intend married women to have. I am convinced that one of the reasons young married couples divorce so readily today is because the wife is not economically dependent upon her husband. (LaHaye 1968:29)

Betty DeBerg (1990), in her discussion of the rise of the first wave of American fundamentalism in the nineteenth century explains that Victorian gender roles were an integral element of fundamentalism. In this ideology, there were separate spheres: the public world of work and politics and the private world of the home.

Men were naturally suited to the battlefield of the public sphere, while women's inherent qualities enabled them to set up the home as a peaceful refuge for the men (Lasch 1977; Welter 1966; Aidala 1985; Ehrenreich and English 1978; Ginsburg 1989; Ryan 1975). According to the Victorian gender conceptions, men, who are meant to be the breadwinners, are aggressive, strong, intelligent, and sexually driven. Women, on the other hand, who are created to be homemakers, have personalities that are submissive, physically weak, passive, spiritual, emotional, and sexually pure. Although there have been some changes and loosening of these roles over the past century, even within fundamentalism, it is this Victorian conception of gender differences that is nostalgically called upon as the "traditional" one to which fundamentalist teachings would like its members to return (Stacey 1990, DeBerg 1990).

Sexuality

The two groups' teachings about sexuality revealed the greatest between-group differences. Certainly there are significant similarities, such as the restrictions both groups placed upon the free expression of sexuality. Common to both are restrictions against any form of extramarital sex. As Timothy LaHaye warns: "All sexual intercourse outside marriage is condemned in the Bible; consequently you will never be a strong, growing Christian while practicing free love" (LaHaye 1976:267).

Another common, interesting similarity is the device of "tabula rasa" employed in both communities, as a way to deal with the issues of worldly formerly secular women, who are supposed to be virginal at their religious marriages. Many adult newcomers to conservative religious communities face the problem of past sexual relations that are seen as unacceptable in their new faith. Born-again theology provides a mechanism by which those past indiscretions can be erased, through the concept of tabula rasa, the idea that one's life before conversion is morally irrelevant (Stacey and Gerard 1990:105; Friedman 1990:90). In this way, those who have participated in the sexual norms of the secular culture can start anew to search for a more satisfying and acceptable sexual lifestyle.

Another similarity between these groups is that both see sexuality as related to Godliness. In a pamphlet entitled "Reunion,"

Pearl Lebovic wrote the following description of sexuality—"serving as the vehicle through which G-d shares His creative power with Man, the union of husband and wife in Judaism, is a sacred act that is blessed by God (regardless of whether a particular union is procreative or not)" (Lebovic n.d.). Timothy LaHaye similarly writes that "the act of marriage is that beautiful and intimate relationship shared uniquely by a husband and wife in the privacy of their love—and it is sacred. In a real sense, God designed them for that relationship" (LaHaye 1976:11).

However, the differences between the two groups's teachings in this area are even more striking than the similarities. The most notable of these differences are the Jewish laws that establish boundaries around the free expression of sexuality even within marriage, the laws of *taharat hamishpacha*. These laws establish that marital relations are permitted only during certain times of the month—they are forbidden during a woman's menstrual period and for seven days thereafter. In describing these laws, Jewish leaders argue that they actually promote passionate love since the required separation gives rise to passion. As Rabbi Friedman wrote,

> After all, husband and wife were once strangers. Male is different from female, so in essence they must remain strangers. Because of this, the love between them can never be casual, consistent, or calm. . . . This acquired love is naturally more intense then the love between brother and sister. When love has to overcome a difference, a distance, an obstacle, it needs energy to leap across and bridge the gap. This is the energy of fiery love. (Friedman 1990:72)

Because the gap between husband wife will never really close, their love for one another will continually have to reach across it. There will be distance, separation, then a bridging of distance, and a coming back together, again and again. This sense of distance intensifies the desire to merge. Writes Friedman,

> When we say "no" to unhealthy situations we are building the walls of our dwelling place. When we thus define our inner life we become capable of intimacy. The real meaning of intimacy is that, under certain circumstances, we can invite someone into our private place. (Friedman 1990:60)

The ultra-Orthodox laws regarding separation and establishment of boundaries include rules that limit the locations in which physical affection may be expressed: husbands and wives may not touch each other in public, not even at home. Rabbi Friedman explained this to his class at Bais Chana as follows:

> In a traditional Jewish home, husbands and wives only touch each other in privacy. Children raised in such a home never see their parents hugging or expressing any kind of physical affection, even playfully. From this, children learn that family love is structured in two ways: the love between man and woman, and the love between parents and child. That's a healthy message.

Pearl Lebovic, reiterated this message in her guest lecture:

> A hug and a kiss is childish; it's what you do with children. A peck on the cheek is for a baby. Adults have more serious, more responsible, more adult forms of affection. Husband and wife need not touch each other casually or in public; they should avoid casual nudity; and vulgarities, which are inappropriate in mixed company, should also be inappropriate for the home.

However, despite these strict regulations on the expression of marital sexuality, Orthodox Jews, including Hasidim, encourage husbands and wives to achieve satisfying sexual relations, as long as they are in appropriate settings and at the proper times. In addition, the tradition states that men are obligated to fulfill their wives sexually. The generations of rabbis who interpreted the law tried to spell out in detail what that meant. But these texts are generally not ones that newcomers to Orthodoxy—or even most ordinary Orthodox Jewish women and men in contemporary society—are likely to regularly refer to as sources. Instead, contemporary Rabbis and Jewish community leaders have written manuals on marriage and sexuality. What is most noteworthy about these manuals is their inexplicitness; the language about sexuality is highly glossed-over. For example, contemporary ultra-Orthodox and Hasidic marriage manuals generally do not even use the word sex but rather employ euphemisms such as "physical union between husbands and wives." Their use of dispassionate language is related to their understanding of Jewish modesty laws, which are based upon the Biblical quotation, "The entire glory of the daughter of the King lies on the inside" (Psalms 45:14).

For example, Pearl Lebovic demonstrated this use of euphemistic language when talking about sex in the Hasidic community. As she wrote in the brochure, "Reunion,"

In Judaism Hashem rejoices when a couple finds each other. We call it a reunion . . . their soul is one to begin with. The physical union of husband and wife is a physical expression of that spiritual union. Hashem is there—the third partner in all unions. Hashem is happy when a couple that is married properly enjoy each other and express their love physically. (Lebovic n.d.)

In contrast, there is a fairly wide selection of Christian sex manuals available which are very explicit and encourage open communication within marriage about sexual pleasure. One can walk into a shopping mall in any suburban community and find these books on the shelves of Christian bookstores. These manuals encourage Christians to

Keep the lines of communication on these matters open between you and your husband so that there is no misunderstanding. Most natural differences can be ironed out and a happy physical adjustment effected if two people will talk frankly about them. (LaHaye 1968:71)

Sexual relationships are explicitly described in the Christian marriage books we examined. T. LaHaye writes that sex is good and that Christianity does not believe in twin beds (LaHaye 1968:153–54). His books actually contain precise guidelines for how to bring one's partner to orgasm, including how to do oral sex. In contrast to the Hasidim, who are enormously reticent about these matters, LaHaye encourages people to not be shy in talking about these matters with their spouses. "When conversation is prohibited on the subject of sex, the act of intercourse takes on the atmosphere of a 'performance,' each partner feeling that he is being critically evaluated by the other." Beverly LaHaye, his wife, who also writes about Christian marriage, was asked by a woman how she can communicate what she likes as a wife, so that her husband understands? She told this woman, "Talk frankly to him. If you are unsatisfied, say so. Most women find it difficult to converse with their husbands about sex which merely increases their frustration" (LaHaye 1976:259).

The significant differences between Hasidim and Fundamentalists in this area are due both to Jewish tradition and the long-standing emphasis upon the laws of modesty, and also to the fact that as a distinct minority in the wider culture, Hasidim are more concerned about creating boundaries. As Rabbi Friedman stated, "when we say 'no' to what is not allowed, we establish a protec-

tive circle of modesty. And within this circle we create for our-
selves a private, peaceful place that says, 'This is who we are and
this is where we belong.'"

Birth Control

The Lubavitcher Hasidim further create boundaries around sexuality by forbidding birth control except under certain circumstances. As Rabbi Friedman told the women in class one day,

> The purpose of marriage is children. That is a polite way of talk-
> ing about the physical relationship between a husband and his
> wife. . . . The Torah sets it up so that the time to renew relations
> is the time she is the most likely to conceive.

On another occasion he told them that

> for a woman to wait to have children would be tampering with
> her native condition. I think birth control, whether it's pills or
> whatever, is a violent violation of a woman's being. Not just
> physically but psychically. It really hurts the psyche to say, plug
> yourself up; don't let it happen. . . . Ultimately the sexual act
> means for a woman, biologically, psychically, emotionally, it
> means opening yourself up to what is and what is; is pregnancy.

The community's strictures against birth control are reinforced by rooting them in women's own biological beings. Just as
women have no choice about whether to pursue their own self-ful-
fillment, because their biology demands that they be selfless and
devotional, so their own bodies demand that they be open to as
many children as God might provide. A Lubavitcher pamphlet
warns members of the group that family planning actually leads
to marital discord:

> Compare now with previous generations, esp. in Jewish homes,
> where family planning was unthinkable. The divorce rate was
> infinitesimal, respect and harmony between spouses legendary
> in the eyes of the world. (Hanitzotz n.d.:21)

In contrast, the fundamentalist Christian groups we studied
do not have such strict norms against the use of birth control. As
Tim LaHaye wrote,

> Virtually every couple practices some form of birth control, for
> otherwise families would be much larger than they are. If the
> partners do not use one or more of the scientific methods

described in chapter 11, they at least practice abstinence during the wife's most fertile time. However, this seems unfair to the wife, because that is the time when she would find lovemaking most enjoyable. Rather than cheat her out of the pleasure God designed for her to enjoy in marriage, it would be better to use a proven contraceptive. But as we warned in chapter 11, though we believe God does not oppose limiting the size of one's family to the number of children one can effectively raise to serve Him, we do think He never intended parents to use birth control devices to exclude children. (LaHaye 1976:256)

Ammerman reports that in the community she studied, women generally saw conception as something outside of their control: "birth control (other than abortion) is not openly condemned. Few members limit or plan their families. Neither do they seek help with infertility" (Ammerman 1987:141). Instead they pray that God will bless them with the families they want, and accept what they receive as God's will.

The differences between the Hasidim and fundamentalists on the matter of birth control can be seen to derive both from the distinct religious traditions they draw upon, and from their disparate statuses in the wider society. In particular, the destruction of millions of Jews by the Nazis earlier in this century is often cited as a reason to not limit family size in Jewish families of the present generation.

CONCLUSIONS

As religious minorities who are attempting to establish sectarian communities within the larger society, the Lubavitcher Hasidim and fundamentalist Christians share some similar approaches. In a society in which the patriarchal family is on its way out and postmodern families are coming in, these groups nostalgically recall better times when gender roles were clear and marriages lasted. Both groups, in their attempts to solve the dilemmas of family life in modern society, provide explicit guidelines for "traditional" gender roles and the maintenance of nuclear families. Their suggestions for achieving happy marriages—ignoring one's partner's faults and respecting her/his privacy—were remarkably alike and suggest that both groups are influenced by contemporary self-help literature.

Despite these similarities, however, there were important distinctions between the Hasidic and fundamentalist teachings in several key areas of family life: the role of singles in the tradition, norms guiding courtship, birth control laws, and the rules concerning the expression of marital sexuality. We can understand these differences sociologically as rooted in the groups' distinct locations in contemporary society, as well as in their different religious heritages. Fundamentalist Christians are numerically dominant and have more political power than do the Lubavitchers. They share more of the values of the dominant culture and see their mission as transforming society so that it better conforms more with their ways of life. In contrast, the Lubavitchers want to "convert" only Jews. As a minority within the culture, the Lubavitchers have to set up strong group boundaries. Arranging marriages for members is one way of maintaining these tight borders and controlling the inflow of divergent worldviews. Their minority status may also affect their desire to promote their own population growth by discouraging singleness, arranging marriages, and prohibiting birth control.

In addition, each religious group has a distinct heritage. Although we recognize that these groups are neotraditional, modern constructs, each group is nevertheless shaped by its heritage and religious legacy. Each religious approach draws upon a body of texts as well as an oral tradition that is there to be worked over—added to, deleted from. These distinct traditions are visible in the different approaches to singleness and courtship in the two communities. The ancient rabbis discouraged adults from remaining single, especially because it prevented them from fulfilling the Biblical commandment to "be fruitful and multiply." In contrast, there are statements in the New Testament supporting single life. Their diverse traditions shape the group's current teachings about singleness and also their customs about arranging marriages. If it is imperative that young members of a community marry, their compliance will be greatly assisted by adults arranging these affairs for them.

Jewish restrictions on marital sexuality are related to the particular content of Judaism as a religion—the ancient rabbis spelled out detailed laws governing every minute aspect of daily life, including the patterns of sexual relations between wives and husbands. The laws of family purity are part of the cultural heritage that Lubavitchers draw upon, even as they legitimize them in terms of the modern concept that individuals will derive satisfaction from them, since enforced separations create a sense of honeymoon each month. The Christian tradition has no such laws and thus does not limit the joint sexual activities of married couples.

The strictness of birth control sanctions in the Hasidic community also relates to another, more recent aspect of Jewish history—the Holocaust. The systematic slaughter of the Jews of Europe has left Jewish leaders with a sense of urgency about replenishing the population. Since it is essential to replace the lost souls with new, Jewish ones, control over the selection of marriage partners is essential.

In this essay we have begun to compare how different sectarian religious groups construct particular neo-orthodox religious cultures that are shaped both by their inherited traditions, and the dynamics of life in contemporary society. Typically, ethnographic studies of religion focus upon one religious tradition or group and do not provide comparisons between groups. By engaging in careful, nuanced analyses of the similarities and differences between religious groups, sociologists of religion will develop more sophisticated analyses of each one, and how it fits into the broader social context.

REFERENCES

Aidala, A. A. 1985. Social change, gender roles, and new religious movements. *Sociological Analysis* 46 (3):287–314.

Ammerman, N. T. 1987. *Bible believers*. New Brunswick: Rutgers University Press.

Bendroth, M. L. 1984. The search for "women's role" in American evangelicalism, 1930–1980. In *Evangelicalism and modern America*, ed. George Marsden, 122–134. Grand Rapids, MI: William B. Eerdmans Publishing Co.

Campbell, B. 1986. Single truth. *Pentecostal Evangel* 3781:12–13.

Clifford, J. 1988. *The predicament of culture: Twentieth century ethnography, literature, and art*. Cambridge: Harvard University Press.

Clifford, J., and G. E. Marcus, eds. 1986. *Writing culture: The poetics and politics of ethnography*. Berkeley: University of California Press.

Danzger, M. H. 1989. *Returning to tradition: The contemporary revival of Orthodox Judaism*. New Haven: Yale University Press.

Davidman, L. 1988. Gender and religious experience. Paper presented at the meetings of the American Sociological Association, Atlanta, Georgia, August.

————. 1990a. Accommodation and resistance: A comparison of two contemporary Orthodox Jewish groups." *Sociological Analysis* 51 (1):35–51.

————. 1990b. Women's search for family and roots: A Jewish religious solution to a modern dilemma. In *In Gods we trust II*, ed, Tom Robbins and Dick Anthony, 385–407. New Brunswick, NJ: Transaction Books.

————. 1991. *Tradition in a rootless world: Women turn to Orthodox Judaism*. Berkeley: University of California Press.

Davidman, L., and S. Tenenbaum. 1990. Towards a feminist sociology of American Jews. Paper presented at the meetings of the Association for the Sociology of Religion, Washington, D. C., August.

Dayton, D. W., and R. K. Johnson, eds. 1991. *The variety of American evangelicalism*. Knoxville: The University of Tennessee Press.

DeBerg, B. A. 1990. *Ungodly women*. Minneapolis: Fortress Press.

Dobson, J. 1975. *What wives wish their husbands knew about women*. Wheaton, IL: Living Books.

————. 1980. *Straight talk to men and their wives*. Dallas: Word Publishing.

————. 1982. *Dr. Dobson answers your questions*. Wheaton, IL: Living Books, Tyndale House Publishers, Inc.

Ehrenreich, B., and D. English. 1978. *For her own good: 150 years of the experts' advice to women*. Garden City, New York: Anchor Press/ Doubleday.

Epstein, B. L. 1981. *The politics of domesticity*. Middletown, CT: Wesleyan University Press.

Evans, A. T. 1991. *Guiding your family in a misguided world*. Pomona, CA: Focus on the Family Publishing.

Falwell, J. 1981. *Listen America*. Toronto: Bantam.

Feldman, A. 1987. *The river, the kettle, and the bird: A Torah guide to successful marriage*. Israel: CSB Publications.

Friedfertig, R. S., and F. Schapiro, eds. 1981. *The modern Jewish woman: A unique perspective*. New York: Lubavitch Educational Foundation for Jewish Marriage Enrichment.

Friedman, M. 1990. *Doesn't anyone blush anymore?* San Francisco: Harper Collins.

Ginsburg, F. 1989. *Contested Lives: The abortion debate in an American community*. Berkeley: University of California Press.

Goldscheider, C., and A. S. Zuckerman. 1984. *The transformation of the Jews*. Chicago: University of Chicago Press.

Greenberg, B. 1983. *How to run a traditional Jewish household*. New York: Simon and Shuster.

Hanitzotz Lubavitch Educational Foundation. nd. Pamphlet.

Harding, S. 1990. If I should die before I wake: Jerry Falwell's pro-life gospel. In *Uncertain terms*, ed. Faye Ginsburg and Anna Lowenhaupt Tsing, 76–97. Boston: Beacon Press.

Harvey, D. 1989. *The Condition of postmodernity: An inquiry into the origins of cultural change*. Cambridge MA: Basil Blackwell.

Heilman, S. C. 1978. Constructing orthodoxy. *Society* 15 (May–June):32–40.

Horowitz, I. L. 1982. The new fundamentalism. *Society* 20 (Nov–Dec):40–47.

Hunter, J. D. 1983. *American evangelicalism*. New Brunswick: Rutgers University Press.

———. 1987. *Evangelicalism*. Chicago: The University of Chicago Press.

Hyman, P., and S. M. Cohen. 1986. *The Jewish family: Myths and reality*. New York: Holmes & Meier.

Kaufman, D. R. 1991. *Rachel's daughters: Newly Orthodox Jewish women*. New Brunswick: Rutgers University Press.

LaHaye, B. 1976. *The spirit-controlled woman*. Eugene, OR: Harvest House Publishers.

LaHaye, T. 1968. *How to be happy though married*. Wheaton, IL: Living Books.

———. 1991. *I love you, but why are we so different?* Eugene, Oregon: Harvest House Publishers.

LaHaye, T., and B. LaHaye. 1976. *The act of marriage*. Grand Rapids, MI: Zondervan Publishing House.

Lamm, M. 1980. *The Jewish way in love and marriage*. New York: Jonathan David Publishers.

Lasch, C. 1977. *Haven in a heartless world: The family besieged*. New York: Basic Books.

Lawless, E. J. 1988. *God's peculiar people*. Lexington: The University of Kentucky Press.

Lebovic, P. n. d. Reunion. Lubavitch Educational Foundation for Jewish Marriage Enrichment.

Lechner, F. J. 1985. Fundamentalism and sociocultural revitalization in America: A sociological interpretation. *Sociological Analysis*, 46(3):243–259.

Liebman, R. C., and R. Wuthnow, eds. 1983. *The new Christian right*. New York: Aldine Publishing Co.

Lubavitch Women's Organization. 1981. *The modern Jewish woman: A unique perspective*. New York: Lubavitch Educational Foundation for Jewish Marriage Enrichment.

Marsden, G., ed. 1984. *Evangelicalism and modern America*. Grand Rapids, MI: William B. Eerdmans Publishing Co.

McNamara, P. 1985. The New Christian Right's view of the family and its social science critics: A study of differing presuppositions. *Journal of Marriage and the Family* (May):449–458.

Mills, C. W. 1959. *The sociological imagination*. New York: Oxford University Press.

Mollenkott, V. R. 1977. *Women, men, and the Bible*. Nashville: Abingdon Press.

———. 1983. *The divine feminine*. New York: Crossroad Publishing Co.

Neitz, M. J. 1987. *Charisma and community: A study of religious commitment within the charismatic renewal*. New Brunswick, NJ: Transaction Books.

Pohli, C. V. 1983. Church closets and back doors: A feminist view of moral majority women. *Feminist Studies* 9(3):529–558.

Ridenour, F., ed. 1989. *The marriage collection*. Grand Rapids, MI: Zondervan Publishing House.

Rose, S. 1987. Women warriors: The negotiation of gender in a charismatic community. *Sociological Analysis* 48 (3):245–258.

Ryan, M. P. 1975. *Womanhood in America: From colonial times to the present*. New York: New Viewpoints.

Scanzoni, L. D., and N. A. Hardesty. 1986. *All we're meant to be*, Nashville: Abingdon Press.

Shaffir, W. 1974. *Life in a religious community: The Lubavitcher Chassidim in Montreal*. Toronto: Holt, Rinehart, and Winston.

———. 1978. Witnessing as identity consolidation: The case of the Lubavitcher Chassidim. In *Identity and religion*, ed. Hans Mol, 39–57. London: Sage.

———. 1983. The recruitment of ba'alei teshuvah in Jerusalem yeshiva. *Jewish Journal of Sociology* 25 (June):33–46.

Stacey, J. 1990. *Brave new families*. New York: Basic Books.

Stacey, J., and S. E. Gerard. 1990. We are not doormats: The influence of feminism on contemporary evangelicalism in the U.S. In *Uncertain terms: Negotiating gender in American culture*, ed. F. Ginsburg and A. Tsing, 98–117. Boston: Beacon Press.

Warner, R. S. 1988. *New wine in old wineskins: Evangelicals and liberals in a small-town church*. Berkeley: University of California Press.

Welter, B. 1966. The cult of true womanhood, 1820–1860. *American Quarterly* 18:151–174.

Wikler, M. 1988. *Bayis ne'eman b'Yisrael: Practical steps to success in marriage*. Jerusalem and New York: Feldheim Publishers.

Wulf, J., D. Prentice, D. Hansum, A. Ferrar, and B. Spilka. 1984. Religiosity and sexual attitudes and behavior among evangelical Christian singles. *Review of Religious Research* 26 (2):119–131.

Yuval-Davis, N. 1991. Fundamentalism, multiculturalism, and women in Britain. Paper persented at the XII World Congress of Sociology. July Madrid Spain.

CHAPTER 5

Engendering Orthodoxy: Newly Orthodox Women and Hasidism

Debra R. Kaufman

GENDER IDENTITY POLITICS AMONG SOME URBAN SECTARIANS

Where are the voices and "text" of Hasidic women in contemporary scholarship about Orthodox Judaism? Indeed, our knowledge about Jewish Orthodoxy, and most particularly Hasidism, is clearly and predominantly from the perspective of males. And beyond Jewish studies the feminist literature also reflects this notable gap. Like other fundamentalist women, Hasidic women are often visible and vocal opponents of feminism. Likewise, as Nancy Ammerman suggests, fundamentalists are clearly the "other" for most feminists, academics, and other "moderns" (1992:1). Yet, gender relations and gender identity are a central community-defining discourse for both groups. If both fundamentalists and feminists remain the "other" to one another, and Hasidic women remain "unvoiced," we will never get beyond the "mutual other-izing" (Ammerman 1992) common for both groups, nor can we hear the more nuanced discourses internal to each community of women. In this chapter I would like to compare and contrast the ways in which newly Orthodox Hasidic women and some femi-

Parts of this chapter come from Debra Renee Kaufman. *Rachel's Daughters: Newly Orthodox Jewish Women.* New Brusnwick, NJ: Rutgers University Press. Reprinted by permission of Rutgers University Press.

nists engender and come to understand the symbols and meaning of their lives in "woman-identified" communities.

I'd like to begin this chapter with the same quote with which I began my book, *Rachel's Daughters* (1991). For I believe that this quote discloses at least one juncture where the boundaries between fundamentalist women and feminists may not be so distinct.

> The big lie of male supremacy is that women are less than fully human; the basic task of feminism is to expose that lie and fight it on every level. Yet for all my feminist militance I was, it seemed, secretly afraid that the lie was true—that my humanity was hopelessly at odds with my ineluctably female sexuality— while the rebetsen (wife of the Rabbi), staunch apostle of traditional femininity, did not appear to doubt for a moment that she could be both a woman and a serious person. Which was only superficially paradoxical, for if you were absolutely convinced that the Jewish woman's role was ordained by God, and that it was every bit as important spiritually as the man's, how could you believe the lie? (Willis 1977:76)

So wrote feminist journalist Ellen Willis after she had visited her brother, a recent convert to Orthodox Judaism in Israel. The paradox Willis refers to suggests that both feminists and these fundamentalist women, as outsiders to the "dominant" patriarchy of which both are a part, share some common themes as they develop the discourse that supports their gendered identities.

In the early and mid 1980s I conducted in-depth interviews[1] in five major urban areas[2] across the United States with 150 once secular and often countercultural women who had become Orthodox in their young adult years.[3] In Hebrew, women who have "returned"[4] to Orthodoxy are called *baalot teshuvah*. Of the 150 women I interviewed,[5] 85 women identified themselves as Hasidic.[6] The women in this study are either from the Lubavitcher or the Bostoner Hasidim. Unlike most other Hasidic sects, these two groups believe in and have active outreach programs.

Although it seems obvious why men might be drawn to religious communities steeped in patriarchal tradition and staunchly opposed to any changes in the clear sex-segregation of religious roles, it is much more difficult to explain women's attraction. Most puzzling to me was the discovery that although many baalot teshuvah openly reject feminism or what they perceive feminism to represent and advocate, they are not without a gender consciousness that seems to incorporate, adapt, revise, and, most importantly, depoliticize some of the central values of those whom we refer to as radical cultural feminists, feminists who celebrate the female, her body, her life-cycle experiences, and her so-called "unique" feminine attributes.[7]

Some authors (Stacey and Gerard 1988) use the term postfeminist to describe women who do not necessarily identify with the women's movement, but who, as inheritors of the women's movement, use its ideological and rhetorical messages to frame their own arguments. The baalot teshuvah I studied do not explicitly challenge or necessarily form a strong critique of patriarchy. In fact, unlike feminists, these newly Orthodox women use patriarchal religion, ideology, and social structure as a way of protecting and enhancing the status of women. However, they do selectively use feminist rhetoric and ideology in framing their experiences and interpretations of Jewish Orthodoxy. We can only hear this kind of internal discourse, however, if we allow these women to speak in their own voices and if we do not focus solely upon their involvement in antifeminist or right-wing activities. The "voicing" of Hasidic baalot teshuvah permits us to develop a more nuanced understanding of how these fundamentalist women come to understand their gender and religious identities. We come to understand better how current cultural and sociohistoric conditions of a postindustrial[8] economy contribute to the need for many of these women for a conservative worldview. And we come to see that the seeming antipathy of Hasidic women toward feminism is perhaps less an antifeminist stance as it is a response to ethnic survival in a postmodern[9] social order, a social order that sets one group against the other in the search for an "authentic" identity amid a multiversity of competing and sometimes conflicting possibilities (see also Morris in this volume; Kaufman 1993).

Until recently most feminists have focused almost exclusively on Religious Right women in the context of their participation in antifeminist activities.[10] More recently, however, ethnographic and other studies have given us a broader, if not more complex picture of Religious Right women.[11] While it may be generally true that women who turn to patriarchal religious traditions reject feminist politics, recent data also suggest that Religious Right women make claims for an enhanced status for women and for greater claims upon men as husbands and fathers within those patriarchal traditions (Kaufman 1991, 1993). Therefore, despite many "born again" women's distrust of feminism, their focus on raising women's status, promoting female interests, and altering gender-role behavior of men as fathers and husbands resonate with issues long of concern to feminists.

POSTMODERNISM AND IDENTITY POLITICS

At the foundation of identity politics, writes Ilene Philipson, is "a fundamental belief in the necessity of expressing an identifiable 'authentic self,' and this belief increasingly has become the means through which individuals interpret their own experience and give it social expression" (1991:51). Currently, in what many scholars term a postmodern period, the search for an "authentic self" proliferates. Philipson writes that in our own society it is assumed that the diversity that makes up our multicultural society is generally ignored by a white, male Protestant ruling class. Therefore, she concludes, the fundamental agenda of a politics of identity, particularly in a postmodern era, insists upon respect for and a greater representation of social diversity (Philipson 1991:51).

Feminists and others on the left increasingly have found themselves caught on the horns of what might be defined as a contemporary dilemma. How do we include different ethnic/religious groups, often inclusive of antifeminist women, in our academic discourse about gender identity without reducing such women, as Stacey might frame it, to "robots," "fools," or "victims" (Stacey 1987)? Indeed, for instance, if represented at all in feminist scholarship, Religious Right women are portrayed primarily as victims of male control and ideology.[12]

Borrowing from Clifford Geertz's (1973) analysis of religion as a cultural system, I'll describe the ways in which the 85 Hasidic women[13] of the 150 newly Orthodox women I studied engender concepts of the Jewish self by celebrating the female and those characteristics commonly understood in our culture as feminine. This celebratory process goes beyond forming a Jewish self-identity. In the strong woman-identified community that emerges from the sex-segregated Hasidic community, the baalot teshuvah negotiate the realities of their public/private lives in ways meaningful and valuable to them. Developing a strong woman-identified community is a tactic used by other fundamentalist women and by many radical cultural feminists as well. Sex segregation helps to shape the normative social structure for each, the Hasidic and the radical feminist, community. The separate sphere of ideology that characterizes both communities of women highlight, in general, some of the complexities of gender-identity politics in what many have come to call a postindustrial, postfeminist, and postmodern period.

HASIDISM, HASIDIC WOMEN, AND ETHNIC SURVIVAL

Contemporary Hasidism is based upon a Jewish pietistic movement founded in eighteenth-century Poland by Israel ben Eliezer (known by Hasidim as the Baal Shem Tov, or the Master of the Good Name). Hasidism broke with the elitist tradition of scholarship common to Orthodox rabbinical academies of that time by making Judaism more accessible and immediate to poor Jews. It did this by incorporating peasant activities and values into the practice of Judaism and by stressing prayer, joy, and religious devotion in all aspects of daily life, and by widely disseminating kabbalistic and mystical thoughts (although attaching different meanings and emphases to them) into Jewish theology (Sharot 1982; Harris 1985; Morris 1990, 1991).

Hasidism is a monistic system where absolute evil has no independent existence (See Scholem 1961; Sharot 1982; Handelman 1984). The key task then of the Hasid is to uncover or penetrate the appearance of evil in order to see and have contact with the real. This places a great emphasis on contact with and transformation of the material world. Many of the Hasidic baalot teshuvah in my study suggest that women's greater association with the physical and material world is support for their claims that through their everyday activities as Orthodox wives and mothers the Messiah will come.

Perhaps, however, the most distinguishing feature of Hasidism is the Hasid's attachment and obedience to a single authority, the man representing their specific sect's rabbinic dynasty, the man known as their rebbe. Like their other Orthodox sisters, Hasidic women have no public voice in the world of Jewish Orthodoxy, they depend upon men for spiritual leadership and theological scholarship. However, all Hasidim, both male and female, have only one person as the central authority in their lives: the rebbe. Both the Bostoner Rebbe and the late Lubavitcher Rebbe[14] (rebbes of the two Hasidic communities in my study) have actively encouraged women to engage in the proselytizing missions of each community. Indeed, women are critical to the proselytizing mission (see, also, Morris in this volume).

Because they represent a well-educated and well-informed population of women, baalot teshuvah often are encouraged by their rebbes to become active in the many outreach and proselytizing campaigns of their respective communities. Since fifteen out of the eighty-five Hasidic women in my study were active feminists before they became Hasidic, many have been targeted as important resources and as leaders in outreach programs. Moreover, the higher their level of secular education, the more likely these newly Orthodox women are to seek Judaic education. They are encouraged to do this in order to become well-informed proselytizers.

By focusing on Hasidic women as agents rather than victims, we can see that they not only are carriers of the Hasidic tradition but, in part, creators of the tradition as well. In this volume, historian Bonnie Morris redirects our focus away from "victim" to "agent" by documenting the active role Hasidic women have played in the growth of Hasidism in the United States since World War II. In addition, Morris focuses our attention on the specific context for Hasidic women's responses to feminism. This puts into perspective some of the seeming paradoxes which emerge when feminist and Hasidic women are compared.

Writing about Lubavitcher Hasidic women, Morris notes: "Long before civil rights and ethnic pride, Lubavitcher women confronted their American Jewish sisters on internalized anti-semitism and spiritually dishonest suburban conformity" (Morris 1991:7).[15] In fact, Morris shows that Lubavitcher women demonstrated leadership roles either as writers for the women's journal, *Di Yiddishe Heim*, or as hostesses and role models for those interested in becoming observant. Morris notes that in the five full-length texts celebrating the role of the Hasidic woman published by the Lubavitcher Women's Organization between 1976 and 1984, the authors place Hasidic culture against the background and "decadence" of Western values and culture.[16] Indeed, many similar themes are to be found in contemporary radical feminists arguments as well. Moreover, as Morris points out, Lubavitcher women never thought of liberation as an undesirable goal, never thought of themselves as sexually oppressed, and were often praised for their worldly skills (see Morris in this volume). Since prejudice against religious Jews has been a constant historical fact, women have been an important economic resource in the Orthodox community. Therefore Morris concludes that "ethnicity rather than gender" informs the Hasidic view of women and secular world activities such as work (1991:13–14).

Ethnicity informs the Hasidic woman's seeming antifeminism as well. Morris sees Hasidic women's antifeminism as rooted in the fear of any revolutionary ideology that threatens minority survival rather than in right-wing political views about women (1991:15). Jewish women's fears about "other" women are not entirely unfounded. Recent feminist works about the role of women in the National Socialist Movement in Germany (Koonz 1987) and in the Ku Klux Klan (Blee 1991) have shown that women, as well as men, have been active participants in the oppression of Jews. Letty Pogrebin (1982) tells of Jewish-identified feminists' sometimes uneasy relationship with second-wave feminism. In that many Hasidic women in my study accept many of the goals, arguments, and gains of the women's movement and use them to their own advantage, it is reasonable to conclude that Hasidic women's negative response to feminism is, perhaps, more a fear of what feminism represents (the gentile world, bourgeois individualism) than what it has to say about women. Morris tellingly notes that while feminism has criticized the white male base of knowledge making, it has not yet come to grips with its own Protestant heritage and the sometimes blatant antisemitism within it.[17]

Second-wave feminism,[18] coming so close on the heels of the Holocaust, posed real concerns for Hasidim, and particularly Hasidic women, who were actively involved with "reviving and reproducing Hasidic culture" (Morris 1991:16). Morris contends that modern Hasidic women are concerned more with sectarian survival than with liberating themselves from Hasidic men. Therefore a narrow focus on patriarchy alone (Hasidic male ideology and control) underestimates the agency of Hasidic women as they formulate a gender identity politics within the context of Jewish ethnic survival.

NEWLY ORTHODOX HASIDIC WOMEN AND RADICAL CULTURAL FEMINISTS

Most of the baalot teshuvah began their journeys toward Orthodoxy during the counterculture, or in its wake. Sixty-six percent of the women (99) were in their late teens and early to middle twenties between 1966 and 1976. Of these women, almost 71 percent identified with the counterculture (70). And a little over 92 percent (65) of those women were Hasidic. For the remainder of the baalot teshuvah, even those who were not politically aware during the sixties, or who had come into their young adult years in the late seventies, and/or who were not from upwardly mobile, middle-class families, similar themes emerged: their search for a moral community of both public and private virtue, and, above all, their need for a moral framework in which to make decisions—the need, as one woman put it, for "official values." Jewish Orthodoxy provided these women with clear ethical guidelines and both historic and transcendental ties. Moreover, it was a tradition with which many of them were, if not knowledgeable, familiar.

Implicit in the complaints of countercultural youth, and among the baalot teshuvah as well, was a discontent with the pluralistic relativism of a modern.[19] Tipton believes that this kind of relativism forces us to migrate through discrepant worlds, so that "the cognitive and normative definitions of modern culture become abstracted and emptied of specific content in order to be flexible" (1982:24). Thus, he argues, no activity has any intrinsic value and each person is set at the center of his/her own universe of calculated consequences. For all the women in this study, the return to Orthodox Judaism constitutes a conscious rejection of secular culture and the relativism of contemporary living. Most baalot teshuvah describe themselves as searching for moral guidelines, absolute truths, and above all a sense of community to counter the individualistic bent of postmodern culture.

The baalot teshuvah share the "official" patriarchal belief system of Orthodox Judaism and a belief system that emerges organically from their everyday lives as women in a highly sex-segregated community. They believe that community is critical if Orthodox Jewish life is to be preserved. For them, female activities and systems of meaning are as vital to Orthodox Judaism as are men's. They do not see their sphere as inferior, but rather as a place where they are free to create their own forms of personal, social, intellectual, and, at times, political relationships. Whether intentional or not, sex-segregated living seems to provide these women with the resources on which they can build a community of meaning and action. By accepting and elaborating on the symbols and expectations associated with gender difference, these baalot teshuvah claim they have some control over their sexuality and marital lives. They seem to transcend the domestic limits set by patriarchal living, not by entering a man's world but by creating a world of their own. In such a sex-segregated community, male control and ideology take on less significance. The solidarity, self-esteem, and strength they receive from their sex-segregated world reinforce them in their celebration of gender difference, their bodies, their reproductive functions, and woman-centered values. Like the Hasidic women whom Morris describes, many of these baalot teshuvah are open advocates of the Hasidic doctrine of separate spheres.

Hasidic women, more than the other newly Orthodox Jewish women in my study, were the most woman-identified in their attitudes and beliefs. In many respects, they were the most likely to develop arguments similar to radical cultural feminists. Despite *radically different politics*,[20] both Hasidic women and radical feminists argue for celebrating women's "unique" biological, emotional, temperamental, psychological, and spiritual qualities.

Drawing on the works of such celebrated radical feminists as Mary Daly and Susan Griffin, Alison Jaggar describes contemporary radical feminists:

> The contemporary radical feminist movement is characterized by a general celebration of womanhood, a striking contrast to the devaluation of women that pervades the larger society. This celebration takes many forms. Women's achievements are honored; women's culture is enjoyed; women's spirituality is developed; lesbianism is the preferred expression of sexuality. . . . Women's special closeness with nature is believed to give women special ways of knowing and conceiving the world. (1983:95)

Ynestra King (1989) expands upon Jaggar's characterization of radical feminists by suggesting that there are essentially two schools among radical feminists: radical rationalist feminists, who repudiate the woman/nature connection, and radical cultural feminists, who celebrate the woman/nature connection. She writes:

> The major strength of cultural feminism is that it is a deeply woman-identified movement. It celebrates what is distinct about women, challenging male culture rather than strategizing to become part of it. (1989:123)

Jane Alpert represents the radical cultural feminist position best in the following:

> Feminist culture is based on what is best and strongest in women . . . the qualities coming to the fore are the same ones a mother projects in the best kind of nurturing relationship to a child: empathy, intuitiveness, adaptability, awareness of growth. . . . (Cited in Jaggar 1983:97)

The radical feminists to whom Jaggar and King refer emphasize and celebrate the biological and psychological differences between the sexes. In general, they wish to develop new values based on women's traditional culture. However, radical cultural feminists tend to ignore (as do the Hasidic women) the complex, multidimensional, and historically different life situations of women (Jaggar, 1983; King, 1989). Consequently, argue Jaggar (1983) and King (1989), radical cultural feminists frame their understanding of human nature, and, consequently their politics, in an ahistorical context.

Not unlike many of these contemporary feminists, the baalot teshuvah frame their understanding of gender differences in an essentialist and ahistorical framework as well. Moreover, newly Orthodox Hasidic women attack many of the same aspects of secular patriarchy that radical feminists combat, such as acquisitive individualism, self-indulgence, and a lack of value consensus (other than individual rights). However, while the baalot teshuvah form a critique of secular patriarchy, they do not challenge religious patriarchy. Interestingly, for the radical cultural feminists described by Jaggar (1983) and King (1989) and the newly Orthodox Hasidic women in my study, gender identity is not independent of separatist and sex-segregated social structure. However, unlike the radical cultural feminists, while many of these newly Orthodox Jewish women acknowledge that secular culture and masculinist culture are essentially the same, they do not associate a masculine ethos with Orthodox Judaism. Rather, many insist that Jewish Orthodoxy is "feminine in principle." This is especially true of Hasidic women.[21]

One Hasidic woman spoke of *tzniut* (modesty) as emblematic of Orthodoxy.[22] "You know," she says, "both men and women have to abide by modesty rules. It is the feminine part of us that applies to all *frum* (observant) Jews. Orthodoxy is the antithesis of *macho*." A Bostoner Hasidic woman notes that, "It's such a wonderful way of representing oneself . . . it means modesty. It means you should present yourself as caring, soft-spoken, gentle, you know . . . in a feminine way. That's what Orthodoxy is really all about." Another woman spoke of tzniut as best translated as having "self-respect." "It is women who teach men to have this self respect," she told me. "They [women] have always been the model for men." In an introduction to an essay about the laws of modesty, Shaina Sara Handelman (also cited in this chapter as Susan Handelman) writes that the culmination of the prayer service is the "Silent Prayer," a prayer where each Jew stands privately before God. This prayer, she writes, known for its modesty, was composed by a well-known biblical woman, Chana (Handelman 1978).

The baalot teshuvah made frequent references in their interviews to the special meaning female imagery holds in Hasidism. Many mentioned the *Shekhinah* (the feminine element in God); almost all noted that the Shabbat is also called the Sabbath Queen. And some pointed out that the Jewish people were the beloved bride of God. One Bostoner Hasid informed me that women are not required to do any of the time-bound commandments because "Men need the discipline; we don't. We are closer to God—we are the Shekhinah. We provide understanding. . . . Our discipline is in the everyday actions of our lives in our intuitive understanding of what is right. In Judaism this is recognized." One woman told me that the Jews' spiritual striving in *Hasidut* (Hasidic philosophy) is often compared to labor and childbirth.

One Lubavitcher woman quoted to me from notes she had from her days at Bais Chana (a seminary for Lubavitcher woman). She was adamant in her belief that a fundamental principle of Hasidic thought is that the woman-identified traits of passivity and receptivity were key to understanding "G-dliness" in this world. It is not surprising that the arguments she made can be found in the writings of her teacher, the principal of Bais Chana, Manis Freeman: "We today need to nurture the G-dliness that exists in the world. We need to develop, master and perfect that quality that is the feminine way of serving G-d" (Freeman 1978:12).

Freeman even hints at women's moral superiority when he writes: "Who has the sensitivity for right? We're all very sensitive about what's wrong, but who still knows what's right? Who still has a feeling for the G-dliness that you can't always explain? Generally, women" (1981:14). More than other newly Orthodox Jewish women in this study, the Hasidic women were most likely to believe that women's spiritual capabilities were greater than men's. Quoting from my book, I cite Chana as a composite representative of her community:

> You know, since the destruction of the Second Temple, the family is like the 'holy tabernacle' on earth. Each week I bring divine presence into this household by preparing for Shabbos, I *make* Shabbos. . . . When I separate and burn a portion of the challah (Sabbath bread), when I light the candles to welcome the Shabbat queen, I am like a high priestess. When I went to Beis Chana (Bais Chana), we learned that women were the *middot* (character formation) of the Jewish people. You know in Hasidus (Hasidic Philosophy), it is said that it is through women's work and efforts that the Mosheach (Messiah) will come. . . . We women take care of the goodness in the world; we nurture and protect it. (Kaufman 1991:41).

Like women-centered feminists, many *baalot teshuvah* and, indeed, other women of the new religious right in America, celebrate gender differences. For many radical cultural feminists and for these baalot teshuvah, women represent a source of special strength, knowledge, and power. Jaggar contends that radical feminists give "special value to women's reproductive functions and to the psychological characteristics that have distinguished women and men" (1983:97). Many of the Hasidic baalot teshuvah claim that there are natural differences between the sexes, and that women's superior moral sensibilities arise from their greater intimacy with the everyday physical world.

This understanding of women's special strengths and unique characteristics is reinforced by a frequent contributor to one of the leading Hasidic women's journals, Shaina Sara Handelman. Throughout Jewish history, she argues, women have had special insights (as evidence for this, Handelman recounts the biblical claims that women didn't believe the false report of the spies about the land of Canaan and that they did not participate in the blasphemous making of the golden calf). "What special strength," she asks,

> do women have that gives them these extra insights? Chassidus (Hasidic philosophy) explains, most interestingly, that woman is from a higher source than man, and in this sense also closer to

the inner essence of God. Her greatness is revealed in the proverb "A woman of valor is the crown of her husband"—and the crown sits on top of the head, higher than the rest of it, giving it its glory. (1978:13)

The comparisons to cultural feminists are sometimes quite striking. For instance, in addition to women's greater moral sensibilities, Jaggar (1983) writes that radical feminists consciously oppose stereotypical models of female beauty and that they give special respect to those parts of the female body and processes that the dominant male culture has considered to be unclean. Rather than being "the curse" of God, for instance, menstruation is viewed as the "blessing of the Goddess" (1983:95).

Like the radical cultural feminists, the Hasidic women also condemn the cultural fixation on self and the focus on women as sexual objects. They see a holiness in women's experiences and bodily cycles. Hasidic women were the most likely to fully discuss their experiences as sexual beings within Orthodoxy. They provided the fullest details about their experiences with the family purity laws. These laws demand a two-week sexual separation between husband and wife during her menstrual cycle. To end the period of *niddah* (exclusion, sexual separation), the baalot teshuvah immerse themselves in a ritual body of water (called the *mikvah*) on the seventh day after they have completed menstruating. For these newly Orthodox Jewish women, the family purity laws allow them to partake in a purity ritual they see as sanctifying and in keeping with their own bodily rhythms. They enter, as one Bostoner Hasid told me, "into a holy cycle of death and rebirth." Hasidic women eschew the term *unclean* as the wrong Hebraic translation for the days of niddah and prefer the word *impure*, for it connotes the proper translation of a sacred act performed for a purity ritual.

In Hasidism there is a unity between the body and the spirit. The Hasidic women often make reference to the Kabbalah.[23] This is especially true of the Lubavitcher women. One woman told me that everything in the physical world has a spiritual counterpart. "Women," she told me, "are the ones who are best able to give spiritual meaning even to the most mundane physical activities." One Hasidic woman told me that the forced separation between her and her husband during niddah signaled the fact that "one-half of the month I belong to my husband, the other half to God." "My husband cannot take me or my body for granted" reasoned another woman as she spoke of the laws of niddah. For these women, all their bodily acts and functions were linked to a spiritual counterpart in the form of purity rituals.

The elevating of bodily functions as part of a purity ritual and the blurring of the distinctions between the body and soul, along with other dichotomies, has some support in the interpretations offered by scholars of mysticism, Kabbalah and Hasidism. Sharot (1982) writes that in the early stages of the Hasidic movement, the distinction between the spiritual and the material was ultimately an illusion. He notes that it was appropriate to worship God in everyday bodily functions and activities (1982:249). Shaina Sara Handelman refines Sharot's understanding. She writes that although the Hasid does not seek to be one with nature, it is also clear that the ultra-orthodox Jew does not "negate nature, the physical, the body" (1978:3). Rather, she continues, the Jew "refines and elevates" nature. To this she compares the Hasidic saying that "G-d takes spiritual things and makes them physical, and Israel takes material things and makes them spiritual" (1978:3). The Jew elevates the "mundane, physical, raw material of nature" (Handelman 1978:4). She later notes, that sanctity is "based on the . . . life of the body as well as the soul" (1978:4). "For the non-Jew," she writes, "there are two opposing realms: body/soul, flesh/spirit, nature/culture" (1978:3).

In comparison to Handelman, Jaggar substitutes the word "patriarchal" for "non-Jew" when she writes that radical feminists

> believe that women's ways of understanding the world contrast with "patriarchal" ways of knowing. According to radical feminism, patriarchal thinking imposes polarities upon reality. (1983:96)

According to cultural feminists, women must trust in their direct and intuitive mode of knowing. A mode of knowing which "perceives the wholeness and oneness of the universe" (Jaggar 1983:96). Therefore, in order to perceive the true universe, "[w]omen must peel off the patriarchal distortions and uncover the reality beneath" (Jaggar 1983:96). The metaphor of peeling though layers used by the cultural feminists is used by scholars of Hasidism as well (Sharot 1982; Handelman 1984). Lubavitcher women believe that it is the job of the Hasid to "lift the veils" which cover up Godliness in the physical world in order that they may reach the essential reality of the spiritual. Women, note these Hasidic women, are particularly qualified to do this.

Almost all the newly Hasidic women mentioned their particular love of lighting the Sabbath candles (one of three ritual obligations falling to Jewish women). One Lubavitcher woman told me that when lighting the candles she represents the light in the world. "We change the darkness in the world to light," she claims. A Bostoner woman told me that by lighting the candles women bring the time of the Messiah closer. Handelman writes: "And through the lighting of the candles of *Shabbat* (Yiddish for Sabbath), one will be worthy . . . to see the lights of Zion which will be revealed very soon in the true and complete Redemption" (1979:6). The emphasis, for many of these women, is on their special strengths in transforming and sanctifying of the world. As Handelman writes, the home becomes a miniature temple, a place where the family serves God (1979:10). And women, as one Lubavitcher reminded me, are like "high priestesses" within that home.

These newly Orthodox women represent an energetic community, strong in a commitment and belief that the female, and those symbols and activities identified with her, are vital and highly valued in the community at large. These women are not incorrect in their assessments that they represent the guardians of the tradition and that in their everyday lives, as mothers and wives, they maintain the vital distinctions between the profane and the sacred for the community as a whole (from maintaining the many dietary laws to purification in the mikvah).

Like those women cited by Michele Rosaldo (1974, 1980) in her overview of women in anthropological studies, the baalot teshuvah seem to use the very symbols and social customs that set them apart to establish female solidarity and worth and to engender male-made symbols with strong feminine imagery. The extra-domestic ties these women share with one another seem to be important sources of power and self-esteem. Through these ties they make claims upon the community, not only as individuals, but as a community of women.[24]

BRINGING WOMEN BACK INTO OUR ANALYSES

In my study of newly Orthodox Jews I have relied heavily on feminist and interpretive epistemological and methodological models.

I described these newly Orthodox Jewish women in their own voices and from their own perspectives. I focused on their everyday world "by taking it up from within," from the standpoint of them as "knowers actually and locally situated" (Smith 1988:3). Had I not presented these baalot teshuvah in their own words and voices, it would be difficult to appreciate, or perhaps even recognize, the paradox their situation presents. What concepts and theoretical schemes explain these women? Are they feminist antifeminists, antifeminist feminists? Are things as paradoxical as they seem? There seems to be, as Dorothy Smith might predict, "a disjunction between how women find and experience the world" and the "concepts and theoretical schemes available to think about it in" (1974:9). I assumed that these women were "minded" social actors, capable of constructing their own systems of meaning and of negotiating both their individual and collective social realities.

Feminist anthropologists have contributed to a burgeoning literature on the ways in which women have actively negotiated their own social and physical space within patriarchal societies (Rosaldo 1974). Feminist historians have pointed to the ways in which the defense of the domestic sphere and "femininity" have served feminist as well as antifeminist purposes.[25] And even more recently, some feminist sociologists have pointed to the ways in which "evangelical theology and institutions may be flexible resources for renegotiating gender and family relationships, and not exclusively in reactionary or masculinist directions" (Stacey and Gerard 1988:2).

A feminist framework does not begin with the assumption that what goes on in the public world of men's relations is the most important focus in an analysis of female relationships or of community relations in general. The epistemological and methodological basis of the majority of feminist research calls for analytic categories as complex as the lives people actually live.[26] Feminist models focus on women's value systems through their own self-understandings. We cannot limit the world to male images of women nor assume that the parameters of women's experiences are set by male exploitation alone. For, as I have argued, here and elsewhere (1989a, 1990, 1991, 1993), even within the most rigid patriarchal parameters, women seem able to develop some interpretive control.

Morris notes that in *Di Yiddishe Heim*, the Lubavitcher women's magazine, women talked to one another, shared their problems, and at times challenged interpretations of Jewish Orthodoxy. Since they had fewer opportunities for higher religious scholarship, the women contributed original essays on aspects of Hasidism to the magazine. These writings were far more creative and varied than those of men, claims Morris, because their essays were practical applications of Hasidic philosophy to their own lives in America, including responses to the women's movement. While they disparaged feminism in their essays, they nonetheless focused on feminist issues and views of women in coming to their own visions and versions of Hasidism. Their strength was in their nonconformity to Western visions of women as sex objects and/or frivolous housewives (Morris, 1990). In a letter to the editor, one Hasidic woman asks:

> Why must we counter the stridency of Women's Lib with 1950ish advice on nurturing the male ego and pampering the tired hubby as he walks in the door after "putting in a full day's work," and never mind how you feel after a whole day in the house with three kids home from school and four unexpected guests in for Yom Tov (holiday)! Is it really necessary to insist that these are "frum" (observant) attitudes? Can't Yiddishkeit (Jewishness) mean mutual respect and interdependence? . . . Let us drop the European modernity of "male chauvinism," . . . and return to the basic Torah way of respect and consideration. (Cited in Morris 1991:12)

What maintains these women's commitment to a past not of their own making and to a patriarchal present? How can one conclude that these women's lives are anything but oppressive and "alienated"? Some feminists have relied upon arguments that stress "false consciousness," or a powerlessness to change the conditions of their existence, to account for women's commitment to patriarchal settings. Theoretical categories, however, cannot distinguish between a woman's "authentic" or "alienated" experiences. When we describe lives according to a series of purely abstract claims we form what Leacock (1977) would call an unwarranted teleology. The portraits and descriptions of these baalot teshuvah come from their own language and self understandings. I have not relied on historical abstractions to explain women's "place" in Jewish Orthodoxy, but rather their immediate and concrete experiences; or, their "local" (Foucault 1976) or time-specific sets of circumstances.

These time-specific circumstances must take into account the socioeconomic conditions as well. A postindustrial economy and its political ideology of individual rights affect men and women differently. In addition to the instability that a postindustrial economy implies, the normative expectations surrounding the sexual division of labor within households have proved resistant to change. Irrespective of paid employment, women maintain the major responsibility for domestic and child care activities (Berheide 1984; Fox and Hesse-Biber 1984). Moreover, we are the only advanced industrial nation that has no public policy of family support. Skyrocketing divorce rates and the lack of enforceable child support payments only exacerbate the difficulties for working women in the United States. The baalot teshuvah have not only inherited the women's movement, but a postmodern cultural order and a postindustrial economy as well. Their choice of a traditional worldview must be placed within that context.

CONCLUSION

Gender identity process and practice are critical to women of the Religious Right. There is the growing recognition that liberal feminism (at least as a popular movement) may have failed a significant number of women because it has not been able to develop a "politics of the personal," particularly for heterosexual women, amid the destabilized family and work conditions of the past few decades.[27] For instance, vigorous legislative reforms aimed at promoting gender equality often fail to bring about real changes in the private arena of life, most particularly, in the role behavior of men. Despite their increases in the labor force and some positive legislative reforms, women still earn less than men in every occupation, irrespective of their training, skills, and qualifications (Kaufman 1989b).

The newly Orthodox Jewish women raise important questions about the meaning of family, the politics of gender identity, religious identity, and feminism. Their stories, and those of other born-again women, reveal more than the antipathy of an antifeminist Religious Right. Their voices are the voices of women trying to cope with the inequities and imbalances of liberal patriarchy in a postmodern cultural and postindustrial economic order. In addition, Hasidic women, and other Jewish Orthodox women, are often responding to what they believe to be the hostility of a gentile world in the form of the Western Protestant heritage that belongs to feminism.

Gender identity, and consequently gender politics, are at the center of the practice of Jewish Orthodoxy. As with other fundamentalist movements, women mark the boundaries of the group and are considered the carriers and transmitters of the tradition. Yet, while "Orthodoxy" is presented as the inviolable, ahistoric, and only authentic voice of Judaism, the focus and the language of these newly Orthodox women set at least some of the terms for ongoing discussions within the Orthodox community. That some challenge has emerged to the patriarchal law is clear from the way feminism has entered into the authoritative discourse, even if only to be railed against.[28]

Gender difference is key in understanding the identity politics of both fundamentalism and feminism. For as Nancy Cott acknowledges: "Both theory and practice in feminism historically have had to deal with the fact that women are the same as and different from men, and the fact that women's gender identity is not separable from the other factors that make up our selves: race, region, culture, class, age" (1986:49)—and, I would add, ethnicity and religion. The question remains whether these newly Orthodox women and feminists can learn ways of using the vantage point of gender difference without stumbling on its clear limitations.[29] Although feminists and fundamentalists differ markedly in the practice of their gender-identity politics, common themes can be discerned if we listen carefully to the internal discourses that are part and parcel of the making of any Orthodoxy—be it feminist or religious.

NOTES

1. Interviews with leading rabbis, lay community leaders, and known baalot teshuvah in each of five major urban cities helped locate baalot teshuvah within the three identifiable frameworks in contemporary Orthodoxy—modern (25), centrist (40), Hasidic (85). Once within these settings, the referral method or snowball technique of sampling (Coleman 1971) was employed, thereby identifying smaller interactive groups of baalot teshuvah in each community. Interviewing ended when no new names were generated. No claims are made that the women under study were randomly drawn as a sample of a defined universe, nor

can the interviewed be considered statistically representative of those who return to Orthodoxy, of Hasidism, or of Orthodoxy itself.

2. The five cities include: Boston, Cleveland, New York City (including Crown Heights), Los Angeles, and San Francisco. The choice to interview in these cities was based on several considerations. According to the statistics in the 1985 Jewish Yearbook, all five cities have recognizable Orthodox-affiliated Jewish populations (ranging from 5 percent in Los Angeles to 13 percent in New York City. Interviewing also occurred in cities where I had Jewish communal contacts who could help me map the Orthodox communities, and who could provide contacts, and where there were known baalot teshuvah.

3. In my study I initially identified a *baalat teshuvah* (f. singular) in any of the following ways: as a woman who never practiced Orthodoxy and who currently practices and believes in Orthodox Judaism; as one who is more traditional in her practice/belief than her parents or early caregivers; or, as a woman who currently practices and believes in Orthodoxy but who had lapsed in that belief/practice for some period of time. Orthodoxy was defined as those who were in strict observance of all the Sabbath and dietary laws.

4. The term *teshuvah* can be translated from the Hebrew to mean either return or repent. Orthodox Jews believe that all Jews who are not currently Orthodox are considered to be in the process of "returning" or "repenting." The term in English is a misnomer in that most of these women had never been Orthodox.

5. The interviews began with a number of predefined topics but were unstructured and in depth, focusing on the history of women's return to Orthodoxy, their current familial and communal life-style, and their views about gender roles and feminism.

6. For the majority of Hasidic women, the range of return was between the ages of 18 and 25. At the time of interviewing, most had been baalot teshuvah for an average of five years. Most came from middle-class backgrounds and currently occupy a middle-class socioeconomic status. Although they are all committed to childbearing and rearing, close to one third of them work outside of the home. Of those who work, the majority are in female-dominated occupations or, if in male-dominated ones, in female-dominated subspecialties. Irrespective of work status, household help and child care, of some sort, is common.

7. For a fuller discussion of second-wave feminism and the baalot teshuvah see Kaufman 1985a, 1985b, 1993.

8. Here I am using the term *postindustrial* advisedly. I am using it in the very specific sense, as does Judith Stacey (1987), to mean that there has been a decline in real wages and in the percentage of well-paid and career-structured jobs available to individuals. Others have referred to the deskilling of the labor market and, more recently, we have seen what

is loosely termed a downsizing of most corporate businesses in the United States. These changes refer to a narrowed and restricted opportunity structure, especially to those most recently entering the labor market.

9. The term *postmodern* has received copious attention in the scholarly literature recently. In this chapter I narrowly refer to a post-modern period as a time in which the once grand overviews from which we understood and interpreted human behavior have given way to much more historically specific and local interpretations (Featherstone 1988). In his introduction to a special issue on postmodernism, Mike Feather-stone synthesizes major writers in the field and links the definition of postmodernity to a postindustrial age. He writes:

> Baudrillard (1983) stresses that new forms of technology and informa-tion become central to the shift from a productive to a reproductive social order in which simulations and models increasingly constitute the world so that the distinction between the real and appearance becomes erased. Lyotard (1984) talks about the postmodern society, or post-modern age, which is premised on the move to a postindustrial order. His specific interest is in the effects of the 'computerization of society' of knowledge and he argues that the loss of meaning in postmodernity should not be mourned, as it points to a replacement of narrative knowledge by a plurality of language games, and universalism by local-ism. (1988:198)

10. See Klatch (1987:9) for a more extensive discussion.

11. See, especially, Stacey and Gerard (1988), Stacey (1989), Brusco (1986), Ammerman (1987), and Klatch (1987).

12. Increasingly, some feminists have revealed a far more complex picture of socially conservative and Religious Right women (Ammerman 1987; Ginsburg 1989; Kaufman 1991; Klatch 1987; Pohli 1983; Stacey and Gerard 1988) than has been evident in previous feminist writings. Stacey and Gerard (1988), for instance, refer to protofeminist attitudes among female members of a pentecostal church (Global Ministries). A strong bent in feminist methodological approaches to ethnographic research is to allow respondents not only to give social expression but also interpretation to their own experiences.

13. The two groups of Hasidic women represented in this study are from the Lubavitcher (45) and Bostoner Hasidic (40) communities. See the next note for a description of Hasidism.

14. Schneur Zalman was the founder of Chabad Hasidism, which became known as Lubavitch Hasidism when its leaders moved to the Belorussian town of Lubavitch, two years after Zalman's death. Zalman (1754–1813) was a blend of talmudist and mystic. Handelman notes that his writings were a "unique synthesis of Rabbinical Judaism, Kabbalah, Rationalism, and applied Mysticism" (1984:3). The Bostoner Hasidim are the only Hasidic group founded in the United States. In a remark to

a *Boston Globe* reporter, the Bostoner Rebbe explains: "My Hasidic movement had to be customized, tailored to Boston. . . . We had to provide our Boston Hasids with an American flavor. That was the job that my father started and I continued it after he passed away" (October 21, 1985, p. 17).

15. See especially the work of Lotte Pogrebin (1982) on antisemitism in the feminist movement for corroboration of the Lubavitcher assessment.

16. In my book, *Rachel's Daughters*, I discuss the antipathy many baalot teshuvah feel toward the individualistic bent in what they call feminism. Indeed, there is a contemporary debate among feminists on this very same point (see, especially, chapter 6 of my book).

17. It is important to remember that first-wave feminism was in membership and ideology as much rooted in the evangelical and the temperance movements of the early to late nineteenth century as it was in classical liberalism and the suffrage movement.

18. "First-wave feminism" refers to the nineteenth- and early-twentieth-century feminist movement most closely identified with the suffrage movement, although not limited to it (that is, it also includes material feminists, some religiously inspired moral reform movements, purity campaigners, etc.; see Banks 1981; Hayden 1982). I have borrowed Stacey's (1988) definition of second-wave feminism as the resurgence of feminist politics and ideology that began in the mid 1960s, peaked in the early 1970s, and as she notes "has been a major focus of social and political backlash since the late 1970s" (1988:7).

19. Or, perhaps more appropriately, what some would call a "postmodern period" (Featherstone, 1988). Or, what may be termed a transition time, from a modern to postmodern period. Or, finally, what the postmodern period shares with the modern period.

20. In this chapter I am focusing on the similarities between radical feminists and these newly orthodox Jewish women. For a full discussion of the political differences between the two, see Kaufman 1993.

21. They hold this belief despite the fact that Jewish Orthodoxy has maintained a religious-legal system that supports only heterosexual marriage, recognizes only the husband's right to divorce, and leaves public religious leadership and devotion only in the hands of men.

22. One of the leading apologists in Orthodox Judaism, Moshe Meiselman, confirms this woman's contention that those characteristics of modesty associated with the female are meant for the religious community at large. "When anyone, male or female, serves G-d, he must concentrate on the inner dimensions of his personality. *Tzniut* is the inner-directed aspect of striving, the essence of the Jewish heroic act . . . (it) is not restricted to women (1978:13-14).

23. The Hebrew word *Kabbalah* means "tradition." It generally refers to a large body of collected mystical teachings and writings accumulated and transmitted over the past two millennia. Kabbalah is considered by its students as the revelation of the inner, hidden mysteries of God, the universe, and the Torah (Handelman 1984).

24. See, especially, chapter 4 of *Rachel's Daughters* (1991) for details on men's household and child-care responsibilities, and chapter 3 for sexual respect and honor.

25. See, for instance, the entire volume of *Feminist Studies*, 6, Spring, 1980.

26. Elshtain (1984) makes this same point. For a fuller discussion of both a feminist and interpretive model of sociology see Cook 1983; Stacey and Thorne 1985; Farganis 1986; Kasper 1986; Kaufman 1989a, 1990; Cook and Fonow 1986; Grant et al. 1987; Stacey 1989.

27. In fact, feminists have been most aware of this problem. Among the earliest to address this concern, without losing a feminist politics, was Zillah Eisenstein (1981).

28. For instance, there is a collective movement within Orthodoxy around divorce suggesting that the case-by-case decision making of authoritative rabbinic decision makers is not working. That the issue of women's prayer groups has forced a virulent attack against "feminist troublemakers" within the orthodox ranks suggests that the patriarchal discourse of religious orthodoxy is being challenged.

29. Could we now speak of the differences that inflect gender, asks Bordo (1990:141), if gender had not first been shown to make a difference?

REFERENCES

Ammerman, N. 1987. *Bible believers*. New Brunswick: Rutgers University Press.

Banks, O. 1981. *Faces of feminism*. New York: St. Martin's.

Baudrillard, J. 1983. *Simulations*. Trans. Paul Foss, Paul Patton, and John Johnson. New York: Semiotext(e).

Berheide, C. 1984. Women's work in the home: Seems like old times. *Marriage and Family Review* 7:37–55.

Blee, K. 1991. *Women of the Klan*. Berkeley: University of California Press.

Bordo, S. 1990. Feminism, post-modernism and gender-skepticism. In *Feminism/post-modernism*, ed. L. Nicholson, 133–156. New York: Routledge, Chapman & Hall.

Brusco, E. 1986. Columbian evangelicalism as a strategic form of women's collective action. *Feminist Issues* 6(2):3–13.

Cook, J., and M. Fonow. 1986. Knowledge and women's interests: Issues of epistemology and methodology in feminist sociological research. *Sociological Inquiry* 56(1):2–29.

Cook, J. 1983. An interdisciplinary look at feminist methodology: Ideas and practice in sociology, history, and anthropology. *Humboldt Journal of Social Relations*, 10:127–152.

Coleman, J. 1971. *The adolescent society.* Glencoe, IL: The Free Press.

Cott, N. 1986. Feminist theory and feminist movements: The past before us. In *What is feminism?*, ed. J. Mitchell and A. Oakley, 49–62. Oxford, England: B. Blackwell.

Daly, M. 1978. *Gyn/ecology: The metaethics of radical feminism.* Boston: Beacon Press.

Eisenstein, Z. 1981. *The radical future of liberal feminism.* Boston: Northeastern University Press.

Elshtain, J. 1984. Symmetry and soporifics: A critique of feminist theories of gender development. Unpublished manuscript, University of Massachusetts, Amherst.

Farganis, S. 1986. Social theory and feminist theory: The need for a dialogue. *Sociological Inquiry* 56(1):50–68.

Featherstone, M. 1988. In pursuit of the postmodern: An introduction. *Theory, Culture and Society* 5(2–3):195–217.

Foucault, M. 1979. *Discipline and punishment: The birth of the prison.* Trans. Alan Sheridan. New York: Vintage Books.

Fox, M., and S. Hesse-Biber. 1984. *Women at work.* Palo Alto, CA: Mayfield.

Freeman, M. 1978. The feminine mystique. *B'Or Ha'Torah* (3–19).

Geertz, C. 1973. The interpretation of cultures. In *Religion as a cultural system*, ed. Clifford Geertz, 87–125. New York: Basic Books.

Ginsburg, G. 1989. *Contested lives.* Berkeley: University of California Press.

Grant, L., K. Ward, and X. Rong. 1987. Is there an association between gender and methods in sociological research? *American Sociological Review* 52 (December):856–862.

Handelman, S. 1979. The Jewish woman . . . three steps behind?: Judaism and feminism; and To the house of Sarah his mother. *Di Yiddishe Heim* 20(4):8–14.

———. 1978. The paradoxes of privacy. *Sh'ma* 9:2–5.

———. 1984. The crown of her husband: The image of the feminine in Chassidic philosophy. Unpublished manuscript, Department of English, University of Maryland, College Park, MD, 20742.

Harris, L. 1985. *Holy days: The world of a Hasidic family.* New York: MacMillan.

Hayden, D. 1982. *The grand domestic revolution.* Cambridge: MIT Press.

Jaggar, A. 1983. *Feminist politics and human nature*. Totowa, NJ: Rowman and Allanheld.

Kasper, A. 1986. Consciousness reevaluated: Interpretive theory and feminist scholarship. *Sociological Inquiry* 56:29–49.

Kaufman, D. 1985a. Women who return to Orthodox Judaism: A feminist analysis. *Journal of Marriage and the Family* 47(3):543–555.

———. 1985b. Feminism reconstructed: Feminist theories and women who return to Orthodox Judaism. *Midwest Sociologists for Women in Society* 5:45–55.

———. 1989a. Patriarchal women: A case study of newly Orthodox Jewish women, *Symbolic Interaction* 12(2):299–314.

———. 1989b. Professional women: How real the recent gains? In *Women: A feminist perspective*, ed. Jo Freeman, 329–346. Mountain View, CA: Mayfield Publishing Company.

———. 1990. Engendering family theory: Toward a feminist-interpretive framework. In *Fashioning family theory*, ed. Jetse Sprey, 107–135. Newbury Park, CA: Sage Publications.

———. 1991. *Rachel's daughters, Newly Orthodox Jewish women*. New Brunswick: Rutgers University Press.

———. 1993. Paradoxical politics: Gender politics among newly Orthodox Jewish women. In *Identity politics: Cross national perspectives*, ed. Val Moghadam. Clarendon/Oxford Press (forthcoming).

King, Y. 1989. Healing the wounds. In *Gender/body/knowledge*, ed. A. Jaggar and S. Bordo, 115–141. New Brunswick: Rutgers University Press.

Klatch, R. 1987. *Women of the New Right*, Philadelphia: Temple University Press.

Koonz, C. 1987. *Mothers in the fatherland: Women, the family, and Nazi politics*. New York: St. Martin's Press.

Leacock, E. 1977. The changing family and Levi-Strauss, or Whatever happened to fathers? *Sociological Research* 44:235–289.

Meiselman, M. 1978. *Jewish woman in Jewish law*. New York: Ktav Publishing House.

Morris, B. 1990. *Women of valor: Female religious activism and identity in the Lubavitcher community of Brooklyn, 1955–1987*. Dissertation, State Unviersity of New York at Binghamton.

———. 1991. Agents or victims of religious ideology? Approaches to locating Hasidic women in feminist studies. Unpublished paper. Harvard Divinity School, Cambridge, Mass. 02138.

Oakley, A. 1981. Interviewing women: A contradiction in terms. In *Doing feminist research,* ed. H. Roberts, xx. London: Routledge and Kegan Paul.

Philipson, I. 1991. What's the big I.D.? The politics of the authentic self. *Tikkun* 6(6):51–55.

Pohli, C. 1983. Church closets and back doors: A feminist view of moral majority women. *Feminist Studies* 9(3):529–558).

Nicholson, L. 1990. *Feminism/postmodernism*. New York: Routledge, Chapman, and Hall, Inc.

Pogrebin, L. 1982. Anti-Semitism in the women's movement: A Jewish feminist's disturbing account. *Ms.*, June, pp. 15–19.

Rich, A. 1976. *Of woman born*. New York: W.W. Norton, Inc.

Rosaldo, M. 1974. Women, culture and society: A theoretical overview. In *Women, culture and society*, ed. M. Rosaldo and L. Lamphere, 17–42. Stanford: University of California Press.

Scholem, G. 1961. *Modern trends in Jewish mysticism*. New York: Schocken.

Sharot, S. 1982. *Messianism, mysticism and magic*. Chapel Hill: University of North Carolina Press.

Smith, D. 1974. Women's perspective as a radical critique of sociology. *Sociological Inquiry* 44:7–13.

———. 1979. A sociology for women. In *The prism of sex: Essays in the sociology of knowledge*, ed. J. Sherman and E. Beck, 135–187. Madison: University of Wisconsin Press.

———. 1988. Ethnographic methods of investigating relations of ruling: Studying the making of a dacum. Paper presented to I.R.C., May 1988, Hamilton, University of Ontario, Canada.

Stacey, J. 1987. Sexism by a subtler name? *Socialist Review* (Nov./Dec.):8–28.

———. 1989. *Brave new families*. New York: Basic Books.

Stacey, J., and S. Gerard. 1988. We are not doormats: Post-feminist evangelicalism in the U.S. Unpublished manuscript, Davis, California, University of California.

Stacey, J., and B. Thorne. 1985. The missing revolution in sociology. *Social Problems* 32:301–316.

Tipton, S. 1982. *Getting saved in the sixties*. Berkeley: University of California Press.

Willis, E. 1977. Next year in Jerusalem. *Rolling Stone Magazine* (April):76–80.

CHAPTER 6

Agents or Victims of Religious Ideology?: Approaches to Locating Hasidic Women in Feminist Studies

Bonnie Morris

It is almost an insult to our beautiful way of life to assume that we are threatened by anything and everything said by the so-called Women's Liberationists. There is no question that this is a viciously destructive movement to all family structure. (Anonymous 1975:19)

One might think that the increased Jewish feminist awareness of the past decade, corresponding to the general "women's movement," would be met with opposition in Torah circles . . . actually, the Torah gives the Jewish woman a lofty status. The times are ripe for a deeper look into the essence of Jewish womanhood. (Lubavitch Educational Foundation for Jewish Marriage Enrichment 1981:x)

Feminism and Hasidic Judaism are ideologies with conflicting approaches to the subject of womanhood. American feminist thought challenges the traditional limitations on woman's role received from generations of Western religious codes; Hasidism promotes ultra-Orthodox Jewish law, infused with mystical inter-pretations on the complementary nature of the (separated) sexes. Feminist thought offers a broad range of secular, legal, political, and socioeconomic interpretations of woman's status; Hasidism steadfastly preserves an exclusive religious vision, wherein sepa-rate roles and expectations for male and female are divinely ordained laws, received as revelation from the Almighty for the

Jewish people. Both feminism and Hasidism claim an interest in the Jewish woman's intellectual and educational potential; but in reality, the perspectives of the Hasidic woman herself are absent from both women's studies and Judaica. Her voice is excluded from feminist texts because she is a traditionally observant Jew, and from the critical texts of her own religious laws because she is female.

While the history and social structure of Hasidism have attracted countless studies by Judaica scholars, the role of the Hasidic woman remains shrouded in mystery, thus permitting myths and stereotypes about her status to flourish unabated.[1] A scholarly dialogue with Hasidic women is not only necessary, but increasingly valuable in this era of multicultural women's studies and research on female spirituality. This chapter begins with the assumption that both Hasidic women and feminist scholars are concerned with female potential, dignity, and self-image, and that rapprochement between them will reveal a shared commitment to issues of Jewish women's agency. In the following pages I will address one Hasidic sect's response to American feminist thought and explore the question of locating Hasidic women in feminist scholarship.

A primary dilemma for feminist historians, both Jewish-iden-tified and non-Jewish, concerns whether Hasidic women are agents or victims of religious ideology. Outside observers who choose to study the modern Hasidic community often focus upon the anachronistic traditions maintained by religious Jews and the phenomenon of such customs flourishing alongside secular insti-tutions and conveniences (Poll 1962; Rubin 1972). To the extent that Orthodox Jewish law circumscribes female choice and agency, the Hasidic community represents old-fashioned Judaism at its most patriarchal, thus inflaming critics of women's limited role. However, the "victim" portrait of Hasidic women must be reconsidered in light of new evidence on Hasidic activism. Often it is the Hasidic woman who actively promotes her own role and who serves as an advocate for the Hasidic ideology of separate spheres. The present-day Hasidic sect most cooperative with research on religious sex roles is the Lubavitcher movement (also known as Chabad), which welcomes critical questions from less observant Jews in the hope of attracting the assimilated or cynical visitor back to traditional practices.

THE HASIDIC WOMAN AS RELIGIOUS ACTIVIST:
LUBAVITCHER ADVOCATES

The Lubavitchers represent a phenomenon of Jewish survival
and expansion unmatched by any other ultra-Orthodox movement.[2] All present-day Hasidic sects trace their roots to the
pietistic revolution founded by Israel ben Eliezer, or the "Besht,"
in eighteenth-century Poland; but only the Lubavitchers can
claim a legacy of Jewish outreach activism and proselytizing
spanning seven generations.[3] The Lubavitcher movement, named
for the region of Lubavitch, Russia, where an influential student
of the Besht named Shneur Zalman transformed Hasidic philosophy into an education movement, is notable for its intellectual
and friendly approach.[4] Where other Hasidic sects preserved
Jewish tradition and virtue by remaining closed to the outside
world, Lubavitchers actively sought to transform that world by
engaging all Jews in the redemptive process through accessible
religious training.[5] Throughout the nineteenth and early twentieth centuries, while much of Europe's Jewish population
remained polarized around the competing values of Orthodox
tradition and Western enlightenment, Lubavitcher Hasidim
steadfastly adhered to an Orthodox agenda by building religious
schools and institutions under the very noses of antisemitic
Tsars. Threats and imprisonment only temporarily fragmented
each successive generation of Lubavitchers, and their movement
expanded throughout Eastern Europe and Israel due to the charismatic leadership and meticulous diplomatic tactics of each
Lubavitcher Rebbe. This expansion ensured a worldwide network of well-informed Lubavitcher emissaries and teachers, who
were able to anticipate the coming destruction of European
Jewry and plan accordingly for their followers' safe passage to
alternative sites.[6] Religious Jews loyal to the Lubavitcher Rebbe
thus survived persecution and pogroms to resettle in Crown
Heights, Brooklyn, just prior to the Nazi Holocaust. Once transplanted to the United States, the prevailing Rebbe and his
devoted followers established a religious headquarters dedicated
to attracting all assimilated Jews back to traditional observance
and family life.[7] The death of this transitional leader in 1950,
and the subsequent takeover by his secularly educated successor,
marked the beginning of the modern American era in Lubavitcher history, the visibility of Lubavitcher activists in the West-

ern media, and the remarkable changes in the status of Lubavitcher women.

While most feminist historians agree that the 1950s were a
period of suffocating limitations in personal choice and political
rights for American women, the same period saw an explosion of
female involvement and education for women of the Lubavitcher
community. Both in Crown Heights and in missionary outposts
worldwide, Lubavitcher women became articulate activists for
female spirituality as defined by traditional Jewish law. In the
Rebbe's holy war on lapsed Judaism, no soldier could be spared,
and such military metaphors of crisis were precisely those used to
recruit women into the campaign sphere (Feller 1963:13; Morris
1991). Well before the impact of the American civil rights movement brought dialogue on ethnic pride into white homes, Lubavitcher women confronted their more-Americanized Jewish sisters
on the subject of internalized antisemitism and suburban assimilation. Resistance to the Lubavitcher platform was considerable: In
an era when real-estate zoning and Ivy League quotas still
declared "no Jews need apply," even the nominally Orthodox
male risked losing certain white privileges by wearing a *yarmulke*
(skullcap) in public (Greenberg 1981:22–28). What the Lubavitcher Hasidim advocated was blatant Jewish resistance to Protes-
tantization and a return to a visible Old World Orthodoxy many
Holocaust survivors associated with enforced ghettoization.

Why, then, were the Lubavitchers so successful in gaining followers and funding in postwar America? Their success must be
attributed in part to the increasing participation of Lubavitcher
women in the promotion of religious education for Jewish children and other campaigns aimed at ambivalent Jewish mothers.
No previous academic research describes this impressive legacy of
female organization in Hasidic subculture; primary materials on
the history of Lubavitcher women are to be found only within the
Lubavitcher community itself. In the Levi Yitzchok Library of
Crown Heights, a surfeit of historical materials by Lubavitcher
women themselves beckons the researcher, materials situated
within the added resource of a living, ongoing Hasidic enclave.

From 1986 to 1988, as a doctoral candidate completing my
dissertation on Lubavitcher women, I sought to uncover the history of women's religious activism by entering the world of
Crown Heights. My research involved studying forty years' worth
of Lubavitcher women's papers and publications, attending

Lubavitcher women's conferences and educational institutions, talking with community spokeswomen and writers, and participating in religious celebrations. The experience of living as a Lubavitcher during those months of archival research and community interviews keenly augmented my perspective—and challenged my own academic and personal feminism.

Lubavitcher women's writing as a distinctive genre of published literature dates from the early 1950s onward, when women's missionary activism became central to the Rebbe's expansionist goals. The Rebbe Menachem M. Schneerson, upon assuming leadership of the sect in 1950, invited Lubavitcher women to uphold their religious convictions from the conference podium and university speakers' table. This exhortation to public visibility and outreach work signified a change in the traditional Hasidic definition of *tzniut* (female modesty). The Lubavitcher activist's tznius continued in her conservative dress, covered hair (all married women wear a *sheitel*, or wig, over their own close-cropped heads), and strict standards of behavior with the opposite sex. Far from implying passivity, however, these significant symbols of Hasidic belief, when presented by an articulate activist, could and did convince many American Jewish woman to reexamine their stereotypes about Hasidic women's lives. Hasidic women who served as Lubavitcher representatives on college campuses set a powerful example of traditional Jewish belief while inviting the unpersuaded into feisty philosophical dialogue—hardly suggestive of a downtrodden or silenced womanhood. With the blessing of the Rebbe, female activists during the 1950s won positions at Lubavitcher outposts around the world. On the home front, women gained three extraordinary advantages between 1955 and 1960 alone—the establishment of a Lubavitcher girls' high school and teacher training seminary, the publication of a quarterly women's magazine entitled *Di Yiddishe Heim* (*The Jewish Home*), and two annual conventions for Lubavitcher women activists.

Education, publication, and organization permitted a three-point platform of agency hitherto denied Hasidic women. The umbrella Lubavitcher Women's Organization, known by its members as *Neshei Ubnos Chabad* (Women and Daughters of Chabad), offered every adolescent and adult woman the opportunity to become involved in the war on American Jewish apathy. The first page of the first issue of *Di Yiddishe Heim* in 1958 made this mission clear:

With the publication of this bulletin we, the women and girls of Chabad are taking another step forward by founding a vehicle wherein to expound, explain, and express the role and the goal of the Jewish wife.

Each moment of history makes its own particular demands upon the people of the time. Today, Jewish life is struggling for its survival, against those outside forces that intrude themselves into the citadel of Judaism, the Jewish home. Who is there to meet this challenge?—the Jewish wife. How can she meet this challenge?

At various periods in our history, we have been known to answer this question in either of two ways. The basic role of the Jewish woman, "bat melech" in her devotion to her household, and her creativity in this inner sanctuary, has been to nurture with care the flower of Jewish Youth. But at times of dire need and stress, the "aishes chayil" has gone out of her four walls, to give of herself, for the strengthening of the structure of the Jewish community. Now at this moment, we have need for both qualities simultaneously. The ways of strangers have insinuated themselves into the Jewish stronghold. (Altein 1958:1)

Subsequent issues of *Di Yiddishe Heim*, the later *Neshei Chabad Newsletter*, and pamphlets and resolutions issued within the Crown Heights Lubavitcher community likewise focused on the female obligations in Jewish law and the preservation of religious integrity in contemporary social contexts. These religious obligations incumbent upon the observant Jewish woman could be expressed generally—faith, prayer, family values, ancestry—or specifically, with careful attention given to the kosher dietary laws and particular Jewish holidays. Without question, the preservation of *shalom bayit* (harmony in the home) and devotion to husband and children were the priorities of Hasidic womanhood.

Traditional Jewish law specifically exempts Jewish women from time-bound religious commandments incumbent upon men so that women are free to care for home and family. Resultant rabbinical interpretations throughout Jewish history, combined with the pertinent *minhag* (custom) from specific communities, guaranteed that "exemption" translated into "prohibition" in the sense that no Jewish woman followed the scholarly path of higher study and public prayer required of her male counterpart. Hasidic philosophy, while upholding this traditional perspective on the division of domestic and intellectual responsibilities according to gender, nonetheless provides positive models of female spirituality and sexuality. The virgin/whore dichotomy of Christian woman-hood is not present in Hasidism; in fact, Jewish law guarantees women the right to *onah* (sexual satisfaction) in the traditional *ketubah* (marriage contract). Pious couples are encouraged to enjoy marital relations on the Sabbath, their earthly union sym-bolically linked to heavenly reunification and repair. Countless other examples reaffirm the healing, rather than destructive, power of the female and the blessings which accrue to the procre-ative (and sexually respectful) couple. The controversial period of separation during the woman's menstrual period and afterwards until her immersion in the ritual *mikveh* is likewise explained by Hasidim as a pleasant marital aid which challenges the husband to view his wife as more than an accessible sexual plaything (Langer 1981:71). These complex tenets of Hasidic family life, much mistrusted by outsiders, were precisely what the two post-war Lubavitcher Rebbes expected female Lubavitcher activists to demystify through dialogue with the uninformed public.

It is hardly coincidental that such a blossoming of institutions and organizations occurred during the simultaneous emergence of the women's liberation movement in the West. But was female activism, as encouraged by the Rebbe, a sign of increasing women's opportunities (and rabbinical tolerance thereof) or a carefully organized antifeminist tactic? In their own writing, Lubavitcher women denied that they were frontispieces for the Rebbe's (male) public relations authorities; instead they con-fronted head-on questions about female status and spirituality. Nor were they reluctant to express criticism of their Hasidic men-folk—within limits. Often the pages of *Di Yiddishe Heim* resounded with lively demands for greater male support in house-hold chores and the development of girls' schools. To the extent that the American feminist movement incited all women to discuss the burdens of housework and the lesser funding allocated to women's institutions, Lubavitcher women certainly joined in ask-ing for recognition and assistance. But this was not equivalent to demanding fundamental *change* in the structure of Hasidic sex roles. What emerges from Lubavitcher women's literature is cer-tainly the kind of antifeminist rhetoric which impedes the location of Hasidic women on the continuum of multicultural women's studies. Birth control, abortion, secular college education, profes-sional careers for women, female synagogue leadership, nonsexist toys, rock music, television, and short skirts received the same treatment in *Di Yiddishe Heim* as in comparable fundamentalist Christian rhetoric. However, an important distinction is that Hasidic women's antifeminism was rooted in minority survival rather than the political pulpit.

As Jews who, throughout history, had seldom experienced more than a grudging tolerance by powerful and oppressive state control, Lubavitcher women never suggested that liberation or choices were undesirable goals. Instead, Lubavitcher women writers and speakers provided an alternative theory which posited that Jewish women were already liberated; that Judaism, unlike Christianity, accorded women neither the Virgin Mary nor unchaste Eve status so problematic to feminists in Christian culture. Jewish women had always worked outside the home, thus enabling their husbands and sons to study; and scholarship, rather than athletic or military success, was the yardstick of a unique Jewish masculinity. These often "reversed" sex roles stemmed in part from limitations on the male breadwinner in societies with antiSemitic statutes; as in African-American culture after slavery, it was the minority woman who found work when exaggerated myths about her spouse's danger to white women closed doors to him. The working woman in Eastern European Hasidic culture received praise, rather than scorn, for her worldly skills. But the male Hasid, too, traditionally viewed his vocational role as secondary to his religious studies, which continued throughout his adult life. Earning a living was a means to economic survival, nothing more. Any discussion of career rights for women must be seen in relation to Hasidic men's lack of career orientation themselves.

Because prejudice against religious Jews often determined the economic standing of the family, ethnicity rather than gender informed the Hasidic outlook on women and work. These arguments, published and circulated by Neshei Chabad activists, offered an ethnocentric rather than politically right-wing position. However, it must be noted that working outside the home, while acceptable, did not historically *enhance* female status in Judaism. The Lubavitcher Rebbe, addressing the topic of equal rights for women, declared in a 1984 address:

> What is false is to replace women's sacred mission with the ideal that having a business or professional career is a goal for itself. But as a means of furthering Torah study, for example, there is a long Jewish tradition of women working to allow their hus-

bands to devote themselves totally to studying Torah. (Schneerson 1984:5)

As male and female outreach activists for the Lubavitcher movement forayed into secular society to make religious conquests, they encountered much feminist resistance to Hasidic philosophy. Less-Orthodox Jewish women, interested in the growing feminist movement, resisted what they perceived to be mere Hasidic proselytizing designed to return women to the home. Consequently, the women of Lubavitch began to offer arguments that did not sidestep feminist critique, but challenged its potential as an ideology to transform the Jewish female experience (Davidson 1981; Handelman 1981). The question Lubavitcher women asked their Jewish feminist critics was whether a Protestant-derived feminism or spiritual Judaism truly liberated a Jewish woman from having to define herself according to Christian majority culture (Handelman 1977).

Throughout the late 1960s and early 1970s, however, Lubavitcher women's writing in *Di Yiddishe Heim* was overtly hostile to feminism, at times almost ludicrously defensive in tone.[8] The reasons for this were not just theological. The American feminist movement's initial attack on patriarchal religious constructs seemed to the Hasidic community to be one more vehicle for anti-semitism. The link between some radical feminist and Marxist-informed writing also created anxiety and reaction in the Hasidic community, only one or two generations removed from religious exile and suppression under Soviet rule. It is important to consider the Jewish community's historical experience with new, revolutionary ideologies. Christianity, Communism, National Socialism in Germany—each defined the Jew as outsider and culpable, requiring conversion, reeducation, or extermination. Many Hasidim feared feminism posed similar threats to the Jewish family.

Some Hasidim located the source of their stance against feminism in the 1970s campaigns for abortion rights and family planning, issues which either contradicted Jewish law or suggested placing limitations on Jewish population growth. The post-Holocaust generation of Hasidim could not have been less receptive to any agenda purporting to reduce the amount of Jewish children born into the world. For the Lubavitcher women of postwar Brooklyn, the survival of the Jewish family was an all-encompassing ethic concerned with both the revival and preservation of

Hasidic culture, and the rebuilding of a religious community nearly extinguished in World War II (Schneerson 1980). If we view the postwar era as a parentheses, with the moral watershed of the Holocaust at one end and the political watershed of the feminist movement at the other, it is clearer how a generation of Hasidic women were forced to recreate their own definitions of freedom and survival.

For the Lubavitchers in particular, repopulating the globe with observant Jews after the Holocaust had an urgent demographic and theological point. The Rebbe and his predecessor had declared postwar America to be the new center from which Hasidic thought and work might be disseminated to other surviving Jewish communities worldwide (Lubavitch Foundation of Great Britain 1970:54). Beyond a basic appreciation of the religious freedom and proselytizing permitted in American society, the Rebbe and his followers had no intention of assimilating into U.S. culture. The ever-present threat of assimilation affected the Lubavitcher woman's relationship to surrounding non-Jewish society and, in this case, to the spectrum of American womanhood. Ironically, the characteristics developed by Hasidic Jewish women to resist physical threat or theological assault over centuries were qualities seldom defined as "feminine" behavior in the West—verbal self-defense, sarcastic humor, economic power within family and community, multilingual academic skills, access to political information. Because of the threats to Jewish men by antisemitic forces, Hasidic women developed a long heritage of self-reliance and capability. Rather than identifying with secular feminists, however, Hasidic women directed their tenacious loyalty and hard work back into the Hasidic community.

During the 1960s and 1970s, as frustration over the slow pace of the American civil rights movement ignited into racial violence and the increasing radicalization of ethnic activists, the Hasidim were politically isolated, their ethnic separatism based on religious convictions rather than a revolutionary socioeconomic agenda. Caught between a white Christian status quo which excluded them, and youth and/or feminist movements seeking to overturn the sex-role codes of religious authority, the Hasidic community redoubled its efforts to preach Judaism to Jews, and increasingly viewed feminism as an outsiders' revolution from which Jewish women needed to be rescued.

LOCATING HASIDIC WOMEN IN FEMINIST STUDIES

Restoring a hitherto unexamined community of women to historical importance is always a victory for feminist scholarship. Yet
Lubavitcher women missionaries and writers, in carefully disasso-
ciating themselves from a feminist agenda, call into question their
own location. In terms of increasing visibility and educational
leadership, Lubavitcher women have experienced a minor
women's movement of their own, yet continue to be less concerned with the politics of gender than with matters of Jewish
authenticity and the coming of the Messiah.

Because Hasidic women are not interested in endearing themselves to feminist critics, my colleagues in women's history seldom
ask, "What have you learned from your research on Hasidic
women?" but readily enquire "Why did you choose *them?*" Buried in the latter question is a familiar challenge. Why, indeed,
would a feminist devote herself to understanding and articulating
the spiritual framework of antifeminist women? While the Orthodox, Conservative, Reform, and Reconstructionist branches of
American Judaism have adapted to many contemporary social
changes and secular structures, Hasidism's survival and definition
stems from unyielding obedience to *Halachah*, or Jewish law.
Hasidic women may not receive rabbinical ordination or serve as
interpreters of Jewish law, may not constitute a prayer quorum or
read the Torah before a congregation, may not testify before religious courts, must cover their hair with wigs or scarfs, and are,
like Hasidic men, otherwise bound to a complex legacy of Orthodox Jewish codes long abandoned by more assimilated and Amer-
icanized Jews. However, Hasidic separatism and Hasidic attitudes
toward feminism reflect a dislike not of women but of non-Jewish
frameworks. Why has there been a general reluctance to examine
the ethnic context of Hasidic separatism as a starting point for
research on Hasidic women's self-image and religious activism?

Women's studies as an academic focus in American higher
education is a fairly recent phenomenon. Like other new and innovative disciplines, women's studies is fraught with internal conflict
from within its own ranks, in addition to charges from external
critics. Perhaps the most crucial debate in academia today concerns the inclusion of studies on women and ethnic subcultures in
the once entirely white, male, and Western canon of historical literature. Certainly, a multicultural approach to the study of history

threatens that established academic canon by introducing an alternative score pad, whereby the achievements of a privileged few are revealed to have perpetrated the oppression of the disenfranchised many. Regardless of the association of women's history and women's studies with "radical" feminist ideology, it is startling to note the white, Eurocentric, and Protestant bias of the scholarly feminist canon itself. Certainly the scope of female experience concerns the contributions of black, Asian, Latina, Jewish, aboriginal, lesbian, and working-class women to the making of history; but their perspectives are not always present in the syllabi or bibliographies compiled by (white) women's history scholars. The challenge for most women's history and women's studies programs, still in their infancy, is to address rather than to obscure the impact of race, class, and ethnic differences between women in comparative social contexts.

Both historians and critical theorists are growing more cognizant of women's ethnic identification, conflicts between ethnic and gender loyalties, and the need to confront ethnic and racial stereotyping in higher education. Afrocentric and bilingual caucuses at feminist conferences attest to this commitment toward fuller representation of women in history and political thought. Despite steps toward the development of more inclusive studies on women, many feminist scholars remain disinterested in documenting the significant activities of traditionally religious women. Yet such women constitute no less of an influential group than any other political segment of women in history. It is women's very involvement in the dissemination of traditionalist and antifeminist rhetoric which poses a unique set of questions for feminist scholars.

What attracts women to religious movements or political ideologies offering them restricted status? Why would a woman participate in the creation and popularization of propaganda advocating that a woman's place is in the home, that her biological functions necessarily limit her capacity for public agency and authority? Furthermore, what academic dialogue might result from the inclusion of works by antifeminist women in a feminist curriculum?

These questions, relevant to feminist scholars in the secular academy, obviously create a context for analysis wherein the Hasidic woman must respond defensively, if she participates at all. But because the Hasidic woman is necessarily bicultural, living and working on the margins of American society while upholding

the values of her own community, she is far more likely to anticipate and respond to feminist criticism than feminists are likely to
have familiarized themselves with Hasidism. Hasidic spirituality
appears controversial and alien because it is, like so much of Jewish culture, virtually invisible in mainstream American media and
academic dialogue. This invisibility is due in part to the fact that
the Hasidic belief system cannot be boiled down to a "sound-
byte" in our age of instant media processing.[9]

Thus the challenge for non-Jewish or secular feminists is to
adopt the temporary perspective that Hasidism is normative, and
to concentrate on *what* Hasidic women do with their lives and
their influence, rather than questioning *why* Hasidic women have
views or values different from those of assimilated Jews. This is a
cultural leap necessary for perceiving Hasidic women's agency
within its correct community context, rather than as compared
with Christian or nonreligious models.

In my research on women of the Lubavitcher community, I
place women in the primary focus as producers and agents of
Hasidic ideology, and examine the possible economic and social
benefits which accrue to them through religious activism. It would
be both inaccurate and patronizing to assume that ultra-Orthodox women have merely been brainwashed or conditioned by the
male leadership of their respective group. Such an assumption
constructs women as passive recipients of religion and shifts the
active focus to the male. While male authority and control often
determine or circumscribe female choice, women still retain
options as ideological consumers. Religious sex-role assignments
may, indeed, oppress all women as a class while still permitting
individual women to attain power and status through the manip-
ulation of the prescribed female role. As more and more women
worldwide are choosing to participate in fundamentalist religious
movements, it is no longer sufficient to dwell upon what they are
not allowed to do in their respective sects. The relevant question
is, again, *what* traditionalist religious women *are doing* with their
permitted influence as religious activists. For perhaps it is the very
alternative of a separate, controlled visibility which offers ultra-
Orthodox spokeswomen in all faiths satisfying, if limited, authority. Certainly, the classification of women as an oppressed group
is qualified by substantial evidence of women advocating their
own restriction (Papanek 1988:69). Any study of Hasidic women
must address not only the role of male authority in suppressing

women's agency, but the role of women in promoting the ideal of sacrosanct male authority.

This "victim" perspective, however, does an injustice to the preservation of a distinctive minority subculture which motivates most Lubavitcher women activists. Distrust of and distaste for non-Jewish society is behind most of the antifeminist sentiment informing Lubavitcher women's writing; historically, the oppression of Jews by non-Jewish women as well as men hardly prepared the Hasidic woman for a global sisterhood irrespective of racial, religious, or ethnic loyalties. The present-day Hasidic construction of the Gentile as opponent/opposite is most significant and illustrates the tension between ethnic and female identity for Jewish women. Because ethnic or religious identity, not gender, was the primary obstacle to Jewish freedom throughout history, it is not surprising to find that modern Hasidic women are more concerned with ethnic survival than in liberating themselves from Hasidic men. The preference is for loyalty to Jewish tradition rather than to a primarily white, Christian feminism; after all, did not Gentile women serve as agents of antisemitic provocation in Eastern Europe, and as Nazi officers in women's death camps? In short, historical and contemporary antisemitism has so uprooted and affected the Hasidic community that Hasidic women cannot afford to consider themselves oppressed by their own people, their male relations and leaders.

But due to the unhappy marriage of Judaism and Christianity in Western moral heritage, these very different cultures are too readily conflated by feminist scholars seeking to challenge sexism in organized religion. Within such a framework any new research on Hasidic women's lives is automatically politicized; the possible glorification of her "oppressive" religious community becomes anything but laudable.[10]

By upholding the virtues of the Jewish home, by constructing those virtues as separate from the realm of Christian experience, Hasidic women believe they are already "liberated"—from Christian ideals of womanhood. Thus, when Hasidic women advocate traditional gender roles and domesticity for all Jewish women, they deny that they are unintentionally reproducing their own oppression. They contend that they are, intentionally, reproducing difference: the difference between a Jewish and a non-Jewish home.

As in the African-American community, where male authority and status have been so limited by the institutionalized racism of the white majority culture, male authority in Hasidic history was consistently undermined by (Christian) state intervention and oppression. In antisemitic European society, Christian women frequently enjoyed higher status than Hasidic men, although both Christian women and all Hasidim lacked political power. The historic condition of the female as Other, as subject, separated the Hasidic woman from the Hasidic man; but the historic condition of the Jew as Other, as outcast, separated the Hasidic woman from the "white" womanhood of Western, Christian society. And the role of the Hasidic woman differed from that of the woman in modern Orthodox Judaism to the extent that Hasidism has a unique spiritual and communal history with specific roles for both male and female. Three times removed, by gender, ethnicity, and sect, the Hasidic woman thrives in a context which has yet to be explored by more than a handful of outsiders.

An appropriate starting point for scholarly dialogue with Hasidic women would have been their inclusion in the wide variety of cultural and academic anthologies on Jewish womanhood which appeared in the past decade (Heschel 1983; Kaye-Kantrowitz and Klepfisz 1986; Schneider 1984). These texts primarily criticized the sex-role limitations inherent in traditional Judaism, while affirming the importance of religious ritual in women's lives. The success of some women and their male allies in overcoming first Reform and then Conservative Judaism's resistance to female rabbis and cantors led a new generation of American Jewish women, in positions of religious leadership and authority, to challenge sexism in Jewish liturgy, hierarchy, and religious education. Texts on the role of the Jewish woman thus expanded to include analyses of this new genre of female participation in the contemporary American synagogue. Yet the resultant dialogue between feminists and male Jewish leadership, however necessary and welcome, continues to marginalize the Hasidic woman because the questions raised are often inappropriate to her situation.

In order to incorporate relevant perspectives by Hasidic women, their own community structures and spiritual self-image must be understood. For example, the relationship between the Hasidic woman and her rebbe is extremely significant. His leadership, authority, and moral platform are the impetus for his adherents. All Hasidim are equal in their attachment and obedience to their rebbe; both male and female receive religious and political guidance from the rebbe's addresses to his followers. The feminist question of women's equal access to community leadership is moot for most Hasidim, as neither male nor female adults seek to displace or succeed the rebbe. Hasidic women are not interested in attaining more congregational power on an individual basis; they consider themselves to be well served by their beloved rebbe. His role as spiritual leader is absolute—and inherited.

Historically, the role of the rebbetzin—the rebbe's wife—provided a model of female dignity and status for wives of specific dynastic leaders or recognized scholars of merit. Some rebbetzins were revered as women of scholarly stature who frequently taught other women and who occasionally taught men. Because it was the rebbetzin who served as the model of Hasidic womanhood and who received female visitors to the Hasidic community, she had considerable influence over those women interested in Hasidism. However, because the chief virtue she was expected to uphold was tzniut, or modesty, her power and visibility hardly rivaled that of her husband. And few Hasidic women historically have enjoyed the rebbetzin role. Unfortunately, the extant essays on Hasidic women in Jewish scholarship have tended to focus on the exceptional woman—as in Rabinowicz's chapter "Lady Rabbis and Rabbinic Daughters," one section of his larger text *The World of Hasidism* (Rabinowicz 1970:202–210). If the leadership dynasty in Hasidism installed men of scholarly renown, models for female leadership came from below—the breadwinning, practical wife who fed, hid, supported, and protected her studious, mystical husband as necessary.

In conclusion, therefore, the Hasidic woman is as likely to be as oppressed by outsiders' misrepresentation as she is to be oppressed by her own community of laws and values. Where there is no white, Western, Protestant model of community, the feminist investigator cannot apply the yardstick of criticism bred by the legacy of white, Western, Protestant feminism. The unique contribution of Hasidic history to feminist studies concerns how gender roles may be manipulated to preserve traditionally patriarchal systems of belief. The Lubavitcher woman activist who flies coast-to-coast with a full speakers' itinerary, lecturing other Jewish women on the virtues of modesty and domesticity, transforms the rules in order to defend them.

NOTES

1. The first book-length work on Lubavitcher women written for a general audience appeared in 1985. Journalist Lis Harris contributed a three-part series about a Lubavitcher family to the *New Yorker* in the fall of 1985, and then published her full text, entitled *Holy Days: The World of a Hasidic Family*, through Macmillan in the same year. Harris concentrated her interviews and anecdotes around one Lubavitcher woman named "Sheina Konigsberg"—the real-life Hensha Gansbourg, a resident of Crown Heights who became somewhat of a celebrity in that community as a result of her starring literary role. "Sheina" was hardly representative of all Hasidic women, however. She discovered the Lubavitcher sect in her late forties, after growing up in a secularized Midwestern family, and her entrance into the Crown Heights social structure was augmented by her marriage to a wealthy and prestigious widower from one of Lubavitch's oldest families. Since 1985, several sociologists affiliated with secular universities have contributed scholarly research on *baalot teshuvah*—women who become involved in Hasidism or traditional Orthodox Judaism as adult seekers. Both Lynn Davidman and Debra Kaufman have received acclaim for their work on the attraction of young and mid-life Jewish women to the Hasidic lifestyle. But aside from this recent scholarship, most existing texts on Hasidic women's history and ideals are those prepared and published by Hasidic presses or educational institutions.

2. Sources differ on the exact size of the present-day Lubavitcher population. An estimate by the *New York Times* in September of 1988 claimed there were 20,000 Lubavitchers in the New York City area alone. In the Crown Heights community where the late Rebbe made his home, a private directory published by the Lubavitcher Youth Organization in 1987 listed over 800 Lubavitcher families for Brooklyn. These numbers do not include the thousands of Lubavitcher affiliates who reside elsewhere in the United States, or abroad in Israel and other countries. While the Lubavitchers are superstitious about suggesting their own numbers, their commitment to placing outreach missionaries in every country where Jews live has resulted in the location—and growth—of Lubavitcher families worldwide.

3. The Lubavitchers are a two-tiered dynasty. Most followers are able to trace their ancestry back to the original founders of eighteenth-century Hasidism. However, a significant and fast-growing minority of Lubavitchers are *baalei teshuvah*, "returning" Jews who joined the Lubavitcher movement as adults. No Jew who sincerely wishes to embrace Lubavitcher philosophy is excluded from the core community; therefore, unlike comparable Hasidic sects which do not recruit outsiders into the fold, the Lubavitchers perpetually welcome and integrate new

adherents. Every Jew is a potential Lubavitcher Hasid, regardless of birth or station. This aggressive outreach policy has drawn criticism from other Hasidic leaders, who contend that Lubavitch is overly zealous in its missionary program. There is also some conflict within the Lubavitcher community about social status; generally, baalei teshuvah marry each other and are considered several rungs below the established Lubavitcher families with *yichus* (ancestry).

4. The outreach movement founded by Shneur Zalman, the "Alter Rebbe" of Lubavitch, is called Chabad—an acronym for the Hebrew words *Chochmah, Binah,* and *Daat,* or "wisdom," "knowledge," and "understanding." These words also correspond to essential principles or divine qualities in kabbalistic mysticism. The Lubavitcher missionary offices located throughout the world on college campuses or in urban community centers are always called Chabad Houses.

5. Hasidic philosophy emphasizes the active role that Jews may obtain in bringing about the arrival of the Messiah. Piety and purity in everyday actions permit the release of divine sparks from the material world, sparks which return to their Source and so restore the divine light above. Other aspects of *tikkun,* or redemption and repair, are explored in the *Zohar,* or *Book of Splendor*; and the highly regarded scholar Gershom Scholem explicates that early text further in his own work *Major Trends in Jewish Mysticism.*

6. The sixth Lubavitcher Rebbe, Joseph Yitzchak Schneersohn, was guaranteed safe passage out of Nazi-occupied Europe by the U.S. State Department. He arrived in New York in 1940 and settled permanently in Crown Heights, Brooklyn.

7. The headquarters of the Lubavitcher movement—offices, meeting rooms, and a huge central synagogue—are located at 770 Eastern Parkway at Kingston Avenue in Crown Heights. Knowledgeable followers refer to this combination house of worship and religious business complex as, simply, "770." There is even a kosher wine, produced under Lubavitcher auspices and marketed to Hasidic adherents, named "770."

8. Examples of reactionary pieces condemning the feminist movement include these articles from *Di Yiddishe Heim*: Rachel Altein, "My Heroines," 1967; Felice Blau, "Women's Lib. Oration," 1971; Chana Sharfstein, "Free To Be . . . ?" 1974; and A. Yerushalmi, "Has It Gone Too Far?" 1978. Note the perennial appearance of these critiques, indicating the ongoing influence of feminist thought in the United States since the late 1960s.

9. I am grateful to Dr. Janet Belcove-Shalin for this apt characterization.

10. The question of Jewish identity and community has also been repoliticized in recent years, due to the Palestinian *intifada*'s spotlight on Israeli occupation of the West Bank and Gaza. While there is consider-

able debate within the Hasidic community on Zionist goals—with some sects such as the Satmar refusing even to acknowledge the modern state of Israel—Lubavitcher support of Israel and influence on religious politics within Israel is not irrelevant. However, in view of the paucity of extant feminist scholarship on Hasidic women, it is inappropriate at present to conflate Lubavitcher women's political views with Israeli military policy. Regrettably, some feminist scholars are now reluctant to explore Jewish women's history because of the controversial association of Jews or Jewish scholarship with Israel. And within the political feminist community, Jewish identity is frequently perceived as an owner/oppressor's identity irrespective of past persecution or American Jewish concerns.

REFERENCES

Altein, R. 1958. Editorial. *Di Yiddishe Heim,* 1(1):1.

Anonymous. 1975. Letters to the editor, *Di Yiddishe Heim,* 17(2):19.

Davidson, G. 1981. The man-woman relationship: Judaism versus Western culture. In *The modern Jewish woman.* Brooklyn: The Lubavitch Educational Foundation for Jewish Marriage Enrichment.

Feller, Rabbi M. 1963. Keynote Address, Souvenir Journal of the Eighth Annual Convention of Neshei Ubnos Chabad. Brooklyn: Neshei Ubnos Chabad.

Greenberg, B. 1981. *On woman and Judaism.* Philadelphia: Jewish Publication Society of America.

Handelman, S. S. [Susan]. 1977. The Jewish woman . . . three steps behind? Judaism and feminism. In *Di Yiddishe Heim,* 18(4):8–11.

1981. On being single and Jewish. In *The modern Jewish woman.* Brooklyn: The Lubavitch Educational Foundation for Jewish Marriage Enrichment.

Harris, L. 1985. *Holy days: The world of a Hasidic family.* New York: Macmillan Books.

Heschel, Susannah. 1983. *On being a Jewish feminist.* New York: Schocken Books.

Kaye-Kantrowitz, M., and I. Klepfisz, eds. 1986. *The tribe of Dina.* Montpelier: Sinister Wisdom.

Koltun, E. 1976. *The Jewish woman.* New York: Schocken Books.

Langer, H. 1981. An interview. In *The modern Jewish woman.* Brooklyn: The Lubavitch Education Foundation for Jewish Marriage Enrichment.

The Lubavitch Educational Foundation for Jewish Marriage Enrichment. 1981. *The modern Jewish woman.* Brooklyn: The Lubavitch Educational Foundation for Jewish Marriage Enrichment.

The Lubavitch Foundation of Great Britain. 1970. *Challenge: An encounter with Lubavitch-Chabad*. London: The Lubavitch Foundation of Great Britain.

Morris, B. 1991. The Tzivos Hashem movement as an aspect of Hasidic identity. *Judaism* 40(3):333–343.

Papanek, H. 1988. *Caging the lion: A fable for our times*. In *Sultana's dream*, ed. Rokeya Sakhawat Hossain. New York: The Feminist Press.

Poll, S. 1962. *The Hasidic community of Williamsburg*. New York: Schocken Books.

Rabinowicz, H. 1970. Lady rabbis and rabbinic daughters. In *The world of Hasidism*, 202–210. London: Vallentine Mitchell.

Rubin, I. 1972. *Satmar: An island in the city*. Chicago: Quadrangle Books.

Schneerson, M. M. [The Lubavitcher Rebbe] 1980. Address to the Annual Convention of Neshei Ubnos Chabad. Translation in *The modern Jewish woman*. Brooklyn: The Lubavitch Educational Foundation for Jewish Marriage Enrichment.

———. 1984. Equal rights. Pamphlet. Brooklyn: Sichos in English.

Schneider, S. 1984. *Jewish and female*. New York: Simon and Schuster.

Scholem, G. 1941. *Major trends in Jewish mysticism*. New York: Schocken Books.

———. 1949. *Zohar: The book of splendor*. New York: Schocken Books.

CHAPTER 7

The Economic Revitalization of the Hasidic Community of Williamsburg

George Kranzler

Since the beginning of the sixties, observers of the American Jewish scene predicted the impending doom of the Jewish community of Williamsburg, one of the foremost Orthodox Jewish communities in this country. A number of serious crises, such as the accelerating exodus of the young and the older, more affluent residents to other neighborhoods in and around New York, the disintegration of whole blocks of streets, and the invasion of large numbers of members of ethnic minority groups, threatened its very survival. In the preface to my book, *Williamsburg—A Jewish Community in Transition* (1961), I pondered the fate of the neighborhood if the massive outmigration of the Orthodox, as well as of the less religious, continued unabated.

The gloomy scenario of the collapse of the Jewish community of Williamsburg, treated as a fait accompli by many (such as Egon Mayer, in *From Suburb to Shtetl*) did not materialize, primarily because of the decision of the Hasidic community of Satmar and other Hungarian Hasidic groups to make a stand and fight for the survival of Jewish Williamsburg. Led by Rabbi Yoel Teitelbaum, the famous Rebbe of Satmar, they rejected the mass exodus to Boro Park and other Orthodox communities. Motivated by their loyalty to their Rebbe, they systematically set about marshalling their forces and resources in a determined effort to cope with the most serious threats and to meet the constantly growing needs of their mostly lower-class population.

Thirty years later, in spite of continuing major and minor crises, the Hasidic community of Williamsburg is larger, more vibrant, and more viable than at any time in the history of this old Jewish neighborhood. Its concerted efforts have assured the survival of the neighborhood and provided a sound basis for the continuity and the future of its three-generational community, in spite of persistent critical housing shortages and the fact that close to 50 percent of the population lives below the general poverty level.

This article is a product of a longitudinal study of Williamsburg that focuses on the social changes that evolved in the past three decades. It is the postscript, if you will, to *Williamsburg—A Jewish Community in Transition*, where I emphasized the crucial role of valuational over ecological and economic factors in the dynamics and structure of a community, which corroborated Robert M. MacIver's claim that social systems are directly or indirectly the creation of cultural values. This article highlights the survival and impressive comeback of this old Brooklyn Jewish community after some social scientists had declared it doomed. It analyzes the relative strength of Williamsburg's economic revitalization and the spirit of enterprise, especially among middle-aged and younger Hasidim, in spite of their sociocultural isolation and scrupulous adherence to the ultra-Orthodox Hungarian Hasidic ideology and lifestyle. To a considerable degree, the regeneration of the neighborhood has been a success because of the Hasidim's loyalty to their leaders, but also on account of the community's relentless pursuit of economic, legal, and political solutions to the serious extrinsic and intrinsic crises that threatened its survival.

THE NEW SPIRIT OF WILLIAMSBURG

Nowhere more than in the economic sphere can even the casual visitor to the new Williamsburg observe the significant changes that have transformed the very appearance and the atmosphere of the neighborhood. Even the once sleepy side-streets that cross the four main avenues from east to west have come alive. Shoppers mix with local residents, craftsmen, workers, and the stream of young mothers who push their baby carriages along the busy streets. They frequent the old and new stores that have opened up on stoops or first floors of private buildings, or in rehabilitated basements. By themselves, neither the flow of heavy commercial traffic nor the loading and unloading of delivery trucks or vans are unusual in the (thriving) neighborhoods that combine business and residential functions. What is different now, and characteristic of the spirit and lifestyle of the Hasidic community, is the fact that the trucks, vans, fork lifts, and hand trucks are frequently handled by young or middle aged Hasidim. These men are dressed in overalls or work uniforms that do not hide their long, dangling *tzitzit* (ritual fringes) and their *peyot* (side curls) under their work caps. In the old Williamsburg there had also been some Jewish menial workers, such as the soda men, glaziers, or shoemakers. Hasidic truck drivers, auto mechanics, or construction foremen, which are a common sight in the eighties and early nineties, would have raised eyebrows and evoked curious comments. Now bus drivers, truck drivers, and the handlers of other commercial vehicles and equipment, as well as craftsmen and shopkeepers, bear vivid testimony to the new spirit of Williamsburg, a spirit which has engendered the lively commercial hustle and bustle, without interfering with the ultra-Orthodox lifestyle. This transformation of the old, sleepy, declining residential neighborhood is reflected in the new look, the result of funds from various neighborhood preservation and beautification programs that were made available with the help of the local Opportunity Development Association (ODA). Grants from the ODA have enabled the residents to repair and install bright new street lights on main streets and to spruce up houses, stores, and properties all over the neighborhood: New trees now replace the old, mostly dead nineteenth-century elms that once lined the avenues; front gardens have been planted; more recently, renovation, weatherization, and new construction are supplanting much of the old, inadequate pre-World War I housing stock. Williamsburg is a community come alive!

WILLIAMSBURG'S *HASIDIC YOUTH*

Key to the neighborhood's new look and throbbing street life is the emphasis on youth, on young people who have become prominent in almost every phase of commercial, organizational, and religious life. According to one woman who had lived in the community for decades:

Our *yunge leit,* the young people are taking over the old stores, start new businesses, and have become the leaders in many activities of our *kehillah.*[1]

The Hasid in charge of running the transportation system for the Satmarer community's educational network of schools said: "I have only two men close to forty working for me. All others are in their twenties and thirties." Another man, a key administrator in Satmar, pointed out:

Young people, our *avreichin,* young married scholars, workers, and entrepreneurs have become the most potent force in our organizational work. They carry much of the burden, and are constantly expanding the scope and range of our activities, as most of our leaders and activists are getting on in age. They are showing the wear and tear of the years of suffering in the Holocaust, of the escape, and of the readjustment and rebuilding in this country.

In point of fact, the source of the new Williamsburg's strength is its three-generational community where the young want to remain and continue the traditions and lifestyle of their elders. Their religiosity and education are superior to what they had been in the small towns of Eastern Europe, in Hungary and Romania, from where most of the Williamsburg Hasidim had originated.

This general emphasis on the young, on rejuvenation of life in Williamsburg, expresses itself most poignantly in the choice of careers and types of skills or enterprises that have become popular. They are quite different from the economic patterns described in the 1961 study. In the first place it must be stressed again that the young confront the same problems as their elders when dealing with the outside world, because of their strict adherence to the ultra-Orthodox life style: the Hasidic garb, the beard and peyot, and the rules of conduct that constrain their dealings with outsiders. Obviously this is not very conducive to their successful participation in mainstream American economic and professional life. Nonetheless, a small number of Hasidim has penetrated the walls of discrimination in the jobs and activities that require little visibility and limited contact with a public that may resent their appearance and conduct. As the spokesman of the Satmar community put it:

Not more than ten percent of our yunge leit are working for the government, in the post offices, in social security, or even in banks or social welfare agencies where they have to face the broader public that is not willing to bear with their being and looking different.

The Hasidim's refusal to mix socially hampers their full participation in the American blend of commercial, academic, and social life. Hasidim will hardly partake in business luncheons, in executive conferences, and in the almost obligatory get-togethers with customers over drinks, at bars or in night clubs. As long as they refuse to make any concessions, such as eating in places that serve nonkosher food, uncovering their heads, or shaking hands with women, their chances of conducting negotiations for deals are severely limited, even if there is no outright antisemitism involved.

There is, of course, a deeper reason why young Hasidim will not even aspire to the careers to which the majority of the American Jewish community's youth has flocked, especially since World War II. The latter have a college education and degrees that open doors to all but the most exclusive institutions and organizations. By contrast, the major factor that determines the economic patterns of the Hasidic community is the almost exclusive concentration of the young on religious education—from nursery to advanced Talmudic studies—even after marriage, with only a minimum of time allotted to the required secular studies. Boys rarely attend general studies classes after Bar Mitzvah, while Hasidic girls schools offer their students mostly vocational courses beyond the required secular studies. This enables them to take jobs as teachers, bookkeepers, secretaries, computer programmers, or sales personnel before and after marriage, and during their child-bearing years. They do so mostly to help pay for their wedding and to supplement the income of their future husbands. This is a necessity in most cases, because the cost of living for Hasidim is much higher than that of the typical American household of four on account of the high rentals, cost of kosher food, and private school tuition for all children. This holds true even though the typical Hasidic family does without much that is standard for most Americans, especially in the areas of leisure and entertainment activities. Lacking a thorough secular education and degrees, the Hasidic self-made man must pull himself up by his own bootstraps as a craftsman or entrepreneur, unless he becomes a religious functionary. Most must start small, work long and hard hours, and endure the ever-present danger of failure, which, incidentally, has increased considerably since the beginning of the economic downturn in the 1990s.

ENTREPRENEURSHIP—HASIDIC STYLE

In *Williamsburg—A Jewish Community in Transition*, I quoted a pre–World War II refugee who had been a successful businessman prior to his emigration from Germany. After years of unemployment, failure, and disappointments, he had worked his way up to the position of foreman in a leather goods factory by sheer stamina, hard work, and dedication to the interests of his boss. As the foreman, he induced the owner to hire several of the Hasidic newcomers. Though they caused him some problems by their ultra-Orthodox conduct that went beyond his own Orthodox standards of religiosity, he retained them and was quite satisfied with their attitude and work. But after little more than half a year, the newcomers had learned enough of the trade to strike out on their own. They did quite well and branched out into new, related lines. "They had the guts," he commented, "the resolve, and the resources to do what I had often considered but never dared do because I had a growing family to support and send through school."

This case is typical of what was to become the pattern for many of the newcomers who had no formal education or commercial experience. After they became thoroughly familiar with a trade, several formed partnerships and set up shops or businesses of their own. The following comment of one prominent leader in the Hasidic community of Williamsburg, speaking to the differences between his generation and that of his grandson, is indicative of this trend:

> I had learned my trade in my father's shop in the small Hungarian town where I grew up. And when we came here I trained my son to become an equally competent craftsman. The attitude of my grandson and his friends is quite different. When I offered to train him, too, and eventually take him also into my shop that can use more help as we are expanding, he rejected my offer. He and his fellow students who have recently married, have a different view than we. They don't want to spend years in a shop learning a trade from the "ground up." They scouted around for

some venture that seemed promising and that would not require tremendous resources to start with. They took the plunge knowing that they took a chance, since they had no knowledge, education, or commercial experience. They are still struggling, but the prospects of their breaking through and building up a successful business are improving daily. I and my son did not have the courage, and the opportunities were not as available, as they are now. Within a few years they have achieved what took us decades of hard physical labor. With the help of the Lord, they hope to broaden their trade into a lucrative enterprise.

Another characteristic illustration of this entrepreneurial trend among the young Hasidim was offered by a Hasid in his thirties. Together, with one of his fellow scholars, he had started a small electric appliance store in the basement of a house on a side street off Lee Avenue. Eventually, they branched out into computer hardware and software, bought a second building, and now have a thriving business. When questioned about the technical details, one of the Hasidic owners with beard and peyot smiled and admitted frankly:

> I know nothing about the technical aspects of computers. All I do is I buy and sell; and if necessary consult the companies with whom we deal. They are only too happy to provide technical guidance to us and to our customers.

While directing the busy traffic of people delivering shipments of merchandise, and of customers purchasing and picking up large packages, he said:

> You see, I have no formal education beyond the basics I learned in the first year of high school. But I have no difficulty communicating with my suppliers or customers, as you can see. The same is true for many of my friends and contemporaries who have started a business of their own. Some have failed. Quite a few are struggling. But others, like my partner and I, have achieved a good measure of success, with the help of the Lord, even without having a secular education. Already I have bought a house for my family in Kiryas Yoel [a Satmar community in Orange County], and my partner bought one right here in Williamsburg. Both of us are very active in *hatzoloh* [the local ambulance service run by the Hasidic community] and in a number of other community organizations. Yet, we still make time for our daily Torah study every morning before we start working in our

business. We are satisfied to operate on a lower margin, and try to satisfy our customers. That is what counts.

It was Hasidic businessmen like this one whom an older Williamsburg Hasid had in mind when referring to a synagogue that is mostly attended by second- and third-generation American young professionals.

Our *yunge leit* have no college education like your people here. But I am willing to bet that quite a few of them make out better than your professionals. And they have large families to feed, clothe, and send to yeshivot.

Though this remark may be somewhat exaggerated, it points to the pride of the older Hasidim in the spirit and achievements of the younger generation, though they have little secular education, limited commercial know-how, and little experience. The knack of Hasidic storekeepers to master the intricacies of their trade first became apparent to this writer when he visited a ladies clothing store in the heart of the garment center in New York that was run by two middle-aged Hasidim. They had started out in a loft of an old building on Eighth Avenue. Now they own the entire corner and have combined its three stores into one, which is divided into various departments. Lines of expensive cars were parked outside, and groups of well-dressed ladies kept moving in and out of the store with large packages. Obviously they had found what they were looking for, here at the edge of one of the busiest commercial areas of Manhattan. The owners and their employees, all of them men and women from the Hasidic community, moved easily among their affluent, native-born customers, referring to famous fashion and style magazines that were everywhere on display. In the mid eighties the two Hasidic owners expanded their ladies garment business to several other locations, including one on Thirteenth Avenue in Boro Park and a store in Miami Beach. Apparently all are doing quite well.

These anecdotal descriptions highlight what has become a significant change in the economic patterns of the new Williamsburg. Young and middle-aged Hasidim are successfully dealing with a clientele that hails from in and outside the Hasidic community, and with suppliers as well as employees. This runs contrary to all the expectations and experiences of earlier generations of immigrants for whom acculturation and assimilation were the sine qua nons of acceptance and success. Obviously, the new generation of Hasidic entrepreneurs blends well into the mainstream of American commercial life, despite the handicaps of their appearance, language, and sociocultural isolation.

COMMUNITY LEADERSHIP

It stands to reason that this breakthrough has not happened overnight. It is largely the result of strenuous efforts of the community leadership to create an environment in which their members, especially their young, would get a fair share of the opportunities. A key organization in opening avenues of training and providing technical assistance in dealing with the various federal, state, and city agencies is the local office of ODA (Opportunity Development Association), a department of the U.S. Department of Commerce Small Business Division. Its staff of technical advisors, specialists, and counselors have succeeded in tapping vital resources and in developing channels for funding, financing, and business procurement in governmental and private commercial sectors. They have successfully cultivated the political connections and technical expertise that produced changes and opportunities not thought possible even a decade before. Foremost among these achievements is the official designation of the Hasidim as a *disadvantaged minority*. It took more than ten years of intensive legal and political maneuvering to overcome the open resistance and legal blocks. In a formal ceremony in July 1984, in the presence of political figures from the U.S. Department of Commerce and White House, the State and City, and heads of other minority groups, the Hasidic community achieved this important recognition.

The record of ODA in the decade and a half in which it helped untrained and inexperienced Hasidim establish themselves and expand their businesses is very impressive. As one of the high government officials pointed out, it provided valuable evidence which attested to the effectiveness of the federal programs that evolved from the War on Poverty and on Inequality. This is evidenced in the brief summary of achievements of the local ODA that appeared in *Minority Business Today,* published by the U.S. Department of Commerce,[2] in an interview with its dynamic director, Rabbi Tzvi Kestenbaum, whose efforts were largely responsible for this major breakthrough on behalf of the local and wider Hasidic community. First and foremost, ODA's officers have systematically located funding sources for training and job development. They guide and sponsor the establishment of new business ventures by Hasidim who have neither the technical know-how nor the skills and experience necessary to start new careers in business, having spent most of their youth on religious studies. Hence they are limited to the trades and commercial ventures that do not require intensive formal education.

Yet, in spite of these handicaps, ODA reports that between 1974 and 1985 it has assisted 2,500 Hasidim in establishing their own businesses. It has processed for them close to $50 million in loan applications. It has prepared $31 million worth of procurement bids for federal, state, and city agencies in 1985 to which Hasidim had no access prior to their designation as members of a disadvantaged minority. Most importantly, ODA has established a Small Business Investment Company that is chartered by the Federal Small Business Administration. Its officers work with hundreds of Hasidic clients, direct their efforts, provide access to funding and management help, and search for new avenues of business and manufacturing. With the help of the MBDA Program, Hasidim are engaged in international trade with such countries as Japan, China, Korea, Italy, Portugal, Spain, Romania, and various Latin American countries. ODA has also been the prime mover in the establishment of the Williamsburg Merchant's Association that has been one of the main forces in the improvement and security of the neighborhood.

The efforts of ODA and other communal organizations continue unabated and are achieving results that have been praised by visiting government officials, such as the late U.S. Secretary of Commerce, Malcolm Baldridge; his successor, Robert A. Mosbacher; Governor Mario Cuomo; Mayor David Dinkins; and other prominent federal, state, and city political figures. All these officials remarked favorably on the determination of the Hasidic community to overcome their social and economic disadvantages and enter the mainstream of American business.

A DISADVANTAGED MINORITY

Some outsiders have criticized the propriety of the efforts of the Hasidic community to draw on governmental programs designed to help minority members who face disadvantage and discrimination. In response, one has only to think of the findings of the update of the classic Middletown studies of Robert and Helen Lynd, especially the volume *Middletown Families—Fifty Years of Change and Continuity*, by Theodore Caplow et al., which points out:

> At least fifty percent of Middletown families received public assistance in one form or another, either directly from federal agencies or from local agencies to which the federal government was the major contributor. (1982:27)

Similarly, Gregory J. Duncan, of the Institute of Social Research at the University of Michigan reports that:

> According to a 1986 report of *The Use of Welfare*, more than one of every four Americans has lived in a family that needed welfare assistance during a 10 year period. (1986:2)

It seems, therefore, quite appropriate that the needy of the Hasidic community in Williamsburg and elsewhere avail themselves of the same types of direct and indirect assistance. This justification is further reinforced by the fact that Hasidic Williamsburg has an average of 7–9 children per household for which to provide. This is difficult to do when close to 50 percent of the population of 40,000 has an income far below the 1985 poverty line of $10,000 for a family of four. And in families in which both husbands and wives work, the joint income is considerably less than the typical $30,000 indicated in a Special Report conducted by the U.S. Census in 1984 and 1986. The need for public assistance is underscored by the fact that about one third of the Hasidic population is either elderly and unable to work, or they are young scholars, businessmen, or tradesmen at the beginning of their family and career building. They have a modest income and live at the most basic level, as the manager of one of the largest public housing projects in Williamsburg pointed out in an interview :

> Many of the Hasidic families here just crowd their six or more children into one room. They sleep in triple bunk-beds or on mattresses stored in the closet during the day. They cannot afford to pay for the extra rooms or for the larger apartments set aside in the project for the large-size families.

The average middle-aged Hasidic family has between seven and eight children squeezed into a project apartment, while the average Hispanic family has between two and three children. According to an article in the 1986 *New York Times*, the average income of the Jewish family in Williamsburg is $9,000, whereas it is $7,000 for the average Hispanic family, a figure that includes the areas adjoining the Jewish Triangle that have a concentration of low income Hispanic families (South Williamsburg 1982).[3]

The seriousness of this situation becomes even more evident when we consider the cost of providing for the basic needs of a typical Hasidic family, such as keeping its young clothed. In my book (1961) I indicated that until World War II (Phase I), the cost of a set of clothes for the average adult in Williamsburg was about $70. In Phase II, 1939–1945, it was about $100. And in Phase III, 1949–1960, it was about $125. The same set of clothes in the mid eighties ranged between $750 to $850, and is still rising higher in the early nineties. Even if we consider the high rate of inflation since 1960, the lifestyle of the Hasidim necessitates a more elaborate attire than that worn by the American adult. The proprietor of a popular shoe store in the heart of Jewish Williamsburg pointed out that among his customers, the average Hasidic family has to purchase at least eight pairs of shoes for its children, at a cost of several hundreds of dollars. Similarly, in 1985, girls' dresses ranged between $52 to $85 for middle-of-the-line apparel in a popular children's clothing store. The proprietor, himself a Hasid, estimates that the typical family among his customers spends about $500 per child on underwear, pajamas, dresses, and coats or jackets. If one adds the cost of adult clothing, one realizes that the $10,000 on which the low income earners must exist hardly suffices to make ends meet. Hence, it is not surprising that the average large Hasidic household cannot do without some form of government support or private help. The situation has become further aggravated since the early nineties, as a result of the growing economic crisis and the resultant joblessness among the Hasidim, as well as the rest of the entire work force.

OCCUPATIONAL DISTRIBUTION

Almost half of the Hasidim work at blue-collar and white-collar jobs. They are machine operators in factories, clerks in stores and offices, mechanics in repair shops, and workers in lumber yards and construction companies. They handle the simple and more sophisticated mechanical and power tool equipment that have become part of the Williamsburg street scene and in other neighborhoods where Hasidim have established their manufacturing centers. They work as locksmiths, carpenters, electricians, and mechanics. The white collar workers are employed as secretaries, bookkeepers, sales personnel, or as low level managers. An increasing number have become insurance agents, financial managers, real estate agents, and brokers. Some even work with stockbrokers and in financial institutions and organizations. About 10 percent work in government offices.

Table 7.1 presents the typical breakdown of one relatively new congregation of younger and middle-aged Hasidim, of which the average member is in his middle thirties or early forties. The youngest congregant has three children. The older members have the typical six or seven children, and expect to have more.

Table 7.2 presents the occupational distribution of a congregation of older Hasidim. Their average age is 55, and their average household has six children. Both congregations are small and of the type one finds on most blocks in the Jewish Triangle. In both congregations the majority of the members are in business as owners or employees - considerably more than in the two congregations analyzed in the 1961 Report, Williamsburg—A Jewish Community in Transition (46, 47). Conspicuously absent are professionals. Most of the members in these Hasidic congregations are business employees or skilled and semiskilled craftsmen. They work as sales personnel or in offices. Many have become quite competent in handling computers and other advanced bookkeeping equipment. Quite a few work for larger Hasidic enterprises, such as 47th Street Photo or the Crystal Clear Company, the largest and best known firm that employs hundreds of Hasidic men and women in their stores, assembly plants, offices, or storages. At least 15 percent of the younger and middle-aged in these congregations (and in the Hasidic work force in general), are employed in some phase of the diamond, jewelry, gold, and silverware business. About 25 percent of the younger and middle-aged Hasidim have established businesses of their own. Some of them are becoming increasingly prominent in the organizational structure, as well as in the economic life of the Hasidic community. As serious budgetary constraints resulting from the growing economic crisis in the early 1990s are limiting the support that the young would-be entrepreneurs have counted on, they must now turn elsewhere and look for other sources of

Table 7.1
Occupational Distribution of a Small Congregation of Young and Middle-Aged Hasidim

7	12.5%	entrepreneurs (manufacturers, wholesale trade, import, export)
10	18%	small business owners
16	28.5%	business employees
8	14.5%	skilled craftsmen
6	10.7%	semiskilled craftsmen
4	7.2%	teachers
3	5%	ritual functionaries
1	1.7%	post office employees
1	1.7%	Kollel scholar
56	100%	TOTALS

Average number of children: 6
Average age: 35

Table 7.2
Occupational Distribution of a Congregation of Older Hasidim

1	3%	factory owner
1	3%	store manager
7	20%	businessmen
17	48.6%	business employees (sales, office)
2	6%	retired blue collar workers
8	23%	white collar workers
36	100%	TOTALS

Average number of children: 6
Average age: 55

funding or for new businesses that require less government support, such as insurance, travel bureaus, financial management, and real estate.

A growing number of these businessmen have chosen to branch into export and import, especially in clothes, crystal, jewelry, linen, and china. Some have become exclusive distributors for a number of European and Far Eastern products that one finds in trade magazines or in the advertisements of *Der Yid*. Williamsburg is crammed with stores that sell lines of apparel for children and adults: A typical one—a child's wear clothing store—inhabits a converted basement in the heart of Williamsburg, and has become a favorite for mothers who are looking for elegant children's clothes. The owner, a Hasidic woman, travels twice a year to Europe to select her imports carefully. Yet another Hasidic woman runs her crystal and lamp wholesale place in an old factory building at the edge of the Jewish neighborhood. Every six months she travels with her husband to Italy and Portugal to make her selections. A real entrepreneur, she also provides goods for wholesale and retail stores in New York and in cities throughout the United States.

As more of the younger Hasidim learn to handle all kinds of simple and more sophisticated equipment and machinery (much of which has been spawned by the computer and laser technologies) they are turning to the skilled and semiskilled crafts. Many of the younger Hasidim, who after spending years on Talmudic study in a yeshivah and, after marriage, in a kollel, are becoming quite adept at handling all kinds of light and heavy equipment and sophisticated machinery, such as computerized bookkeeping, iron and steel processing machines, or metal casting. They drive heavy trucks and do not mind wearing the standard work uniforms until they know enough, earn enough, and gather the resources needed to start their own trades and hire "menial workers," as several said frankly. Above all, they aspire to have their children grow up in the intensively Orthodox spirit, marry into a *baale-battishe* (socially respectable) Hasidic family, and become scholars or choose a baale-battishe career. This does not take away from the fact that they are plumbers, locksmiths, carpenters, or repairmen who wear work uniforms or handle construction jobs. They wear beards and peyot unabashedly, and take pride in their crafts and skills, and quite a few earn a good living. "We make as much as your government employees," said one of these middle-aged Hasidim who started his own notions business on the Lower East Side and who is quite satisfied with a trade that affords his family a good living and a decent lifestyle, and allows him to accumulate a library of talmudic and Hasidic books which he studies before and after work.

EMPLOYMENT IN THE YESHIVAH OR AS A RELIGIOUS FUNCTIONARY

Of course, a major source of employment, especially for the young scholars of the Advanced Talmudic Studies Institutes, are the constantly growing Hasidic educational systems for boys and girls in Williamsburg and other Hasidic centers. There is a constant need for teachers, supervisors, administrators, bus drivers, cafeteria managers, and maintenance workers as new schools are built to accommodate children from day-care centers to the institutes of advanced studies. In contrast to the yeshivah teachers of the earlier pre– and post–World War II period, who were poorly and often irregularly paid and who had to look for other work during the summer months, today's Hasidic yeshivah teachers are given regular twelve-month positions once they have proven their competence over a two-year trial period. They also have fringe benefits, not the least of which are free tuition for their children and special consideration in the communal food stores, such as the Satmarer butcher store. Moreover, they are the recipients of new housing and are allotted bungalows during the summer months in the Catskills when all classes above the primary grades move to summer camps. Today's Hasidic *melamdim* (elementary school teachers) can no longer be considered the proverbial schlemiels of the old Hebrew schools, who had no other means of sustenance or who used teaching as a temporary job while they went to school or trained for better paying work. *Chinuch*, the field of education, has become a prime occupational goal for the students of the institutes of advanced talmudic research who want to dedicate themselves to lifelong study and Torah learning, unlike their predecessors in the earlier decades of the century.

A number of similar occupations have also opened up as a result of the growing need for religious functionaries. Besides the usual ritual slaughterers (*shochtim*), the Hasidic community trains capable young scholars to become religious judges and arbitrators (*poskim* and *dayonim*) not only in matters of ritual laws but for a broad spectrum of civil and business matters. Teams of dayonim routinely convene at regularly announced hours in the *Beyt Horaah* (the court of the Hasidic Rabbinic organization) on Division and Bedford Avenues. A number of these bright, still relatively young scholars and judges have made a name for themselves as experts in difficult divorce or desertion cases, or in matters of personal conflicts or business disagreements that are usually brought before the public courts. One of the prominent non-Hasidic rabbis who is still in Williamsburg, when questioned about the crucial differences and changes in the religious life of the old and the new Hasidic Williamsburg, said:

> Our yeshivot never really focused on producing poskim, the rabbis who were competent to judge not only questions of "kosher and treyf" [fit and not fit to eat] chickens or meat, but who devoted themselves systematically to deal with the daily problems that confront a functional community. We were educated on the model of the classic Lithuanian yeshivah, whose major goal was to produce *talmidei chachomim* [talmudic scholars] above all else, to perpetuate the chain of the scholarly tradition that has largely been destroyed in the Holocaust. Our yeshivot succeeded in training the American *lamdan* [outstanding theoretical scholars]. Little attention was paid to the applicability of the theoretical subject matters studied, except for those who wanted to become rabbis and devoted the required time to the study of the sections of the *Shulchan Oruch* [the code of religious laws] that were required to get *Semichah* [rabbinic ordination]. There is now a definite shift toward producing specialists in various areas of practical *halachah* [Jewish law] in our yeshivot. But there is no comparison to the systematic training of the Hasidic yeshivot, which initiates every student since early youth into the various branches of the vast halachic literature. Thus they have now *baalebatim* [lay members of the community] who can look up the laws in the standard codes; but they have produced a generation of competent poskim who are qualified to handle all matters of vital concern to a community like Williamsburg.

Indeed, Williamsburg and the other Hasidic communities have little use for the polished orators and social directors that have dominated many of the Orthodox synagogues in the last half century. They demand poskim (rabbis) who are not only talmudic scholars, but who have mastered the vast halachic legal literature that equips them to function as judges in all realms of individual and collective life, not only in questions that relate to ritual and religious concerns.

There are a number of other occupations that offer careers to the graduates of the Hasidic yeshivot besides those of teachers, rabbis, dayonim and poskim (religious judges and arbiters), or shochtim (slaughterers). Among these are *sofrim* (scribes) who produce, check, and repair *Sifrei Torah* (Torah scrolls), *tefillin* (the leather phylacteries worn by Jewish males on their heads and left arms during the daily morning prayers), *mezuzot* (the small parchment scrolls attached to the doorposts of Jewish homes), and *megillot* (parchment scrolls on which books of the Bible are inscribed, and which are used on such holidays as Purim. They also write the *ketubot* (Hebrew marriage contracts) or *gittin* (divorce documents). The large Torah scrolls which are used in the synagogues for the reading of the weekly portions of the Torah take even the most skilled scribe years to write properly and command an average price of $25,000 in the United States and in Israel. There is now the STAM organization of scribes that certifies and reviews the qualifications of professional sofrim. Their number has increased in recent years, commensurate with the demand and the price paid for this painstaking work. Yet, there is still a great need for competent scribes, especially in cities and communities outside of New York. These have to be satisfied with occasional visits of traveling sofrim.

As the yeshivah organizations expand, there is a growing need for competent officials to administer them. The head of the Satmarer community recently remarked:

> We thought we would have to go outside to find effective administrators and workers for our offices. Yet, right here among our own young we discovered the kind of talents, the dedication to the needs and needy, and the resourceful men and women who master not only the technical difficulties of this work. They have the spirit, as well as the devotion, the *mesirat nefesh* (readiness to make sacrifices) that makes up for some of them lacking broader education and make us proud of our *chinuch*, our education.

As a result, these young and middle-aged Hasidim have moved into the front ranks of the leadership of the Hasidic Community of Williamsburg.

EXPANSION OF THE BUSINESS DISTRICT

The most significant transformation of the economic scene in Williamsburg itself is the expansion of wholesale and retail shops into the formerly quiet side streets, not just in the major business avenues. Almost every edition of the weekly *Der Yid* announces the opening of a new store, a new shop, or a trade office in one of the cross streets that stretch from Brooklyn Broadway to Whythe and Kent Avenues along the water front. There are new business centers, such as the plaza off Bedford Avenue, at the confluence of Bedford Avenue, Rodney, and Keap Streets. Even more significant is the expansion south and southwest, into the formerly blighted areas that range all the way to the blocks cleared for the sprawling Pfizer Drugs and Chemical Corporation. A former public school building on Throop Avenue has been turned into a large yeshivah center of Satmar for the intermediate boys division. The entire area between the Jewish residential core and Throop Avenue is gradually being acquired for commercial, industrial, and residential purposes. Also, some of Williamsburg's institutions that are outgrowing their original locations, such as Pesach Tikvoh—the mental health facility—are moving into this extension of the Jewish Triangle.

Interestingly enough, a large number of the new stores opened in Williamsburg are devoted to infant and children's wear, as well as to adult clothes. In an informal shopper's survey of sixty women, conducted in the summer of 1985, most of the people who come from as far as Flatbush, Boro Park, and beyond are interested in shopping for clothes for their children and for themselves. The respondents indicated that they preferred to visit Williamsburg stores rather than going to the fancier and considerably more expensive stores in Manhattan. Among these are not only Hasidic women who naturally would prefer to shop in a setting closer to their own lifestyle, but the well-to-do patrons from the suburbs, or even from out of the state. One well-dressed woman from a city 200 miles south of New York stated that she had been used to coming to New York to do her shopping at Bloomingdales and Saks Fifth Avenue for herself and for her grandchildren. Now she has learned that she gets equally stylish and frequently better quality clothes at more reasonable prices in Williamsburg. Not that she cannot afford the higher prices. But, as she put it, "it goes against her grain" to spend more for something that is worth less.

At the initiative of the local ODA, about 120 retailers have joined in an active Williamsburg Merchants Association, of which only 2 are not Jewish. In a 1983 survey done by an official of ODA, only about half of the stores had been in existence twenty-five years or more. Between 20 percent and 30 percent are ten years old, and 28 percent had been established in the past ten years. In 1987 their numbers had increased dramatically. Though some do not survive the keen competition, the majority seem to do relatively well, judging by the improvement in appearance and the traffic of customers in the main shopping streets at all hours of the day, even during the hot summer months. Currently, the number of qualified Hasidic enterprises is considerably greater, as evidenced by the recently established *Business Directory Yellow Pages* that is published and updated every year in Williamsburg. It reflects the unabated growth of local retail, wholesale, and manufacturing establishments in the waning eighties and early nineties. Although clothing is still the dominant industry, there is a marked increase in electrical appliances stores; in linens, silver, and jewelry stores; and in a variety of food lines never before available in Williamsburg and other Hasidic communities: these include Kosher health foods, new dairy products, wines, juices, liqueurs, condiments, and candies.

Also increasing are a number of services that are announced in practically every issue of the weekly *Der Yid*. There are automotive shops, car leasing companies, real estate agencies, and financial management and brokers offices. Furthermore, there is a growing number of medical services offices opened by specialists and legal services by lawyers who emphasize their Orthodox religious orientation and their ability to communicate with the Hasidic population. New stores specialize in baby carriages, baby furniture, and other items that reflect the baby boom.

DREAMS AND REALITIES

The American dream of "making it," of transcending adversity and succeeding against all odds, is critical to the Williamsburg mindset. In the words of one woman:

> Our parents and many of our older brothers and sisters came to this country from concentration camp and years in D.P. (Displaced Persons) camps with little more than the rags on their

backs. Now, after years of privation and hard work we want to live like others and enjoy our homes. Where else can a woman like myself express her sense of beauty and aesthetics.

This frank attitude of a woman who lives in one of the larger apartments in a public high rise building expresses the desire especially of the younger women who want to create an environment in their own homes that is more pleasant than the ones in which they have grown up. The vast majority of homes in Hasidic Williamsburg (except for those of the 5–10 percent of Hasidim who have become successful in their enterprises, and who can afford a more comfortable residence) are furnished simply. Most people cannot afford greater displays of luxuries than the ever-present bookcase filled with the standard talmudic, halachic, and Hasidic literature, and a china closet that contains the usual silver candlesticks, menorah, esrog box, and other ritual vessels and bowls necessary for the proper celebration of Sabbaths and the holidays. Most of the other available space is used for bedrooms and sleeping facilities for the many family members. This cramped life style is what some of the middle-aged women are trying to leave behind. The woman previously cited showed her visitor how she replaced most of the appliances and refurbished the rooms to accommodate her growing family. This attitude of lavishing much attention on the home is shared by many of the middle-aged and younger women and their husbands. It makes the furniture and appliance stores and home renovation companies among the busiest in the new Williamsburg. Similarly, shopping and providing for the constant needs of their large and growing families is a major outlet for the young Hasidic women, as for many women everywhere. Hence the streets are usually crowded with mothers pushing their baby carriages up and down the major avenues while simultaneously holding on to one or two toddlers. These outings are one of the few outlets that women have from their busy schedule of handling the endless household and child-care chores.

Fortunately, a growing number of the Hasidic women are able to leave the dusty, hot streets of Williamsburg during the summer months for a bungalow in the Catskills. The women live there in July and August with their younger children. The boys and girls above Grade 3 live and study in the well-appointed summer camps nearby. Typically, the Hasidic men spend the weekdays in the city on their jobs and join their families in the mountains during the weekends. It is, incidentally, one of the by-products of the Hasidic revival of Williamsburg and similar Hasidic communities that they have saved the "Jewish mountains" from total ruin: While a number of hotels have gone bankrupt, the better ones have been taken over by Hasidic yeshivot for their boys and girls school camps. Others have become centers of bungalow colonies that crowd the famous old resort centers. What is new is the opening of numerous stores, most of them branches of those in Williamsburg and other Hasidic neighborhoods, that provide the type of food and other necessities that the Hasidic population requires for their intensively Orthodox lifestyle. Thus, Hasidic Williamsburg and other communities make sure that their families are properly taken care of while in the mountains as during the rest of the year in the city.

SUMMARY: THE ECONOMIC REVITALIZATION OF THE HASIDIC COMMUNITY OF WILLIAMSBURG

The effectiveness of the Hasidic leadership in stemming the collapse of Williamsburg emerges boldly in the economic revitalization. Counter to the pessimistic predictions, the Hasidic community has developed new economic patterns that enabled it to overcome the serious handicaps and difficulties inherent in their Hasidic lifestyle. By the early nineties, Hasidim have become part of the mainstream of American business in the spirit of free enterprise and competition.

Instead of following the masses of earlier residents who left the neighborhood during the fifties and sixties, the Hasidic community, led by the Rebbe of Satmar and his associates, undertook a multi-phased attack on the most pressing problems that threatened its survival. Foremost among these were the economic depression, a critical housing shortage, unemployment, and poverty, especially among the elderly survivors of the Holocaust. Most important, the Hasidic leaders were able to succeed because of the loyalty of their followers. These men and women were willing to overlook the serious disadvantages of remaining in Williamsburg in order to be close to their rebbes and to the milieu they had created, though other neighborhoods, such as Boro Park and Monsey, New York, offered "greener pastures."

First and foremost, the leadership of the Hasidic community explored various avenues to locate private and public resources to help them meet the urgent need for adequate housing for the large families of its growing population. The most strenuous efforts were devoted to developing a sound basis for the survival and economic future of the neighborhood. Drawing on municipal, state, and federal programs, the community leadership searched for avenues that allowed their mostly low-income members to gain access to opportunities available to the members of other ethnic and racial minorities. After a decade of political and legal negotiations, pressures, and preparations, they succeeded in achieving a major breakthrough when, in July 1984, the Hasidic community was officially designated a disadvantaged minority. This prime requisite helped its members overcome numerous obstacles and problems inherent in their strict adherence to their ultra-Orthodox lifestyle. Their hard work and spirit of enterprise enabled many of the Hasidim to break into new lines of business and trade. This contributed to the process of economic growth and the revitalization of the entire neighborhood, though close to 50 percent of the population is still living far below the official poverty line. It is particularly the middle-aged and younger American-born Hasidim who, despite their lack of formal education, skills, and experience, have turned to business and trades rather than to the academic and professional careers chosen by the majority of the non-Hasidic American Jewish youth. Aided by various training and counseling programs initiated by the local office of ODA, hundreds of young and middle-aged Hasidim have benefitted from government resources and programs and qualified for various funding and procurement opportunities that are available to the members of other American ethnic and racial minorities.

Williamsburg Hasidim have increasingly become part of the American business world without compromising their ultra-Orthodox lifestyle. They have established themselves in a number of commercial and trade areas in spite of their lack of formal education. Jewish Williamsburg is still primarily a low- and low-middle income neighborhood, yet indications of the economic revitalization are in evidence everywhere. Less than a generation after predictions of the disintegration of Jewish Williamsburg as a major community, the prospects of a sound socioeconomic future of the three-generational Hasidic community are promising. It remains to be seen, however, whether the economic crisis of the nineties will seriously impede or turn back the level of progress achieved before the end of the eighties.

NOTES

1. Most of the direct quotes cited in this essay are the author's translation from Yiddish or an admixture of English and Yiddish spoken by the majority of the residents of Hasidic Williamsburg.

2. *Minority Business Today.* 1985 pp. 13–15. Washington D.C.: The United States Dept. of Commerce.

3. See *South Williamsburg*, 1982. p. 3. New York: Opportunity Development Association. According to the '80 Census, the median income is $8,046, compared to the median income of $16,818 in all of New York City.

REFERENCES

Caplow, T., et al. 1982. *Middletown families—Fifty years of change and continuity.* Minneapolis: University of Minnesota Press and Bantam Books

Duncan, G. 1986. Welfare use in America. *Winter Bulletin Institute of Social Research.* Ann Arbor: University of Michigan

Kranzler, G. 1961. *Williamsburg—A Jewish community in transition.* New York: Feldheim Books.

Mayer, E. 1979. *From suburb to shtetl-The Jews of Boro Park.* Philadelphia: Temple University Press.

Minority Business Today. 1985. Washington, D.C.: The United States Department of Commerce.

South Williamsburg. 1982. New York: Opportunity Development Association.

CHAPTER 8

Home In Exile:
Hasidim in the New World

Janet S. Belcove-Shalin

Home is a sacred symbol of universal import. Panculturally, "home" signifies familiarity, centeredness, spirituality, and wholeness. It is the beginning and the ultimate return, a sanctuary and a place of redemptive suffering. It is the key symbol of what postmodernist writers term "presence"[1] (Derrida 1970:248).

Layers of experience surrounding our homes are rich and tangled. Home is the familial dwelling, the street on which one lives, community, country. For our age of ecological awareness, home is planet Earth. Whether home is construed as a castle or just the place to hang one's hat, there is no place quite like it, except, perhaps, for the eternal peace to be found in the world to come.

Traditionally, studies exploring the rich symbolism of home have deciphered its cosmic import (Heine-Geldern 1943; Rapoport 1969; Griaule and Dieterlen 1954), analyzed the key oppositions ingrained in kin and gender structures (Bourdieu 1971;

I am indebted to a number of people who reviewed earlier versions of this paper: David R. Dickens and Laurence Loeb for their editorial comments; Naomi Loeb and Zalman Alpert for their ethnographic observations; Dmitri N. Shalin for his suggestions on substance and style; Joel Schwartz for his data on Boro Park demographics; and Rabbi Shea Harlig for his informative remarks on the nature of *galus* for Hasidim.

On August 8, 1990, my good friend and colleague, Martha Biggar Anders, was killed in an automobile accident on the Panamerican Highway in Canete, Peru. As her *yahrzeits* come and go, I think of her often. I would like to dedicate this article to Martha—to her decency, generosity, and dedication. With Martha I always felt quite at home.

Hugh-Jones 1979; Cunningham 1965), or traced its astrological significance (Dahl 1982; Skinner 1982). More recently, the symbolism of home has attracted the attention of geographers and sociologists who write about it in the context of social time and space (Zerubavel 1981; Mazey 1983; Kellerman 1989; Sack 1980), as well as students of communication interested in the media's impact on global linkages and space contraction (Myrowitz 1985; Massey 1992; Spigel 1992). This paper explores the Jewish quest for home, as exemplified by a Hasidic community transplanted from the Old to the New World. My discussion centers on the Hasidic community of Boro Park, Brooklyn, with special attention given to Bobov, a Hasidic dynasty that originated in the Western Galician town of Bobov but eventually sunk roots in Boro Park and became the third-largest Hasidic group in the United States. Bobover Hasidim are a model case of *Klal Israel* (the people of Israel) rebuilding home after yet another round of expulsion and exile. By the same token, Boro Park represents a sanctuary where these post-Holocaust survivors live as Orthodox Jews, Hasidic style, relatively free from outside hostile interference. Home building in this Brooklyn neighborhood has proven to be so successful that Boro Park has been characterized as the most vital Jewish community in the country (Mayer 1979). Understanding reasons for this success is one of the objectives of this study.

I deliberately use the term *home* rather than *house* in this text. Although the latter presupposes no particular otherness and can be thought of only as a singular object in time and space, the former is inextricably bound to its antithesis—a place where you are only a guest, a visitor, an alien. Home signifies both the personal niche one carves out in a given communal space and a transhistorical reality imbued with sacred meaning. It is a replica of the beloved homeland—Eretz Israel—and, ultimately, of paradise lost and regained. What makes the Hasidic Jews of Boro Park an interesting case study is the radical manner in which they have set out to domesticate public space through the expansion of domicile boundaries. As they take control over sidewalks, streets, buildings, and local facillities, the Hasidim alter the ecological balance btween the sacred and the profane space in their neighborhood. This appropriation has had profound implications for the performance of ritual. Moreover, it has also served to empower its inhabitants, as clearly seen in the influence Hasidim have on their

Jewish neighbors and in the control Hasidim have over the political pulse and economic well being of the environs. I would like to point out that this vigorous quest for home and the desire to expand its boundaries correspond to the ancient tradition of *eruvin*,[2] which allows Jews to merge the private (reshut hayakhid) and the public (reshut harabim) domains. Whenever an *eruv* is established in the adjacent courtyard, alley, or even around one's community, profane space is sanctified when home boundaries are expanded. Objects that could be carried only within one's home on the Sabbath can now be transported within the confines of the symbolically enlarged domestic space. Although a lack of rabbinical conseneus has so far prevented the construction of *eruvin* in Boro Park, its spirit is unmistakably there.

My discussion begins with a general overview of the meaning that the terms *home* and *exile* have acquired in the Jewish tradition. Then, I show how the Hasidim have molded their neighborhood into a community that enables its members to maintain their distinct lifestyle.[3] Next, I demonstrate how Hasidic leaders have reasserted their charismatic authority in exile, focusing in particular on the critical role that the Bobover Rebbe played in gathering his Hasidim and rebuilding the Bobover community in the New World. Finally, I share some thoughts on the meaning of home and exile in the postmodern age.

JEWS AND EXILE

Jews are known as the "People of the Book," but they might as well be called the "People of Exile." Expelled from the proverbial garden, driven from the land of their forefathers, Jews have repeatedly suffered from historical reversals that transformed safe havens into Hell. Exile and text, the longing for home and the devotion to Torah, have been inextricably linked in Jewish history since the destruction of the Second Temple. This ancient linkage, in turn, was inscribed in the Jewish calendar and ritualized in sacred canon. In the annual cycle, the holiday of Passover dramatizes the return to the promised homeland and at the same time powerfully reminds us about the hardships of exile. *Sukkoth* memorializes the temporary dwellings built by the Israelites during their wanderings in the desert. *Tishah b'Av* marks the destruction of the temple, home to the holy of holies. *Purim* and *Hanu-*

kkah celebrate the successful defense of home. *Shmini Atzeret* commemorates the rains and *Tu-Be-Shvat* celebrates the flow of sap that make the homeland fertile and life-sustaining. *Shavuot* celebrates the giving of Torah, the home manual par excellence for all the Jews, while *Simchat Torah* marks the old and new cycle of Torah reading.

In the sacred texts, home and exile are twin concepts, tied to each other as two sides of the same coin. The Talmud treats the Jewish home as a symbol of the destroyed Temple, and the family table as the Temple altar. According to scripture, the Garden of Eden is the original home from which Jews were exiled. When the Messiah finally comes, Klal Israel will be spiritually redeemed, heaven and earth will be reunited once again, and humanity will have regained its place in the garden.

The historian Arnold Eisen notes that "Paradise, it seems, has never preoccupied the Jewish imagination nearly so much as exile" (Eisen 1986:xi): "The loss and leaving of home stamp all the narrative of Genesis. . . . Indeed, they predominate throughout all five books of Moses" (ibid.). In Deuteronomy, he points out, Moses discourses on the promise of home, though the image is "overwhelmed" by the continuous threat of homelessness (Eisen 1986:25). This sense of homelessness, coupled with the painful memory of the home lost, resonate in the experience of Jews wandering through the vast stretches of space and time in search of a home in exile. The traditional home on the *yiddishe gas* (Jewish street), in the *yiddishe shtetl* (Jewish town), in the midst of the *kehiles kodesh* (corporate Jewish community) was provisional, a protected island in a sea brimming with latent dangers, but made meaningful "by reference to the Center which they had left behind" (Eisen 1986:xi).

Forcibly removed from the ancestral sources of their religious life, the wandering Jews initiated new, mobile centers. Over the centuries, Torah served as "movable territory"—a "symbolic substitute for the loss of real territory" (Maier 1975:18). In Emanuel Maier's words, Torah "seems to perform the function of territory, standing upon which the people, like Antaeus, are constantly renewing their strength.[4] This kind of symbolic territory gave rise to the social and political structure of the ghetto, so typically internalized and isolated from the political reality of the outside world" (ibid.:21–22). More than the source of spiritual edification and canonical law, Torah offers Jews a paradigm for the reconstruction of home: "The memory of the beginning and the anticipation of the end are located in the sacred text, which inevitably becomes the only 'home' to the exile, for here the original site is cited, and anticipation is clarified" (Tigerman 1988:125). Like the proverbial tortoise carrying his home on his back, the wandering Jew took his home into exile and preserved it in lore and customs handed over from one generation to another through Torah learning. The Jewish experience, in essence, is that of perennial home-leaving and home-rebuilding, with Torah furnishing guidance and instruction.

Boro Park is just the latest incarnation of home that is built on Torah[5] precepts, recovering what Rashi, the great Torah scholar, referred to as *derekh hashas* (The Way of the *SHaS* or Talmud) (Weinreich 1980:208). Along with the traditional Jewish agenda of homebuilding, we also find here the uniquely Hasidic cosmological mandate to restore the cosmos to its pristine unity. For the Hasidim, home is not just "an object, a 'machine to live in'; it is the universe that man constructs for himself by imitating the paradigmatic [re]creation of the gods, the cosmogony" (Eliade 1959:56–57). The quest for home, then, is yoked to a sublime agenda—no less the rescue of God himself from exile. This world view requires further explanation.

From the time of Rabbi Akiva it was believed that "in every place where Israel was exiled the *Shekhinah* [the divine presence among mankind] was exiled with them" (*Mekh.*, *Pisha* 14; *Meg.* 29a; TJ, *Ta'an.* l:l, 64a; etc.). This notion was elaborated in the Lurianic Kabbalah, in its doctrine of the *nitzotzot* (holy sparks), and then taken up by the Hasidim who believed that the liberation of holy sparks through worldly pursuit enables God/the universe to return to its pristine harmony. The exile of the Jews, according to Hasidic doctrine, mirrors the exile of the Shekhinah from the Godhead. By carving out a home from *galut* (exile), therefore, Hasidim help God return to his primordial source (Jacobs 1987).[6]

As one might surmise, the Hasid is no puppet or helpless actor in the divine drama of history; the restitution of the cosmos's ruptured wholeness, referred to as *tikkun*, is achieved when man and God become coauthors of the historical script. This divine-human collaboration cannot be overemphasized, for tikkun is only realizable if man maintains a close relationship with the Almighty. God needs man as much as man needs God. Both are participants in a cosmic drama by which man assists God in bringing the holy sparks to their divine source while creating heaven on earth. By rebuilding home in exile, Hasidim liberate holy sparks and assist cosmic reunification; they are metaphorically "imitating the paradigmatic creation of the Gods, the cosmogony" (Eliade 1959:56–57). Hasidim do this by engaging in deceivingly mundane chores of homebuilding, by investing in what they themselves call a "Torah-true" infrastructure built to last for generations to come.

This intense community-building has proven to be inimical to the forces of acculturation and assimilation that characterized much of Jewish history in the United States (Heilman 1982:141; Zenner and Belcove-Shalin 1988:24). It has even confounded those social scientists who prophesied that Boro Park would succumb to a "third wave of succession," displacing the Jewish community with new ethnic groups (Mayer 1979; Rosenthal 1980). To date, Boro Park remains a thriving American Hasidic neighborhood, a model for their brethren worldwide.

NEIGHBORHOOD

Before the Second World War, most Hasidim viewed America as a *treyf land* (nonreligious country), inhospitable to their religious needs.[7] No wonder that few made concerted efforts to come to the New World.[8] Those who arrived in the 1920s had not, for the most part, planned to stay for good, hoping instead to earn some money and return home to Europe. Not that home was a promised land: Poached upon by secularists and ravished by the First World War, the Hasidim nonetheless preferred to live in the communities of their forefathers. All of this changed after the Holocaust, for the Hasidim, like other Jews, had simply no community or family to which they could return. Among the first Galicianer-Polish rebbes to have come to the United States was the new leader of the Bobover dynasty, Rabbi Shlomo Halberstam. Most of the other rebbes who had arrived on these shores came from further south in Europe, particularly from Hungary. These rebbes, among them the Klausenberger and Satmarer, put down roots in Williamsburg and nearby Brownsville rather than in the Lower East Side.[9] The Hasidim's worst fears for this *treyf land* were readily confirmed. Although America appeared to be a land of relative economic opportunity and religious tolerance, it had nurtured a permissive Jewish community, unable to sustain a robust *Yiddish-*

keit. "What happened to your young people?" they queried. "Where are the youth of your synagogue, where is the second generation?" The Hasidim quickly set about to reverse this trend. In the 1950s their progress was most evident in Williamsburg, home to many of the newcomers. The sociologist George Kranzler (1961) writes that as early as 1949, the Hasidim, mainly Hungarians, assumed leadership in this community. Thanks to the unifying power of their rebbes, they were able to seize the initiative in many areas of communal and religious life that had been neglected by others. In the years directly following World War II, the community of Boro Park was by and large untouched by this new wave of refugees. With the exception of the Blueshover Rebbe, who came directly to Boro Park, the renowned rebbes settled elsewhere.

Boro Park is located in the Southwest corner of Brooklyn, bounded by Bay Ridge, Flatbush, and Bensonhurst. It runs a mile in length and a mile-and-a-half in width.[10] In the 1950s, it was described by one resident as a thriving community set among lush, tree-lined streets, straddled by private residences and modern apartment buildings, "totally American in appearance and outlook" (Kaminetsky 1953). The complexion of Boro Park changed dramatically following the social and cultural changes that swept the nation in the 1960s. The most immediate cause of this transformation was the ever-increasing presence of an alien Hasidic population. Schick (1979) writes that in the 1960s, "the early steady trickle of Chassidim into Borough Park grew into a stream which has continued to this day." This migration was related to the decline of two other Hasidic centers in Brooklyn—Crown Heights and Williamsburg—due for the most part to the influx of poor Blacks and Puerto Ricans.

With the arrival of Hasidim into Boro Park in the mid-1960s, these newcomers could no longer be considered anachronistic oddities by the community's long term residents. Not since the 1920s had the neighborhood changed so much. A real estate boom ensued.[11] Old-timers lamented that the avenues' beautiful mansions and manicured grounds were being replaced by "unappealing, unimaginative brick structures"—multifamily apartment buildings crowding a single lot to accommodate an escalating population" (Kipust 1981). In her article, "Cultural Transition," Bertha Beck describes the changes which occurred in Boro Park when the Hasidim arrived. Her children have begun to call 13th

Avenue, the major business street, "Rue de la *peyot* [side curls worn by the ultra-Orthodox]" on account of all the Hasidic shops and shoppers. Most of the stores on 13th Avenue have been bought out by Hasidic entrepreneurs.[12] Above them, in the space which once housed business offices, are now boys' and girls' yeshivot. All are closed on Saturday and open on Sunday. In no time at all, Sunday mornings have become the busiest shopping time on the avenue. While walking down the side streets, Beck encounters signs on private homes bearing the names of the new Boro Park rebbes. And on every block she discovers there is usually a *shtiebl* (prayer room). The author suspects that her husband is rather resentful of the changes the Hasidim have brought to his community, for he fondly remembers Boro Park as it was: the spacious private homes, the wide lawns, the high hedges. Yet even she and her family have been influenced by the Hasidic lifestyle and customs, specifically those of their new next-door neighbors— Shmeeyul, his wife Chavah, and their six children—Hungarian Hasidim from Williamsburg. In the past, her husband used to run through his morning prayers at home. Now he prays with Shmeeyul at his prayer room where they need an extra man for the minyan. Beck finds herself reciting more and more often Chava's stoic formula: "Don't worry about tomorrow; the Lord will help" (ibid.:8). But miracles of miracles, her eldest son has finally begun to pray without being coaxed, no doubt influenced by his pious friend next door. Beck writes, "I am delighted—and alarmed. Will my son be wearing *peyot* [side curls] next week? Will he demand that I shave my head and wear a *sheitl* [wig] and that his father wear a beard" (ibid.:6)?

Beck's fears are not entirely ill-founded; they foreshadow a cultural dynamic which Marvin Schick calls "Chassidification" (1979). The term characterizes the way in which "American Orthodox Jews from relatively 'modern homes' (which means, among other things, a positive attitude toward college and secular education) have adopted Chassidic dress and life styles," reflecting the strong Hasidic presence in the neighborhood (ibid.:27). This process of Chassidification has had a profound effect on the neighborhood by engendering a reversed form of assimilation: While normally it is the newcomer who is absorbed into the mainstream and, in the process, moves away from his roots and traditions, the Hasidim, due to their strong moral presence, have inverted the trend. Not only have Hasidic Jews been successful at resurrecting their way of life, but they have traditionalized the ethos and world view of much of the non-Hasidic Orthodox population that lived in the community before their arrival. The Chassidifaction of the non-Hasidic, American-born Orthodox Jews (*Baale-Batim*, as they are called in Boro Park) is most evident in the transformation of American religious practices, synagogues, and yeshivot. One of the most profound changes has been in the observance of *kashrut*. Thanks to the Hasidim, a wider selection of kosher products today exists, with more stringent supervision of the final product. For example, when the Hasidim came to the United States, the milk was not *Cholov Yisroel*. That is, there were no Jewish supervisors on farms to guarantee that cow's milk would not be mixed with that of other animals. Today, for the most part, both the Baale-Batim and Hasidim drink Cholov Yisroel milk and eat Cholov Yisroel milk products, despite the fact that the latter do not have the *halachic* (legal) imperative of the former. The Hasidim also reintroduced strict European standards for kosher meat, since they considered the regular kosher butchers to be unreliable. These days, the lung of the cow has to be completely smooth or *glat*. Any imperfection which rubs off is considered *treyf* (non-kosher). Today, both communities make it a point to eat only glat kosher beef.

The Hasidic influence is also felt in a more stringent separation of the sexes. No longer do American Orthodox Jews participate in mixed dancing or coed swimming. A *mechitzah* (divide) at weddings is now common. To assure this separation, the American Orthodox women, like their Hasidic counterparts, dress modestly. Virtually all married women these days wear wigs; none wear pants. Their children and husbands have also begun to resemble the Hasidim more closely. All small boys wear yarmulkes, and in growing numbers, the children at *Litvish* (non-Hasidic Orthodox)[13] yeshivot sport side curls up until their bar mitzvah or school graduation. One informant termed this style "Boro Park chic." In parallel fashion, fathers are more apt to wear a beard. And should they begin to identify with Hasidism, they may opt to wear a *gartl* (a belt worn during prayer). Although prayer rooms were never part of the American-born tradition, Americans do worship at them, either as a matter of convenience or because they prefer the particular company of worshippers and manner of worship. At the prayer rooms, Litvish men inevitably adopt Hasidic customs. Thus, every morning at 6:00, Isaac Tanner studies and prays in the prayer room of the Gerer Hasidim. He likes the punctuality, the mix of people, and the intellectual rigorwhich led him to embrace some Hasidic customs: he goes to Hasidic rebbes for a blessing and "celebrates" a yahrzeit rather than solemnly marking the occasion. His father-in-law, who he describes as a real "*Yeke*" (German Jew), and who comes from a long line of *Misnagdim* (opponents of the Hasidim), is appalled. But in Boro Park, such close associations inevitably foster cultural and religious pollination.

As Hasidim transform Boro Park into home, even the Litvish yeshivot are turning more Hasidic in their orientation:less emphasis is placed on Hebrew grammar, Jewish history, and *Eretz Israel* (the Land of Israel); greater weight is given to demonstrations of piety, such as customs, blessings, and the manner of praying, than is given to erudition; more time is devoted to Talmud and less to bible studies; the mystical is favored over discursive commentary; teaching in Yiddish takes precedence over both English and Hebrew. While many of the students would have normally gone to college, very few choose this route today. It is doubtful, one informant told me, that his own children will even bother to finish the secular studies program at their yeshivah, for a secular education is simply not esteemed. In the Orthodox world view, "making it" means becoming a sage, not a yuppie.[14]

Yeshivot have traditionally been the preserve of the *Litvak*. Yet Chasidification in Boro Park owes a great deal to the yeshivah network that the Hasidim themselves constructed. Said one informant, "The only Hasidic movements that took hold in America, and for that matter in Israel too, were the ones that built a yeshivah." Other Boro Parkers concur. In the words of a local historian:

> In order for a rebbe to sustain a following after World War II, he must have built a yeshivah. Before the war many rebbes did not have one.[15] Their followings were maintained in other ways: through people living at the court of the rebbe; through informal study of the dynasty's Hasidism. After the war when few links existed to a traditional way of life, the yeshivah became vital for it attracted the young who were without attachment to any dynasty. The rebbes who did not set up yeshivot were left without a youthful following and with only the nostalgic. It is the young people in each Hasidic group who are the rebbe's soldiers.

Indeed, according to the son of one prominent rebbe, the younger generation of Hasidim, the ones who learned at the neighborhood yeshivot, are the most zealous in their allegiance to the rebbe. "The older generation remembers many prominent rebbes. Perhaps they also lost their own and took on a new one in the United States for whom they can't form the same attachment. They particularly can't be devoted to someone they bounced on their lap or saw playing stickball."

The Blueshover and Stuchiner Rebbes are examples of two eminent pre–World War II rebbes who never established yeshivot in this country, and hence, never attained the prominence of their less sage and august peers. The Blueshover in particular was regarded in Europe as a great scholar, serving as a member of the revered Agudath Israel's Council of Torah Sages. Before his recent death, his following consisted of the elderly who knew him in Europe, some of their children, and a few non-Hasidic admirers.

That yeshivot have played such a critical role in the success of Hasidism in Boro Park is due in large measure to the new function with which they were endowed by the Hasidic community. Today's yeshivah is not just an institution of Torah instruction; it is also a center for perpetuating and disseminating the Hasidic way of life. Bred into the students' bones, the dynasty's customs and teachings turn an initiate into a devotee of the rebbe whose yeshivah it is.[16] Today all Hasidic groups of any distinction in Boro Park have established educational facilities: Bobov, Krasna, Ger, Skver, Munkacz, Pupa, Karlin-Stolin, Spinka, even Satmar (based in Williamsburg) all compete for the loyalty of this neighborhood's youth. This competition extends to summer camps. Since parents prefer their children to be formally supervised the entire year, the most popular yeshivot are those affiliated with a camp.

There are other reasons why Hasidic efforts at home-building in Boro Park have succeeded so well, some having little to do with Hasidic endeavors. One factor that may account for the success of Hasidim in Boro Park is the religious infrastructure they found in place there. The Hasidim benefitted from the fruits of an Orthodox community, such as its schools, *mikvahs* (ritual baths), and self-help organizations, while they established their own institutions. It should also be noted that unlike the Lower East Side, which swelled with impoverished *griners* (newcomers), the community of Boro Park was a middle-class neighborhood as well as a second and a third area of settlement. By the time Hasidim moved into Boro Park, some individuals had acquired great affluence and contributed handily to the community building that transformed Boro Park into a bastion of *Hasidus* (a Hasidic way of life). Bobov, for example, had a large number of individuals employed in the diamond industry. When diamonds commanded a high price, Bobov was a beneficiary.

Home-building in Boro Park should also be understood in the context of the times which promoted the goals of minorities. Designated a disadvantaged minority under Lyndon Johnson's "Great Society," Hasidim benefitted greatly from government programs aimed at strengthening their "underprivileged" community. The floodgates of federal aid were opened even wider in July of 1984 at a ceremony at the Manhattan Federal Plaza when the government expanded the Hasidim's minority designation by including them in a privileged group of six other disadvantaged minorities recognized by federal agencies. More recently, a coalition of Hasidic groups that calls themselves the Council of Jewish Organizations of Boro Park (COJO), has developed Business Outreach Centers that link their neighborhood with economic-development organizations throughout New York City. A bona fide success, COJO has already been awarded over a million dollars to invest in the community's economic life (The Forward 1993). Owing to this largess, the Hasidim have acquired much of the power and influence, mainly in the areas of business and education, that have long been held by non-Hasidim. They have also worked hard to master their political fate, having made significant political strides on the home and national front. In Brooklyn, Hasidim dominate the Boro Park Community Council and serve as advisors to the mayor. On account of their strength as a voting block, Hasidic communities are courted by political candidates, from senators to councilmen. In cooperation with the police, they operate their own neighborhood safety patrols. Hasidim aggressively compete for funding and exemptions, sometimes provoking animosity from rival ethnic communities.[17]

The total Chassidification of Boro Park is nearing completion. Today, Boro Park is a community that is 85 percent Hasidic,[18] and the feel of the neighborhood reflects this statistic. It is hard even for old-timers to believe that some ten years ago, Boro Park had been a heterogeneous community, composed of non-Hasidic Jews and other ethnic groups. In his discussion of Boro Park prior to the depression, Egon Mayer describes what a different community it was then. He astutely points out that the Yiddishkeit then taught was "primarily a system of special practices rather than a world view" (Mayer 1979:28). Judaism was taught around the school day, functioning as an extracurricular pursuit. Nothing was taught that would compromise the students' secular goals. "That mentality, typically, sought to make the meaning of 'being a good Jew' consistent with 'being a good American,'" and a well-to-do one, no doubt (ibid.). Boro Park at this time exemplified the Horatio Alger story. It was a rung on the ladder of upward mobility, leading to the American dream. The religious posture adopted by these Jews was defensive. Yiddishkeit was acceptable to American culture only insofar as it remained in the closet—practiced at home but invisible on the streets. In the words of Mayer, there was the distinct "desire to contain those values and practices within the finite boundaries of privacy" (ibid.:29).[19]

Judaism has a very different meaning for Boro Park's current inhabitants. The Hasidic way of life leaves nothing outside the religious purview. Its domestic life, business activities, schooling, and friendship networks are permeated by Hasidic ideals. Being a "good Jew" is clearly something very different from being a "good American." Very simply, a good Jew is a Torah-true Jew. Success is measured by a yardstick other than that favored by yuppies. What Hasidic mother, after all, would not prefer to have her son grow up to be a *talmud chocham* (sage), and her daughter to marry one!

Correlatively, neighborhood has also a different significance for today's Hasidim. Under the Hasidic influence, public space has been transformed into private space—neighborhood streets have been assimilated into home in "the desire to live in a pure and holy cosmos" (Eliade 1959:65).[20] I am not just referring to the emergence of stores, schools, and shuls ubiquitous throughout the area that are emblematic of the Hasidic way of life. What I have in mind, rather, is a cheerfully transparent attitude of comfort and familiarity totally unknown to their non-Hasidic predecessors. These newcomers do not hesitate to perform their rituals outside the walls of their apartments, whether it means dancing in the streets on Simchas Torah (a celebration marking the end and beginning of a cycle of Torah reading), burning *chometz* (leaven) on your block before Passover (a celebration marking the exodus from Egypt), being married under a canopy of stars, performing the expiation rites of *tashlikh* at a local lake and *capores shlogan* in an empty lot for the High Holidays, or constructing *sukkahs* (temporary dwellings constructed for the holiday of *Sukkot*) on the balconies which are de rigueur for all new three-family brick apartment buildings. Moreover, while few Jews of the 1930s and even the 1970s would wear a yarmulke outside the home, the Hasidim with their distinctive appearance literally wear their Jewish identity on their sleeve. No longer put under wraps, Yiddishkeit is proudly displayed like a badge of honor.

It has been noted that with the destruction of the second commonwealth in 70 C.E., Jews lived in the dimension of time rather than space (Levine 1986; Heschel 1951; Bowman 1960). Without a land of their own on which to build, the Jewish people cultivated the rich landscapes of historical time. "Thus, rather than concretize abstractions, symbolize values, memorialize history, or reinforce aspirations by spacial means—for example, architecture, sculpture, painting, or tapestry—the Jews created artistic moments, poignant hours, and evocative days" (Levine 1986:3). After two millennia of living at the caprice of a host culture, of bowing one's head to Christianity and Islam, space is reemerging as a key dimension of Jewish existence. What makes the quest for home in Boro Park so signally important is that it is an excellent example of Jews succeeding in the reunification of time and space. The courts of their rebbes, thriving yeshivot, bookstores, butcher shops, and all their numerous political and social institutions are the reward that territory has to offer: They are monuments of presence that simultaneously anchor Hasidim to a physical and a spiritual realm.

The Hasidic presence has become so strong that non-Hasidic Jews who no longer feel comfortable in Boro Park have chosen to move out in droves. Some social scientists are convinced that this new Boro Park will decline and go the way of so many other Jewish neighborhoods of the past—yet another garden bespoilt (Rosenthal 1980; Mayer 1979)! This generation of Hasidim, however, has dug in and is resolute in its desire to make Yiddishkeit flower. Far from being a stepping stone to the American dream, Boro Park has become a bridge to God.

DYNASTY

"America is a *Gan Eden* [Garden of Eden]," the Bobover Rebbetzin (the Rebbe's wife) pronounced, with apparent satisfaction for the home Bobov has made for itself in the United States. She has reason to feel proud. When the Rebbe, a Holocaust survivor, made his way to New York City in the late 1940s, America had been an inhospitable terrain for Hasidus (Hasidic thought and life). Prior to World War II, many of the Hasidim who had emigrated here saw themselves as the last of their kind. Most let their Hasidic heritage lapse with a heavy heart, never dreaming that their children could follow in their spiritual path. The Bobover Rebbe was determined to reverse the trend. The Rebbetzin, who married the Rebbe in New York in 1948, recounted the Rebbe's anguished yet hopeful proposal to her:

> Why do I remain alive? Am I such a *zaddiq* [righteous man]? Am I better than others? Hitler ruined what my grandfather and father started. What remains is a tree with the branches cut off, but the roots are still there. Please help me, I want to take you with me.

The post-Holocaust transition to the United States proved successful not only due to the mass immigrations of Hasidim, but also because full-fledged rebbes, around whom Hasidic communities were built, followed suit (Robinson 1990; Poll 1962).[21] A rebbe's stature, charisma, familiarity with his Hasidim, and connections within the Jewish community were crucial factors for home-building. He was a sanctuary for the forlorn and homeless Holocaust survivor; he served as a bridge from the home of their birth to the home of their adopted land. Home was simply where the rebbe was.

Bobover Hasidim have recounted for me the critical role their rebbe played in locating his followers and in recreating a Hasidic community after the war. Soon after arriving in the United States he sent visas to the orphans he had taken under his wing in the Italian transfer camp at Bari, later enrolling them in his newly founded yeshivah and trade school on the Upper West Side. In the following years the Rebbe arranged hundreds of visas for Bobover families and individuals scattered throughout D.P. (Displaced Persons) camps.

The Rebbetzin vividly remembered those early and difficult years in Manhattan. "There were Jews" she said, "who tried to convince the Rov [a title Bobover Hasidim use for the Rebbe] to abandon his Hasidic ways and become a rabbi in a synagogue with plush velvet. But the Rebbe would tell them, 'I will not learn from you, you should learn from me!'" Of considerable help to the Rebbe were some local philanthropists who were delighted to see Bobov flourish. With the help of these committed individuals, the Rebbe acquired two buildings in Manhattan on West 85th Street. One was converted into a trade school where men learned to repair watches, cut diamonds, and engaged in other trades. Another building was multipurpose: it was the residence of the Rebbe's family and the war orphans for whom the Rebbe acted as a surrogate father. There was a mikvah in the basement and a *besmedresh* (a place of prayer and study) with a small sukkah on the first floor. It housed the Rebbe's office, which on Shabbat became the women's besmedresh. The building had dining rooms for men and women, and, of course, a kitchen.

Many of the Hasidim who came to the Rebbe's American court were alone and rootless, stripped of everything but their memories. These very memories of their fathers and grandfathers, of how life was before the war, were evoked when the Rebbe donned his *shtreiml* (festive fur trimmed hat), presided over a *tish* (festive holiday and Sabbath table), or gave a blessing. In the figure of the Rebbe, the Hasid found a father, while in his *chaverim* (comrades), he found new brothers. Indeed, a rebbe and his Hasidim functioned as a surrogate family to the orphaned Hasid. What Jacob Katz writes about the relationship between the Hasid and a Hasidic community at the onset of Hasidism is equally true of the movement after the war:

> membership in the emotion-packed Hasidic congregation and the strong attachment of the Hasid to his mentor served to some extent as a substitute for family ties. (Katz 1961:243)

Recovery was slow, but steady. An informant of mine recalled Bobov's first seder in the United States, one in which all twenty-five or so Bobover Hasidim gathered together in celebration. What a curious Hasidic fete it was! Nobody had a beard except the Rebbe. No one could even afford *yom tov* (holiday) clothes (much less Hasidic ones), and what they did wear did not match. That night, instead of giving his traditional Torah, the Rebbe told a tale:

> Once there was a Jewish farmer. And the Jewish farmer had everything a farmer should have, he even had ducks. Now you know Jews, if you own animals, you yourself aren't allowed to eat until you've fed them first. This is the law. So these ducks were fed quite well. And they looked fine too. Whereas gentile

farmers would pluck the duck's soft feathers to make pillows, Jews weren't allowed to do this. No wonder the Jewish ducks felt better and looked nicer.

Now this farmer had a gentile neighbor who was very jealous of his happy animals, and so, decided to steal them. He waited until the farmer went away for a few days, took his ducks, and hid them away from him. In time, he thought, perhaps they wouldn't recognize each other. But one day sometime later the gentile opened the duck's gate so they could walk around. Remembering the good times with their old master, the ducks waddled straight home. As they approached their master's house, they started to quack. Startled by the commotion, the farmer opened his door and looked down at them. "They don't look like my ducks," he said, "but they sure sound like them." And when he saw that they recognized him, he took them in and gave them food and water.

The Rebbe concluded:

Because the gentile didn't feed the ducks well, and because he plucked their nicest feathers, the real master shouldn't let them return? They're his!

Explained my informant:

Now the Rebbe was very happy to welcome everyone again. You see, the story was really about himself and his Hasidim, but perhaps too, about himself and the Almighty. Maybe we all don't look like we did before that war, but we're still your children!

Both the Rebbe and God welcomed home their long lost children and together built an oasis of Yiddishkeit in this treyf land. Some thirty years have gone by, and a Bobover tish in Boro Park is now an altogether different event. On holidays, it is attended by hundreds of Hasidim from within and outside the community. Dignitaries also pay homage to the Rebbe. One Purim, Mayor Koch was in attendance: having just attended a St. Patrick's Day parade, he cut an odd figure—a speck of kelly green in a sea of black coats and hats, worn by clapping, singing, and dancing bearded Bobover Hasidim.

Through his impressive pedigree, strength of character, and plain good timing, the Bobover Rebbe inspired many to join his community, offering his Hasidim a total environment—job advice/training, a yeshivah education, a congenial place to worship, as well as his ear and encouragement. With regards to the newly founded Bobover yeshivah, the case of Leah is typical. Coming from a Galicianer background (in her case, Bobov), she wanted her son to get a Hasidic *bren* (burning religious enthusiasm), and so, sent him to Bobov, but not before the Rebbe had personally reassured her that he would also receive a fine English education. "I gave instructions to the teachers," the Rebbe explained, "that this is America and not to press too much for Hasidic appearances. We must instead stress education so our children can be well informed." Despite his willingness to accommodate to a new land, old ways were not easily forsaken. Sometimes the Rebbe would tease her small son, who had short wispy side curls: "So what happened to the rest of them?" "Yet even the Rebbe," Leah thought, "must have been amazed by how Hasidic the yeshivah became in later years."

A key factor in Bobov's success at community building was that it was among the first of the Hasidic dynasties to establish Hasidic schools. Indeed, shortly after arriving in Manhattan, the Rebbe founded a small yeshivah to teach those whose education had been arrested by the Holocaust. Today, Bobov has yeshivot (among other educational institutions) in Israel, London, Toronto, Antwerp, and Boro Park. Their Brooklyn organization for boys consists of a preschool, the Bobover Yeshivah *Bnei Zion* (nursery school to tenth grade), and Mesiftah *Etz Chaim D'Bobov* (high school). They offer both *limudei kodesh* (religious subjects), and a fully accredited "English" (public school) curriculum. Their facilities include lunchrooms, kitchens, a dormitory, a library, a Passover matzah bakery, and a besmedresh (a place of study, worship, and socializing). Married men study in the *kollel,* where the tuition is free and where they are guaranteed a small weekly stipend. In September of 1981, Bobov inaugurated the new site of *Bnos Zion*, Miriam Locker School for Girls. Its modern and spacious facilities educate unmarried girls from preschool through high school. All together, Bobov educates more than 2,000 students with an annual budget that exceeds $5.6 million. A fleet of eleven busses and four vans transports the thousands of youngsters to and from school. Classes, however, do not end in June; they continue throughout the summer in camps located in the Catskills. The girls attend Camp *Gila* in Ferndale. Boys of 5–13 years of age go to Camp *Shalvah* in neighboring South Fallsburg.

Their older brothers (13–18) are enrolled at Camp *Etz Chaim* in Thompsonville.

As in Galicia, most of the children who attend Bobover schools today become Bobover Hasidim, for they learn Bobover Hasidic songs, and the *nusakh* (manner of praying), and, most importantly, cultivate a fidelity to their leader, the Bobover Rebbe. Other Hasidic communities, eyeing the success Bobov has had in recruiting new members through the yeshivah, have emulated Bobov's ways.

As the history of Bobov in New York City clearly shows, the role of the rebbe cannot be underestimated in Hasidic efforts at home-building. What signally distinguished the successful postwar growth of Hasidim was the presence of major rebbes. Mintz writes that prior to World War II, American Hasidism never took off precisely because the rebbe, "the focal point of Hasidic life had been missing" (Mintz 1968:37). What further distinguished postwar Hasidim in this country was the unprecedented arrival of thousands of Hasidim, in desperate need of a spiritual and emotional center.

It is in this context that the Hasid–rebbe relationship can be understood. Hasid and rebbe must be viewed as flip sides of the same coin—master and disciple. The term Hasid begs the question: "Hasid of Whom?" (Green 1987:127). Hasidic philosophy likens the rebbe to the head of the social body and the Hasid—to the feet. A variation of this theme pictures the rebbe as a tree and his Hasidim as the leaves and branches (recall the Bobover Rebbe's marriage proposal to the Rebbetzin). Together they form a community. That rebbes occupy exalted positions within the Hasidic community is unquestioned: their charisma, wisdom, piety, and ability to work wonders are well known to the faithful. In word and in deed, the rebbe is, for his followers, Torah incarnate. The Hasid learns Yiddishkeit from the rebbe not only through his discourses, but by observing his daily interactions. The well-known statement by the Hasid Leib, son of Sarah, vividly demonstrates this point: "I came to the Maggid [successor to the founder of Hasidism, the Baal Shem Tov] not to listen to discourses nor to learn from his wisdom; I came to watch him tie his shoelaces" (Wiesel 1972:61). Most critically, the Hasid relies extensively on his rebbe's skill to commune with God and elevate sacred sparks. As one Bobover Hasid put it: "Bobov has no people who fly in space. You want your rebbe to have the direct line [to

God] and that's that." Rebbes are virtuosos at sanctifying the profane. They are thought to be at such a high spiritual level that all
activity, even that as mundane as tying one's shoelaces, becomes a
way to worship God and liberate holy sparks.

In his article, "Zaddiq as Axis Mundi in Later Judaism,"
Arthur Green argues convincingly that Hasidism transferred *axis
mundi* symbolism from place to person, from the temple to the
rebbe (1977; 1987).[22] The rebbe's court has the aura of a new
Jerusalem, site of the Temple Mount where the portable Ark of
the Covenant was deposited by the Israelites. The rebbe's rab-
bistva (court) had replaced the *beis ha-mikdesh* (temple mount);
his tish, the temple altar; and the rebbe himself has become the
high priest for his Hasidim. Hasidic lore reflects this. The town of
Sadegora where Israel of Rishin held court was described as "the
place of the Temple" (Green 1977:330). The Hasidim of Menachem Mendel of Kotsk use to sing a song while on pilgrimage to
their master's court that utilized axis mundi symbolism:

> To Kotzk one doesn't "travel"
> To Kotzk one may only walk.
> For Kotzk stands in the place of the Temple,
> Kotzk is in the Temple's place.
> To Kotzk one must walk as does a pilgrim. (Green 1977:330)

A disciple of Jacob Isaac of Lublin put it this way:

> He who comes here is to imagine that Lublin is the Land of
> Israel, that the master's court is Jerusalem, his room is the Holy
> of Holies, and that the *shekhinah* speaks through his mouth.
> (ibid.:339)

As axis mundi, the rebbe is the channel through which his
Hasidim may be in communion with God, and through which
God's blessings descend to the people. "The zaddiq," Green
writes, "stands at the center of the cosmos, the place where the
four directions meet. He is thus the earthly extension of that element within the Deity that is called *zaddiq*, a this-worldly continuation of the Kabbalistic *amunda de-emza ita*, the central pillar of
the universe. He is in a highly spatial sense the earthly counterpart
to the pillar of the sefirotic world" (ibid.:336). In this role, the
rebbe is regarded as both priest and king to his Hasidim. As temple priest, he intercedes with God on their behalf and acts as their
spiritual mentor; he heals his Hasidim spiritually and physically.

As king, his office is dynastic; he performs the duties of his office, and presides over a regal court. He may even claim descent from King David.

Both roles blend perfectly in the Bobover Rebbe. His Hasidim regard him as a zaddiq, a saintly, pious person of rare vintage, and seek him out for blessings and advise. The "superabundance of reality" (Eliade 1959) that emanates from the Rebbe, is evident in the words of one Bobover who described for me what it means to be a Bobover Hasid:

> It's simply one of the greatest things you can be, for when I see my rebbe, even just his face, I feel better. I cannot explain it to you, but I simply feel better for I know there is a God in the world. You observe this man, how he works, talks, and how he worships, so you sense the Almighty's presence.

For his part, the Bobover Rebbe thinks of his Hasidim as his flock (to this day he affectionately refers to them as *mine kinderlech*—my children), whom he skillfully shepherds toward *and* through the life of ultra-Orthodoxy. Not only has the Rebbe led a multitude of souls to Hasidism, but he stands ready to direct them (at least those of the men) through all major life-cycle rituals: When a Bobover boy is three years old, the Rebbe ceremoniously cuts his hair and teaches him his aleph-bes (Hebrew alphabet). At the bar mitzvah the Rebbe puts on the young lad's first *teffilin* (phylacteries). In due time the Rebbe blesses the young man's engagement. At the *aufruf* (the Sabbath festivities proceeding the wedding), the Rebbe lends the groom his *chalat* (festive coat) and places the groom's new shtreiml (fur-trimmed hat) on his head. Come the wedding, the Rebbe accompanies the bride's father to *bedeck* (veil) the bride, a most solemn occasion.[23]

The Rebbe infuses Hasidic life with pomp and circumstance. His resplendent appearance, tish, sukkah (temporary dwelling constructed for the holiday of Sukkoth), and purimshpil (a play commemorating the victory of Persian Jews over the evil Haman) are well-known throughout the community. Perched on the wall of his office behind his desk is a genealogy which traces the Rebbe's ancestry to the House of David. A crown is Bobov's logo.

When the Hasidim made a home of Boro Park, they introduced a new form of religious authority into the neighborhood which altered what Peter Berger calls the "ecology of the sacred" (1954:475). With the recent "irruption of the sacred"[24] throughout the profane landscape, Hasidic Boro Park has become a community dotted with sacred centers bearing the names of Bobov, Munkacz, Karlin-Stolin, Novominsk, etc. These centers display a series of concentric circles at the heart of which are the rebbes, the axes mundi, the focal points of meaning/sanctity/reality for their respective Hasidim.[25] Mr. Endstein, a Bobover Hasid, recounts:

> When I see a different rebbe I see a very great man, who is doing, like my rebbe, a lot for the Jewish nation, but just as Jacob had twelve sons, and each son worshipped the Almighty in different ways, that's the way for the rebbes in this world. What I see by my rebbe, a Gerer sees by his rebbe, a Lubavitcher sees by his rebbe, the Belzer sees by his. When I gaze upon the Lubavitcher or the Gerer or the Belzer, or all the other rebbes, I see outstanding people, but because I am connected to my rebbe, I am inspired.

Each rebbe is surrounded by his confidants and the community's religious functionaries who form the first and closest circle of power in the community. The next circle is that of the faithful, who, according to Hasidic philosophy, have a soulroot in common by virtue of the fact that they are Hasidim of a particular rebbe (Green 1977:339). These Hasidim strive to live in close proximity to the Rebbe's home. The Rebbe is the "Center of the World," to whom his followers wish "to live as near as possible" (Eliade 1959:43). Further out are those people who frequent the Rebbe, but are not devotees, and beyond them, the rest of the community.

The lifestyle that these centers follow is never complacent. Home-building is an ongoing task of intensifying one's Yiddishkeit, expanding the influence of your rebbe, attracting newcomers to Hasidism. As I have argued above, it also has its own special cosmic agenda: As the Hasidim reclaim their own homes, they, with the assistance of their rebbe, assist the divine sparks that had fallen away from the Almighty in finding their way back to the primordial home. Home-building, then, mends community and restores the fractured universe to its original wholeness.

CONCLUSION

The Hasidim have transformed Boro Park into yet another incarnation of the Garden, though with the building boom that accompanied their influx into the neighborhood, it has become shorn of the lush park-like appearance that once attracted so many Jews prior to the 1950s. The "dust of the earth," a passage from Genesis (Gen. R. 41:9) which symbolized the Jews in exile, has become an index of the community-wide construction since Hasidim settled there.

The original home of mankind, the Garden of Eden, is the ultimate dwelling place for all the righteous of the world. The biblical story of the Garden serves as a "living memory" (Plaskow 1989:39): It "calls to mind and recreates the past for succeeding generations," as generations of Jews make their way through the diaspora (ibid.). "Eden represents the first in a series of divine displacements that are all iterations of the original and that all involve relocation to a new and different, but eventually the same, site of exile" (Tigerman 1988:125). To be sure, each recreation is bound to be different (Boro Park is no replica of an Eastern European shtetl). Still, Boro Park is an incarnation of the Garden insofar as it helps sustain an ancient and yet forever new hope for atonement and return to a paradise lost. Hence, the Bobover Rebbetzin's telling reference to "Boro Park as a Garden of Eden." For the Rebbetzin, communal living in Boro Park afforded the Hasidim an opportunity to live and worship as Jews, a chance for "Hasidim with large families, wealthy and happy," to enjoy the fruits of a "thriving [Bobover] yeshivah" (seat of Torah learning) and to prosper. Boro Park, like the Garden, has its share of temptations and dangers, but it provides the backdrop by which the faithful can behold God's handicraft and observe his commandments.

Far from being parochial and ethnocentric, the exile of the Jews and their longing for home has become a metaphor for humanity in the twentieth century. Max Weber, a prophet of the modern era and its discontent, was the first to draw an instructive parallel between modernity and exile. To be a modern, for Weber, is to be alienated, dispirited, living in the world without God, where ultimate religious values are supplanted by conflicting secular beliefs. In his essay on "Science as a Vocation," he pointedly invokes Isaiah's prophecy of the home lost and a subsequent return to Zion as symbolic of "the loss of ultimate meaning in the modern 'disenchanted' world" (Eisen 1986:xiii). In the waning years of the twentieth century, Weber's critique of the modern era has been appropriated by those who refer to themselves as "postmodernists." Following Weber, postmodernists view the present age as a kaleidoscope of competing values—the result of alienation from ultimate truth. It is typified by fragmentation and ephemerality (Harvey 1989), the superficial hodge-podge of pastiche (Jameson 1984), where any semblance of unity is undermined by radical perspectivism (Dallmayr 1987; Dews 1987; Dreyfus and Rabinow 1982) and the dissolution of a shared morality and metatheory (Lyotard 1984). Postmodernism, David Harvey writes, "does not try to transcend it [modernism], counteract it, or even to define the 'eternal and immutable' elements that might lie within it. Postmodernism swims, even wallows, in the fragmentary and the chaotic currents of change as if that is all there is" (1989:44).

In her thought-provoking article, "A Place Called Home?" (1992), Doreen Massey analyzes the loss of place that so typifies the postmodern era marked by the trend toward globalization, the fragmentation of local cultures and disorientation of its residents. The process of globalization is twofold: "Home-grown specificity is invaded—it seems that you can sense the simultaneous presence of everywhere in the place you are standing"—when boundaries are rendered meaningless (ibid.:7). A key attribute of this brave new world is the compression of time and space, a result of the increasing irrelevance of distance and "meaning-endowed durations" (Emberley in Massey 1992:7). Moreover, as context-specific social forms and relations spill over community borders, fewer of them are contained within the place itself. We are more like the other precisely because we least resemble our former selves.

This postmodern topography of fragmentation and ephemerality has engendered a reactionary drive for home and homeland so evident in the emergence of worldwide localisms and nationalisms. Massey points to the pursuit of security and permanence through a sense of place (Harvey 1989), to the longing for an existential compass (Jameson 1984), and to the quest for clear and distinct identities—"placed identities for placeless times" (in Massey 1992:7), as delineated by Robbins (1991). It is in this context that we can situate the Hasidim's quest for home. To paraphrase Weber, the Hasidic quest for home is a "reenchantment" of the world. It is "an irruption of the sacred" into profane space through which communication with the Almighty is established (Eliade 1959:63). If exile is paradigmatic of the alienation from the God, as it certainly is for Hasidim, then home symbolizes the reinstatement of a relationship with God through the building of a new center in which Torah is the privileged value and where the Rebbe, who serves as Torah incarnate, links his flock with the Almighty. "To be home now means to be at or near that Center, and as such to have the security, the lasting name, the contact with Heaven that the builders of Babel have sought in vain through their Tower" (Eisen 1986:25).

Eden, Jerusalem, Babylon, Vilna, Bobov—these are renowned centers of past Jewish life decimated by the harsh winds of history. The Bobover community in Boro Park has now taken the torch. As its predecessors, it thrives on living memory, it longs for spiritual life, it builds a better future for its children here in exile without losing hope of the pending return to their ultimate home. In the end, Boro Park may be yet another home that is built on shifting sands, but it is no sandcastle. Bobov, in the words of its proud inhabitants, is "the new fortress of Torah" (The Miracle of Bobov n.d.:5). And it is designed to protect the Jews from the chaos of modernity and postmodernity.

I conclude this paper with a passage from a Bobover publication, "The Miracle of Bobov," that celebrates the achievements of Bobov in America while yearning for an ultimate resting place:

> Bobov. Krakow. Kotovitz. Tarnov. Auschwitz. Charznov. Bilitz. Such . . . once proud Polish cities boasting flourishing Talmud Torahs and Jewish communities. Now part of a roster of victims of the Holocaust, decimated, devastated beyond belief. But the Bobover Rebbe has taken a sacred vow that neither we nor our children nor our children's children will ever forget the millions of innocent men, women and children who suffered and were slaughtered.
>
> To this end, we of Bobov are creating a living memorial to the cities and yeshivos that could have been, should have been part of our beautiful future. Here, in our new Boro Park Torah Educational Complex, we are having the names of each city, each yeshivah engraved upon the walls . . . where they will be seen and remembered by all for generations to come. It is our hope, our fervent belief, that this will be an everlasting tribute for all who walked with their heads high through recorded history's darkest chapter.
>
> May Hashem [The Almighty] bless us that, in the very near future, we may be able to sing and dance with fervor in our holiest of holy cities, a Yerusholaim rebuilt. Amen. (n.d.:16)

NOTES

1. Jacques Derrida writes that "all names related to fundamentals, to principles, or to the center have always designated the constant of a presence—*eidos, arche, telos, energeia, ousia* (essence, existence, substance, subject), *aletheia,* transcendentality, consciousness, or conscience, God, man, and so forth" (Derrida 1970:249).

2. *Eruvin* were of particular importance to Hasidim because they facilitated the celebration of festive meals (specifically, the transportation of food and drink) to honor a visiting *zaddiq* (pious leader). Moreover, Hasidim were instrumental in spreading the concept of eruvin. The founder of the Hasidic movement, the Baal Shem Tov, said: "This is one of the three things which I came to rectify in the world: *zevihah . . . eiruvin* [an alternative spelling to eruvin], *mikveh . . .*" (Wertheim 1992:219).

3. The different conceptions of home that Hasidim and other Orthodox Jews have of Boro Park do not reside in alternative understandings of their apartments/houses. Actually, the physical appearance of the Orthodox domicile in Boro Park, for Hasid and non-Hasid alike, is rather standard: a *mizrah* (painting, plaque, or any kind of wall hanging) hung on the eastern wall, the direction in which one prays; *mezuzzahs* on the door posts; ritual objects displayed in a breakfront overlooking a large dining-room table for holiday and sabbath meals; a library of religious texts; a patch of undecorated wall (symbolizing the destruction of the Temple); and pictures of Torah scholars, though in Hasidic households they are often of the rebbes (past and present) from the Hasid's dynasty. Even a great deal of the ritual observance is identical in substance (though varying in style). Differences in the meaning of home lie largely in how this concept is extended to community.

4. Torah, as described here, combines the model "of" and "for" sense of home. It is both a surrogate home and a blueprint for home (Geertz 1973).

5. While in its most specific sense, the Torah refers to the Five Books of Moses, I am using this term in its most general sense to symbolize all of Jewish learning.

6. The Hasid is able to perform this herculean task if his daily activities, even the most mundane, are performed with the intention of serving the Lord. Yaacov Yoseph of Polnoye, an early Hasidic writer, characterized this manner of communion in the following way:

> man can perform the deepest meditations and acts of unification (with God) even through his most mundane actions such as eating, drinking, sexual intercourse, and business transactions. (Weinryb 1972:271)

So when the Hasid eats with the motive of strengthening himself to serve the Lord, when a special garb is worn on the Sabbath to honor that holy day, when charity is given to help clothe and feed God's creatures, when the Hasid abandons himself to a heartfelt prayer or joyous song in celebration with his rebbe and does this joyfully with the intention of reuniting the universe, the Almighty is restored while a Torah-true community is built.

7. Poll writes that a number of positive images were used by Ashkenazim to portray America, including *goldene medinah* (golden land) and *frei land* (free country), which symbolized its bounty and liberty. Yet America also symbolized loose, uncontrolled, a-Jewish behavior. Poll describes the Hungarian attitude which held that "in America even the water is not kosher, and even the air can defile a religious man" (1962:37).

8. *Treyf* literally means torn, and usually refers to "nonkosher" food. When it refers to other objects, it connotes unfit.

9. The historian Zalman Alpert has related to me that although there were hundreds of Hasidim living in the Lower East Side in the 1950s, it did not evolve into a Hasidic community on par with those of Brooklyn because the major rebbes chose not to settle there.

10. The Boro Park Community Survey, 1992–93, defines the boundaries of Boro Park as follows: from 9th Ave. (west) to 19th Ave. (east), and from 37th St. (north) to 60th St. (south). Boro Park is not delineated by any official administrative jurisdiction, though it does fall within Brooklyn's Community Planning Board Twelve and the 66th Police Precinct. The community is composed of twenty-five contiguous census tracts (Mayer 1993).

11. The real-estate boom would build up steam in the decades to come. In 1980, from January to October, Boro Park added over 80 new houses, the overwhelming majority of these being three-family brick buildings, each unit containing three bedrooms. This statistic compares with a total of 200 houses built in all of Brooklyn during the same time frame (Boro Park Voice, 1980, p. 1).

12. A 1989 study of "The Boro Park Business Community" by the Council of Jewish Organizations of Boro Park finds that 68.6 percent of businesses in Boro Park are Orthodox/Hasidic-owned.

13. While the term *Litvak* traditionally referred to the Orthodox Jews from Lithuania who did not join the Hasidic movement, in Boro Park the term is applied to all Orthodox non-Hasidic Jews.

14. While scholarship is the time-honored way of achieving high status, making a good *shidduch* (marriage match) for your children and earning a large income are also symbols of status in the Hasidic community—in Boro Park as well as in prewar Europe.

15. Lubavitch, Bobov, Radomsk, and Slonim were among the Hasidic communities that had yeshivot.

16. It is interesting to note that in the 1950s, Boro Park had to export its yeshivah students to schools in other neighborhoods, as the local schools were limited to the elementary-school level (Schick 1979:26). Today, with the florescence of Hasidic yeshivot, Boro Park has become a magnet for yeshivah students.

17. See Mintz's "Ethnic Activism: The Hasidic Example" (1983) and *Hasidic People* (1992) for elaboration of the point.

18. Based on private correspondence with Mr. Joel Schwartz, Director of Research, Council of Jewish Organizations of Boro Park (COJO). Mr. Schwartz pointed out that in his judgment, as well as in that of his colleagues, the Hasidic population of Boro Park is burgeoning, as evidenced by the expanding yeshivot and synagogues, the increased traffic and pedestrian congestion, and the many more Hasidim they spot on the streets. For these reasons, they doubt some of the figures in the Boro Park Community Survey, 1992–93 (Mayer 1993), as they paint a different demographic picture of the neighborhood. The statistics show that while the overall population of Boro Park changed little over the past decade, from 82,593 residents in 1980 to 84,079 residents in 1990, the Jewish population actually declined by 7 percent—from 87 percent of the population in 1980 to 80 percent of the population in 1990 (Mayer 1994:13). Members of COJO feel that the figures reflect the underrepresentation of the Jewish community in the 1990 U.S. Census, on which the survey is based. They also point out that the average household size has increased significantly over the decade, from 2.86 persons in the 1980 census to 3.18 persons in the 1990 census. These numbers, they believe, reflect the growing number of Jewish households in the neighborhood (most of which are Hasidic), which have larger average sizes than that of the non-Jewish households: 4.88 and 2.90, respectively (ibid.:18).

19. Schick reports that the complexion of Boro Park changed little in the 1930s, despite the depression. In the 1940s and 1950s there was an incremental growth of Orthodoxy. The 1960s proved to be a watershed decade for Jewish life in Boro Park with the influx of a large Hasidic population.

20. To cite a very literal example, in a ceremony that marked the fortieth anniversary of the Bobover community's rescue from Poland following the Holocaust, 48th Street between 15th and 16th Avenues, where many Bobover institutions are located, was renamed Bobov Promenade (Jewish Press 1985).

21. Robinson and Poll write that in the 1920s and earlier, a few *eynikleh* (descendants of rebbes) or *shtikl rebbes* arrived in North America, taking on the title of rebbe and the name of their ancestor or the town from which they had emigrated. While they attracted some followers, they were never able to catalyze a Hasidic movement (Robinson 1990; Poll 1962:63, 21).

22. Green writes that rebbes claimed authority on the basis of being a zaddiq, a righteous or holy man, rather than as the bearer of learning or traditional authority. Prior to 1800, the term zaddiq, however, did not uniformly designate the leader of Hasidic communities (1987:130, 134).

23. Due to the Rebbe's advanced age and ever-increasing community size, the Rebbe is not as hands-on as he once was. His role in many of these rituals has been delegated to his eldest son, Naftoli.

24. This is Mircea Eliade's spelling and usage (1959:63).

25. The former community rabbis who led the Reform, Conservative, and non-Hasidic Orthodox congregations taught Torah, adjudicated legal issues, offered pastoral care, and participated in philanthropic ventures. They never were regarded as Torah nor even necessarily as *zaddiqim* (plural of zaddiq).

REFERENCES

Beck, B. 1966. *Cultural transition: Impact of Chassidim on their Jewish neighbors. The Jewish Digest,* September, pp. 5–8.

Berger, P. 1954. The sociological study of sectarianism. *Social Research* 21:467–485.

Bosk, C. L. 1979. The routinization of charisma: The case of the zaddik. *Sociological Inquiry* 49:150–167.

Bourdieu, P. 1971. The Berber house. In *Rules and meanings,* ed. Mary Douglas, 98–110. Harmondsworth: Penguin.

Bowman, T. 1960. *Hebrew thought compared with Greek.* Philadelphia: The Westminster Press.

Council of Jewish Organizations of Boro Park, 1980. Boro Park keeps growing. *Boro Park Voice.* Brooklyn, New York: Author.

———. 1989. The Boro Park business community: A study. Brooklyn, New York: Author.

Cunningham, C. 1965. Order and change in an Atoni diarchy. *Southwestern Journal of Anthropology* 21:359–382.

Dallmayr, F. 1987. *Critical encounters: Between philosophy and politics.* Notre Dame: University of Notre Dame Press.

Dahl, O. C. 1982. The house in Madagascar. In *The house in East and South-East Asia,* ed. K. G. Isikowitz and P. Sorensen, 181–187. London: Curzon Press.

Davidman, L. 1991. Women's search for family and roots: A Jewish religious solution to a modern dilemma. In *In gods we trust: New patterns of religious pluralism in America,* ed. Thomas Robbins and Dick Anthony, 385–407. New Brunswick: Transaction Press.

Derrida, J. 1970. Structure sign and play. In *The structuralist controversy*, ed. Richard Macksey and Eugenia Donato, 247–272. Baltimore: Johns Hopkins University Press.

Dews, P. 1987. *Logics of disintegration.* New York: Verso.

Dreyfus, H., and P. Rabinow. 1982. *Michel Foucault: Beyond structuralism and hermeneutics.* Chicago: University of Chicago Press.

Eisen, A. 1986. *Galut: Modern Jewish reflections on homelessness and homecoming.* Bloomington: Indiana University Press.

Eliade, M. 1959. *The sacred and the profane: The nature of religion.* New York: Harcourt.

The Forward. 1993. Chasidim flout separatist image. *The Forward*, January 8.

Geertz, C. 1973. Religion as a cultural system. In *The interpretation of cultures*, ed. Clifford Geertz, 87–125. New York: Basic Books.

Green, A. 1977. The zaddiq as axis mundi in later Judaism. *Journal of the American Academy of Religion* 45:327–347.

———. 1987. Typologies of leadership and the Hasidic zaddiq. In *Jewish spirituality: From the sixteenth century revival to the present,* ed. Arthur Green, 127–156. New York: Crossroad.

Griaule, M., and G. Dieterlen. 1954. The Dogon of the French Sudan. In *African worlds: Studies in the cosmological ideas and social values of African peoples,* ed. Daryll Forde, 83–110. London: Oxford University Press.

Harvey, D. 1989. *The condition of postmodernity.* Oxford: Basil Blackwell.

Heilman, S. C. 1982. The sociology of American Jewry: The last ten years. *Annual Review of Sociology* 8:135–160.

Heine-Geldern, R. von. 1943. Conceptions of state and kingship in Southeast Asia. *Far Eastern Quarterly* 2:15–30.

Heschel, A. J. 1951. *The sabbath.* New York: Farrar, Straus, and Giroux.

Hugh-Jones, S. 1979. *The palm and the pleiades: Initiation and cosmology in North-west Amazonia.* Cambridge: Cambridge University Press.

Jacobs, L. 1987. The uplifting of sparks in later Jewish Mysticism. In *Jewish spirituality: From the sixteenth century revival to the present,* ed. Arthur Green, 101–115. New York: Crossroad.

Jameson, F. 1984. Postmodernism, or the cultural logic of the late capitalism. *New Left Review* 146:53–92.

Jewish Press. 1984. Hasidic Jews designated as disadvantaged by U.S. July 6, p. 1.

———. 1985. The Bobov living memorial marking the 40th anniversary of the Holocaust. Nov. 15, p. 26a.

Kaminetsky, J. 1953. Boro Park. *Orthodox Jewish Life* 21:18–23.

Katz, J. 1961. *Tradition and crises.* New York: Schocken Books.

Kaufman, D. R. 1985. Women who return to Orthodox Judaism: A feminist analysis. *Journal of Marriage and the Family* 47:543–555.

Kellerman, A. 1989. *Time, space, and society: Geographical societal perspective.* Dordrecht, The Netherlands: Kluwer Academic Publishers.

Kipust, P. 1981. I remember Boro Park. *Boro Park Community News,* Jan. 15, p. 3.

Kranzler, G. 1961. *Williamsburg: A Jewish community in transition.* New York: Philipp Feldheim.

Levine, E. 1986. Introduction: Jews in time and space. In *Diaspora: Exile and the contemporary Jewish condition,* ed. Etan Levine, 1–11. New York: Steimatzky Publishing of North America, Inc.

Lyotard, J.-F. 1984. *The postmodern condition: A report on knowledge.* Trans. G. Bennington and B. Massumi. Minneapolis: University of Minnesota Press.

Maier, E. 1975. Torah as movable territory. *Annals of the Association of American Geographers* 65:18–23.

Massey, D. 1992. A place called home? *New Formations* 17:3–15.

Mazey, M. E., and D. R. Lee. 1983. *Her space, her place: A geography of women.* Washington, DC: The Association of American Geographers.

Mayer, E. 1979. *From suburb to shtetl: The Jews of Boro Park.* Philadelphia: Temple University Press.

———. 1993 *The Boro Park community survey, 1992–93.* New York: Council of Jewish Organizations of Boro Park.

Meyrowitz, J. 1985. *No sense of place: The impact of electronic media on social behavior.* New York: Oxford University Press.

Mintz, J. R. 1968. *Legends of the Hasidim: An introduction to Hasidic culture and oral tradition in the new world.* Chicago: University of Chicago Press.

———. 1983. Ethnic activism: The Hasidic example. *Judaism* 28:449–464.

———. 1992. *Hasidic people: A place in the new world.* Cambridge: Harvard University Press.

The Miracle of Bobov. n.d. *The miracle of Bobov.* Brooklyn: United Bobov International.

Plaskow, J. 1989. Jewish memory from a feminist perspective. In *Weaving the visions: New patterns in feminist spirituality,* ed. Judith Plaskow and Carol P., 39–50. San Francisco: Harper and Row.

Poll, S. 1962. *The Hasidic community of Williammsburg.* New York: Free Press.

Rapoport, A. 1969. *House form and culture.* Englewood Cliffs, NJ: Prentice-Hall.

Robbins, K. 1991. Tradition and translation: National culture in its global context. In *Enterprise and heritage: Crosscurrents of national culture,* ed. John Corner and Sylvia Harvey, 21–44. London: Routledge.

Robinson, I. 1990. The First Hasidic rabbis in North America. Paper presented at the Association for Jewish Studies Meetings.

Rosenthal, E. 1980. The Jews of Boro Park. *Jewish Journal of Sociology* 22:187–191.

Sack, R. D. 1980. *Conceptions of space in social thought.* Minneapolis: University of Minnesota Press.

Schick, M. 1979. Borough Park: A Jewish settlement. *Jewish Life Magazine,* Winter. New York: Union of Orthodox Jewish Congregation of America.

Scholem, G. 1941. *Major trends in Jewish mysticism.* New York: Schocken Books.

Skinner, S. 1982. *The living earth manual of Feng-Shui.* London: Routledge and Kegan Paul.

Spigel, L. 1992. *Make room for TV: Television and the family ideal in postwar America.* Chicago: University of Chicago Press.

Tigerman, S. 1988. *The architecture of exile.* New York: Rizzolie International Publications.

Weinreich, M. 1980. The language of the way of the SHaS. In *History of the Yiddish language,* trans. Shlomo Noble, 175–246. Chicago: University of Chicago Press.

Weinryb, B. D. 1972. *The Jews of Poland.* Philadelphia: The Jewish Publication Society of America.

Wertheim, A. 1992. *Law and custom in Hasidism,* trans. Shmuel Himelstein. Hoboken, New Jersey: Kvav Publishing House.

Wiesel, E. 1972. *Souls on fire.* New York: Random House.

Zenner, W. P., and J. S. Belcove-Shalin. 1988. Persistence and flexibility. In *Persistence and flexibility: Anthropological studies of American Jewish identities and institutions,* ed. Walter P. Zenner, 3–38. Albany: SUNY Press.

Zerubavel, E. 1976. Timetables and scheduling: On the social organization of time. *Sociological Inquiry* 46:88–90.

———. 1977. The French Republican calendar: A case study in the sociology of time. *American Review* 44:868–877.

———1981. *Hidden rhythms: Schedules and calendars in social life.* Chicago: University of Chicago Press.

CHAPTER 9

The Bobover Hasidim Piremshpiyl: From Folk Drama for Purim to a Ritual of Transcending the Holocaust

Shifra Epstein

The paper explores the Bobover Hasidim folk drama for Purim, the *piremshpiyl*,[1] as a ritual transcending the experience of the Holocaust. The paper opens an inquiry into the potential of the festival by showing the adaptability of Purim: Not only are daily events turned topsy-turvy, but merrymaking events become occasions to encounter the abyss of the Holocaust. In addition, the paper also delineates how such encounters are not fixed to a specific time and place, nor to a specifically serious or humorous performance genre. Given that relatively little has been written about the complexity of emotions and beliefs that the Holocaust holds for Hasidim, this chapter is perhaps the first effort to explore the mode of confrontation with the abyss within a specific Hasidic community.

Purim plays, known in standard Yiddish as *purimshpiln* (*purimshpil*, sing.), were the most popular folk plays among Yiddish-speaking Eastern- and Western-European Jews up until the Second World War.[2] The Second World War for the most part brought an end to the folkways of Ashkenazic Jewry, and performances of full-fledged purimshpiln in Yiddish have become scarce in number, the property of a few Hasidic communities in the United States and Israel who continue to use Yiddish as their lingua franca. Among these communities are the Bobover and Munkaczer Hasidim of Brooklyn, New York; the Vishnitzer Hasidim of Bne-Braq, Israel; and the Reb Arelech Hasidim (known also as Toldot Aharon[3]) in Jerusalem, Israel.

The Bobover Hasidim, today of Boro Park, Brooklyn, the focus of this study, is a community of Holocaust survivors which originated in the town of Bobowa in Western Poland more than a hundred and fifty years ago. The Bobover who survived World War II first settled on the Upper West Side of New York. In the early 1960s they moved to Crown Heights and later to Boro Park, Brooklyn, New York, where they established a thriving community. With satellite communities in Israel, Canada, and England, the Bobover number approximately one thousand families.[4] As in the past, the production today is the domain of the males. The crew, including the playwright, the director, the set designer, and actors, are all amateurs and members of the Bobover community.[5] Although women do not participate in the production, they may view the event from the women's section in the *besmedresh* (the house of study and worship), where the performance takes place.

The production of a piremshpiyl was always a part of the Bobover celebration of Purim. Bobover who survived World War II and settled in the United States have been performing piremshpiyln annually and without interruption since 1948, perhaps the only community today that has continued this tradition so continuously. Among the non-Bobover Hasidim, there is no continuity in performing their plays each Purim as the Bobover do, nor do they make it such a key event in their cosmological life as do the Bobover. By comparison, the Bobover piremshpiyln are more elaborate, with more attention to the details of plot, costume, music, and acting.[6]

Pre–World War II Eastern-European Jews viewed Purim plays mainly as a means of entertainment and a temporary release from the harshness of everyday life. The Bobover Hasidim, however, consider the pirimshpiyln central to their belief and practice of Purim. Inspired by studies of the imagery of the rituals and festivals,[7] this paper views the yearly performance of the Bobover piremshpiyl as a moment of extraordinary self-display in which the participants enact and transmit their own visions of their sacred world. Drawing upon the dramatic qualities of the piremshpiyl and depicting themes from the Bible and Hasidic life, moralistic stories are highlighted and elaborated. As such, basic Bobover beliefs and practices "are actually constructed, reconstructed, and they are fundamentally re-established" (Ortner 1978:2).

As mentioned, this chapter follows the transformation of the purimshpil from an all-encompassing Ashkenazic Jewish tradition to a key and extraordinary Bobover ritual for Purim. In the second part of the chapter, examples from two contemporary piremsh-piyl, *Tzayt in Farnumen Poyland* (Times in Occupied Poland), the first Bobover piremshpiyl in the United States, performed in 1948, and *Hananiah, Mishael, Azariah ve-Daniel in Kivshon haEsh* (Hananiah, Azariah, Mishael and Daniel in the Fiery Furnace[8]), performed in 1977 and again in 1987, show how the piremshpiyl has been reestablished in New York and redefined with a newer context, as a ritual transcending the abyss of the Holocaust.

THE BOBOVER PURIM AND *PIREMSHPIYL*

Purim is a Jewish holiday observed annually on the fourteenth and fifteenth of the month of Adar (February/March). Chronicled in the Biblical book of Esther, the holiday celebrates the deliverance of the Jews of Persia during the fifth century B.C.E. from a plot by Haman, the vizir of King Ahashverus, to annihilate them. The second day of the holiday is called Shushan Purim, "The Purim of Susa," celebrating the triumph of Jews of Susa, the capital of Persia. In contrast with other Jewish holidays, there are relatively few precepts associated with Purim, whether injunctions or prohibitions. The main requirement on Purim is to be merry. As a result, from early accounts of its celebrations, Purim emerges as the most enigmatic of all Jewish holidays, an occasion for feasting, masquerading, drinking to the point of intoxication, mockery, and performing and participating in purimshpiln.[9]

Within Judaism there is a continuum of "great" and "small" traditions. Great traditions include rituals, customs, and ideologies shared by all Jews; small traditions encompass those variations which are particular to a Jewish community such as the Hasidim. The Bobover meticulously observe a number of activities required by the Jewish code on Purim: the fast of Esther on the day before Purim, the reading of *Megillat Esther* (Scroll of Esther) in the synagogue, the giving of money for charity, an exchange of presents, and eating a festive meal at home. Since there is considerable freedom from the major prohibitions and the atmosphere is more relaxed than on other occasions during the year, Hasidim have been able to develop their own theology and their own distinct Purim activities.

Drawing upon the inversion and reversal of Purim embedded in the Purim story and elaborated by the theology of the mystics of sixteenth-century Safed, Hasidim have elevated the importance of Purim, a minor festival, to that of Yom Kippur, the most important day of the year.[10] Hasidim, who were influenced since the beginning of their movement by the mystical ideas of the Kabbalists, also adopted the mystics' articulation of Purim. Like the Kabbalists, they found a connection between the Hebrew word *Kippurim* (atonement) alluding to the holiday of Yom Kippur, and *KiPurim*, which means "like Purim."[11]

Barbara Babcock defines the activity of symbolic inversion "as any act of expressive behavior which inverts, contradicts, abrogates, or in any fashion presents an alternative to commonly-held cultural codes, values, and norms, be they linguistic, literary, or artistic, religious, social, or political" (1978: 14). In the Jewish tradition, Purim and Yom Kippur are diametrically opposed to each other, especially in the modes of behavior required. Theologically, by elevating the status of Purim to that of Yom Kippur, Hasidim have created a world for themselves, founded on a temporary reversal and inversion of the normative Jewish code. The inversion quality of Purim, which gives rise to a separate Bobover Hasidic theology for Purim, one shared with other Hasidim but not with non-Hasidic Jews, extends also into the domain of the piremshpiyl. For the Bobover, on Purim as on Yom Kippur, God is more attentive to supplication and repentance.

Galician branches of Hasidim, including the Bobover, have always been known for their mystical beliefs and practices, including belief in miracles performed by rebbes. On Purim, they extend these beliefs and rites into the performance of a piremshpiyl.[12] Since for the Bobover Hasidim, Purim also connotes Kippur (kiPurim), the piremshpiyl with its "sacred words" has become for Galician Hasidim a sacred play, a mystical means to get closer to God.

The Bobover believe that at certain troubled times, God can endow the actors of the piremshpiyl with power to change the course of disastrous events by enacting a reversal of them in the course of the play.[13] From what I have been able to observe, in recent years this "scheme" has never been used for communal needs, but rather in very modest ways to cases of personal need.

For example, in the Daniel Play, the name of a person from the contemporary Bobover community who recently suffered great economic problems was inserted as part of a joke. The Bobover believe that if his name is mentioned during the performance, the problem will disappear.

The variety of moods inherent in the holiday in conjunction with the inversion of the frivolous Purim to that of contemplative and solemn Yom Kippur allows the Bobover Hasidim yet another inversion. They have taken their paradoxical linkage of Yom Kippur with Purim even a step further by incorporating the Holocaust, the most abject of their experiences, into their celebrations of Purim, the most joyful of all their celebrations.

Like many other survivors, both Hasidim and non-Hasidic Jews, the Bobover Hasidim have not fully come to terms with the Holocaust. Evidence for that lies in the fact that themes, images, and beliefs connected with the Holocaust experience still appear in many of the contemporary Bobover piremshpiyln. For Hasidim, man's limited perspective does not permit a full grasp of the Holocaust, and therefore, no human being can create an appropriate ritual to commemorate the Holocaust. Hence, Hasidim prefer to commemorate and remember individual members of their families who perished in the Holocaust. Individual Hasidim observe private *yortzaytn* (memorial services) for close family members who perished. Hasidim refuse to participate in the Holocaust Memorial Day on the twenty-seventh of the Jewish month of Nissan, which was established by the State of Israel and observed by world Jewry today. They also do not accept as a special day the tenth of the Jewish month of Tevet, a fast day in Jewish tradition in which observant Jews remember the Holocaust. For Hasidim, *Tishah b'Av* (the ninth day of the month of Av), when Jews commemorate as a community the destruction of the First and Second Temples, has become an appropriate occasion to commemorate the victims of the Holocaust. However, recently even Hasidim have started to compose their own liturgy for the victims of the Holocaust to be recited on Tishah B'av.[14]

More than on any other occasion in the Bobover yearly calendar of events, including Tishah b'Av, it is during Purim that public laments and mourning for the Bobover victims of the Holocaust are communicated and elaborated in a variety of activities. The Rebbe's sermon during the *trink siyde* (drinking banquet) on the afternoon of Purim is devoted to remembering the "old country" and those who perished in the Holocaust. Songs of lament composed and sung by individuals and the community have become part of the event. As will be shown in the course of the chapter, the Holocaust is also the theme of many of the various Bobover piremshpiyln.

THE *PIREMSHPIYL* AS A RITUAL TRANSCENDING THE ABYSS OF THE HOLOCAUST

The Bobover piremshpiyln are incorporated into the *groysen siyde*, "the great banquet," the central Bobover event on the night of Purim, already Shushan Purim, which takes place in the besmedresh. The Purim/Kippurim frame articulates the event: A special Purim *Rav* presides over the event, and the Rebbe becomes part of the audience. A large chocolate cake in the shape of a fish, the zodiac sign for Purim, is broken into pieces and distributed by the Rebbe to all the audience; large quantities of beer are drunk; songs from the Yom Kippur repertoire are sung both at the beginning and the end of the event; and the piremshpiyl is performed.

The annual performance of the Bobover piremshpiyl is an event involving the sacred and the profane, the everyday and the extraordinary, in a very unique way. Using Harvey Cox's notion as people's celebration of religious faith (1969), we can see that by incorporating the piremshpiyl into their religious observation of Purim, the Bobover communally celebrate their relationship with God using the rich methodology of the folk play (Cox 1969).

The piremshpiyl belongs to a category of rituals which moves or transforms human behavior via space and time different from that experienced everyday, that is, into what Victor Turner calls the liminal state, a stage of ambiguity between the real and the unreal in everyday life (Turner 1969: 96–97). According to Johan Huizinga, the Dutch scholar of play, *play* is "a free activity standing quite consciously outside 'ordinary' life as being 'not serious' but at the same time absorbing the players intensely and utterly" (Huizinga 1972:13). More than any other event in Bobover religious life, the piremshpiyl engages the community in ludicrous, playful behavior antithetical to everyday norms. In effect, it is the only occasion in which their world order is temporarily inverted—young men become actors and wear costumes, and the physical separation between males and females is relaxed: women chide men and draw aside the *mekhitse* (room divider) in the besme-dresh. In accordance with the inversion quality of Purim, a Purim Rav replaces the Rebbe, and the Rebbe's sermon is replaced by the performance of the piremshpiyl. The members of the besmedresh, now the audience, view a dramatic event on this one and only occasion of the year. By inverting norms, the piremshpiyl also defines those norms with special clarity. They are highlighted and dramatized for the community.

Since 1948 the Bobover have produced and performed close to twenty different piremshpiyln. The majority of them are new, as they were written in the United States. Looking closely at their different texts and plots, two main categories of play emerged: pirem-shpiyln which are totally devoted in their plot, themes, and setting to the Holocaust experience; and piremshpiyln in which general themes in Jewish and Hasidic history are highlighted. In the first category, to date, there has been only one play, *Tzayt in Farnumen Poyland* (Times in Occupied Poland), the first piremshpiyl pro-duced and performed in New York in 1948. It is a quintessential piremshpiyl for the Holocaust in that it focuses on the Holocaust, and was produced and performed by Holocaust survivors only three years after the atrocities, before an audience composed of sur-vivors. Post-1948, however, the Holocaust as the focus of the piremshpiyln has been replaced by immediate and nonimmediate threats from past and present enemies of Jews and Hasidim. Themes from the Holocaust may appear to exemplify survival by faith and suffering. This transformation of the piremshpiyl from a psychodrama for the Holocaust to a ritual of survival in general is in line with Sherry Ortner's observation that "rituals do not begin with the eternal verities, but arrive at them" (Ortner 1978:2–3).

Two plays from the Bobover repertoire, *Tzayt in Farnumen Poyland* and the *Daniel Play*, will be used to illustrate how the piremshpiyln "begin with some cultural problem (or several at once), stated or not stated, and then work various operations upon it, arriving at 'solutions'—reorganizations and reinterpreting of the elements that produce a newly meaningful whole. The solution (and the means of arriving at them) embody . . . the fundamental cultural assumptions and orientations . . . " (Ortner 1978:2–3).

What follows are the text and context of *Tzayt in Farnumen Poyland*. In this psychodrama, the Holocaust experience is reversed in the miraculous survival of Yankele literally out of his own ashes. This was an appropriate psychodrama three years after the war, providing survivors with the opportunity to act out their emotions, anxieties, and beliefs connected with the Holocaust.

It was the contemporary Bobover Rebbe, R. Shlomo Halberstam, himself a survivor, who was personally responsible for the revival of the Bobover piremshpiyl in the United States. Around the time of Purim in 1948, he requested that R. Moses Aftergute, then a young yeshivah student, produce a piremshpiyl in Yiddish so that the Bobover piremshpiyl tradition would not be forgotten. The result was production of *Tzayt in Farnumn Poyland*. *Tzayt in Farnumen Poyland* reflects how, for a community of survivors, the piremshpiyl continued to be an appropriate form to celebrate Purim, three years after the atrocities.

Reconstructed from memory by Moses Aftergute almost thirty years after the first performance, the following account best illustrates how, with its theme, plot, setting, and mode, *Tzayt in Farnumen Poyland* is a powerful psychodrama reversing the Holocaust. Since the text of the play has not survived, I include an entire account of the play as it was written in Yiddish by Moses Aftergute (my English translation).

The first scene takes place in a ghetto in Poland during World War II. A Jewish woman named Bila Yakobowitz, whose husband has already been sent to a death camp, "clings to her sleeping child, Yankele, caressing him, as if the sixteen-year-old lad were a small child who could not even walk, trying to reassure herself that the SS officers will not carry him off 'to work.'"[15] Talking to herself, and remembering her home (her parents, brothers and sisters, relatives, friends, and acquaintances), from time to time the mother gives a deep sigh, telling herself that she will not, God forbid, awaken the child. Reliving names and episodes, she suddenly cries out as footsteps are heard in the background. Hearing the footsteps, Yankele wakes up and asks her: "Who goes, mother?" The mother answers "Sleep, my child, nobody walks."

In the background the steps of the SS officers are heard. They break into Yakobowitz's home, cruelly grab the mother and ask: "Are you Bila Yakobowitz? And this is your son? His sentence is stamped." The soldiers throw the mother cruelly to the ground, and leave taking Yankele, her child, with them. She fights desperately and unsuccessfully for her child, who is taken away, leaving the mother alone, lying on the ground.

She then falls into a trance. In a trance, she talks to herself, starting to fantasize. The next scene takes place several years later when an SS officer with a sack in his hand appears at Bila Yakobowitz's door. When she answers the question "Is your name Bila Yakobowitz?" positively, he gives her a small sack, and says: "Here is your child. . . . " Delighted, she clings to the sack, presses it fast to her heart, smiling and not able to take her eyes from what is inside the sack. Nothing within it responds to her tenderness and heartfelt affection. Then she sees the inscription on the sack—ashes. She opens her large eyes and starts to shiver. She presses the sack once more to her heart, and then throws herself on the ground, still holding it. She opens it, put her hand inside and takes out the ashes little by little. She cries, "These are the ashes of my Yankele, these are the ashes of my father, my mother, my brothers and sisters." The world seems to tremble and the skies are torn apart. She starts chattering and becomes nauseated, as everything that happened passes before her eyes. She takes a match, runs outside her home, and races from house to house, lighting houses and trees, shouting at the SS officer: "If you have made ashes from my Yankele, I will light everything which is lightable, and let burn everything that is burnable! . . . Now I have one request: Put me to death so I can be with my child in the same small sack of ashes." (While she is speaking, the American national anthem is heard).

The last scene takes place at the end of the war, with the American liberation. The place is full of American soldiers; some of them provide first aid to Bila Yakobowitz. A knock is heard on the door, and Yankele, her son, hurries inside. Broken in spirit and emaciated, the mother stands dumbstruck, unable to say a word. "Is this not a dream in the valley of death?" she asks. It takes a while before she realizes that it is not a dream, that her son has returned. Her dimmed eyes start to shine with a maternal light. She learns from Yankele that he ran away from a transport in the forests, where a group of partisans found him and brought him to their camp. Yankele embraces and kisses his mother. They both cry about the miracle.

While sitting closer to her, Yankele says, "Mother, just as the rushing streams which create little islands are incapable of tearing themselves away, so will Yankele never tear himself from his mother."

By cheating death, *Tzayt in Farnumen Poyland* inverts the Holocaust experience and provides a ritualistic channel to publicly proclaim belief in God and His miracles even during the

Holocaust. Thus, *Tzayt in Farnumen Poyland* provides the Bobover with the opportunity to celebrate together their survival as individuals and as a community.

According to eyewitnesses, the audience was very moved by *Tzayt in Farnumen Poyland*. Men and women sobbed and one woman even fainted. It was the Bobover *Rebbe* who requested that the actors not perform *Tzayt in Farnumen Poyland* the following year, but rather return to more traditional piremshpiyln. The Rebbe felt that *Tzayt in Farnumen Poyland* was too emotional and too sad for Purim, too close to the Holocaust. As a result, unlike other piremshpiyln, which are often repeated, *Tzayt in Farnumen Poyland* has never been performed again.

The celebration of the first Purim after World War II, in 1947, by the Jewish members of the Landsberg Displaced Persons Center in Germany is an important source of insight into the reversal quality of Purim. Like the performers-survivors of *Tzayt in Farnumen Poyland*, the performers-survivors at Landsberg reversed their Holocaust experience by masquerading as SS officers, death camp detainees, and even as Hitler himself. Toby Blum-Dobkin (1979:52–58), who studied the unique community at Landsberg, elaborates on the ritual of the Holocaust reversal in the Landsberg Purim. According to her,

> Although imitation may be at times a form of flattery, it can also be a powerful weapon and a strong form of ridicule. By assuming the persona of Hitler, a liberated Jew can illustrate his complete power over his former opposer. The masquerader dictates and controls the actions of the character he is playing; in performing the exaggerated Nazi Salute, the Jew can mock the Nazi and emphasize the transfer of power. When the liberated Jew donned the striped suit of the concentration camp, this dramatized the change of status that had taken place. He wore the striped uniform not as a slave, but as a free person, not in the Nazi death factories, but upon a speaker's platform. Those wearing the uniform memorialized those who had died and at the same time emphasized the reversals that had come about. (Blum-Dubkin 1979:57)

Thus, Purim provided the Landsberg survivors with the opportunity to reverse their Holocaust experiences. The celebration was therapeutic, positively affecting their ability to go on after the war.

Post-1948 plays with Biblical and Hasidic plots have replaced *Tzayt in Farnumen Poyland*, utilizing settings far removed from the Holocaust to enact survival. *Akeydas Yitzkhak* (The Binding of Isaac) (1968 and 1976), *Mekhiras Yosef* (The Selling of Joseph) (1969 and 1976), *Yalde Teheran* (The Children of Teheran) (1974), *Yetzias Mitzrayim* (The Exodus from Egypt) (1971), *Di Trirn Hobn im Zurik Gebrakh* (The Tears Have Brought Him Back) (1972), *Hananiah, Mishael, Azariah ve-Daniel in Kivshon haEsh* (Hananiah, Azariah, Mishael and Daniel in the Fiery Furnace) (1971, 1977, and 1987), *Mayse di likht Shtroan* (A Story about the Torch) (1974), *Der Zayde is Gerekht* (Grandfather is right) (1978 and 1988), *Shlomo haMaylekh und Ashmedai* (Solomon and Ashmedos) (1979) are examples of these plays. They provide the community with the opportunity to transcend the Holocaust experience into psychodramas of paradigmatic survival in Babylon, Egypt, and even in Brooklyn, New York.

The Play of Daniel, performed first in 1971, is an example of the post-1948 piremshpiyln, where survival is the focus and where themes from the Holocaust are employed to strengthen the belief in survival. It focuses on the Babylonian Exile and the attempts of King Nebuchadnezzar to convert to idolatry three Jewish children—Hananiah, Azariah, and Mishael. When they refuse to convert, Nebuchadnezzar throws them into a fiery furnace. In the last scene of the play, they are saved by God, and the King acknowledges that their God is the most powerful.

A number of episodes from the Play of Daniel may illustrate how post-Holocaust Bobover piremshpiyln have been transformed into a ritual transcending the Holocaust experience. The play consists of seven scenes. The setting for the majority of the scenes, Nebuchadnezzar's palace in the ancient city of Babylonia, is very far from Europe and the Holocaust. The ability of the Play of Daniel to infuse the Holocaust into its Biblical setting makes the enactment of survival even more powerful.

In the last scene of the play, just before Daniel, Hananiah, Mishael and Azariah are thrown into the fiery furnace, Nebuchadnezzer attempts for the last time to persuade them to become Babylonian. He says:

> Children, children, what are your names? Hananiah, Mishael and Azariah? You probably know about me. How many people have I killed already? Thousands, tens of thousands, and still . . . and I will . . . three such young and beautiful children, I'm about to hear their last breaths, here in the fiery furnace. I

feel myself shivering, for what, for what? Do you remember your home? Your parents, your fathers and mothers, your brothers, your sisters, all were hurt. Why? What remains of them? What? Ashes. And you survivors, such three lonely children, about to take the same stupid step? Why? Why did I call you here? I ask you to bow. Why don't you bow down, why not bow, for such a silly thing is it worth your lives? Children, you're still so young. You have just barely started your life. I beg of you, break your shackles, be one of us, look at what's happening, look what stands before you, a bright world, a golden world. I still want to elevate you. I want to make you the greatest masters in the entire land. Children, I know what's good for you. I love you, I've raised you, I beg of you, be sensible about this drastic step you are about to take. See that I won't fail you. . . . Children, children, I beg you, don't do such a silly thing. I'll give you a few more minutes, to reconsider what you're about to do.

It is quite obvious that underlying Nebuchadnezzer's speech is also a theological question regarding the purpose of the death not only of Hananiah, Mishael, and Azariah, but also of those who perished in the Holocaust. When Hananiah, Mishael, and Azaria refuse to bow to the idol and eat nonkosher food, Ashpenaz, Nebuchadnezzar's prime minister, ties them with a rope before throwing them into the fiery furnace. They say "throw us into the oven, we don't fear for our blood and skin/This happened before in another time." References to the fiery furnace call to mind images of the Holocaust.

Especially powerful is the usage of both lyrics and melodies of Yom Kippur in the play, recalling the sanctity of Yom Kippur and Purim in the Bobover belief. Before entering the fiery furnace, Hananiah, Mishael, and Azaria sing a version in Yiddish of Avinu Malkenu, "Our Father, Our King," a petition to God recited on Yom Kippur, with specific additions that refer to both the Babylonian exile and the Holocaust.

HANANIAH: Our Father, Our King, do look down from heaven
Act on behalf of those who are dying
and comfort your people on this day
In your name: give them comfort.

MISHAEL: Our Father, Our King,
For the honor of heaven
We are hurt and broken
Act for those who die for your Uniqueness.

AZARIAH: Our Father, Our King, for me take action
when I am thrown into the fiery furnace.
Act for those who enter the fire,
Sanctifying of your Name.
Your wrath from them turn.

HANAN., MISH., and AZAR: Our Father, Our king
Vindicate your people.
Revenge your faithful nation,
The blood of your chosen people
Your flesh and blood children
O Lord are burnt to ashes.
Revenge the blood of your slaves.

Strength of faith as exhibited by Hananiah when singing
Avinu Malkenu recalls the strength of faith by the Bobover Hasi-
dim facing the Germans during the Second World War. Hananiah,
Mishael, and Azaria end Avinu Malkenu with the ultimate decla-
ration of faith by reciting the *Sh'ma* "Here O Israel, Our God,
God is one."

However, the ultimate act of devotion is expressed in the
readiness of Hananiah, Mishael, and Azaria to sanctify the Name
of God rather than commit idolatry or eat nonkosher foods. In the
play performed in 1987, Hananiah, Mishael, and Azaria sing
before entering the fiery furnace, saying:

Truthfully we state we are ready
To give our soul to our Creator.
It's what we are taught at home:
To give oneself to sanctify His name.

In the version of the play performed in 1977, Azariah even
recited the martyrdom blessing: *al pi din maizn mir makhn a
brukhe, aniy mekadesh shmo berabim* (according to the law we
must recite: I sanctify the Name of God in public). Apparently, the
recapitulation of the blessing on stage was too powerful and even
considered sacrilegious by some Bobover; hence, the blessing was
not repeated in full in a more recent version of the play performed
in 1987. When Azaria recites the *Kiddush haShem* blessing, men
and women experience an intense feeling of sadness—they can be
seen wiping tears away with their handkerchiefs.

The readiness of Hanania, Mishael, and Azaria to become
martyrs and to sanctify the divine name by committing themselves

unreservedly to death rather than give up their faith is a central tenet in the Jewish religion, known as *Kiddush haShem* (the sanctification of God's Name).[16] In Jewish tradition, martyrdom has become a major thematic element in a variety of literary genres in every period: elegies, dirges, poetic narratives, *selihot* (penitential prayers), historical chronicles, and folk songs.[17] In this way heroic acts are commemorated, recommended, reenacted, praised, and lamented. The ideology of martyrdom has continued from an early formation in the second century B.C.E. through the Middle Ages and into the modern period. Kiddush haShem was a call to close ranks especially when persecution threatened to destroy the whole community. New martyrs sanctified the Name in the course of such catastrophes as the slaughter of the Jews in the Rhine Valley during the First Crusade, and the blood libels and subsequent pogroms in the Ukraine and Poland at the time of Chmielnicki (1648–1649), when countless thousands were massacred.

In Hasidic tradition, the Hasidic victims of the Holocaust are considered holy and martyrs and their death is considered to have been by Kiddush haShem.[18] In Bobover chronicles, individual victims of the Holocaust are depicted as followers of Abraham, Hanania, Mishael, and Azariah by continuing to sanctify the Name of God in the same spirit as those martyrs who preceded them.[19] Those who died are referred to as "innocent martyrs," and praised for their acts as well as for taking their own lives rather than letting themselves fall into the hands of the Germans or the Ukrainians.[20] Pesakh Schindler, in his study of the Hasidic religious response during the Holocaust notes that "the privilege of Kiddush haShem enabled the Hasid to anticipate his tragic fate with some sort of dignity . . . in defiance of the enemy's objective to degrade and terminate life" (Schindler 1990:117). As in the literature of martyrdom, the Bobover piremshpiyl serves as a model for the ideal martyr preparing the Hasid for the possibility of Kiddush haShem in the future.

While Hananiah, Mishael, and Azariah are tied, a furnace is pushed on the stage. Its base is drawn to look like stone, and the flames coming from within it are represented by red, white, and black cellophane, resembling a fire because of a light within the structure. The furnace, of course, calls to mind the incinerators at the death camps in Poland. When Hananiah, Mishael, and Azariah and thrown into the fiery furnace, a fiddler plays the melody of *Ani Maamin* (I Believe in Perfect Faith in the Coming of the

Messiah), which continues through the end of the scene. In modern times this hymn became the credo chanted by the Jews before their deaths in the ghettos and concentration camps.[21] As connoisseurs of Jewish tradition, many Bobover immediately recognize the words as a sacred incantation which probably was first pronounced during the First Crusade (1096).[22] The themes of martyrdom and survival have strong emotional associations for the members of the audience who recall the tragic events of past and recent Jewish history. The Bobover, a majority of whose members over the age of forty-five are survivors or children of survivors, are moved by the fiddler who plays *Ani Maamin* during the scene where the children are thrown into the fiery furnace. Many of them actually heard this credo chanted by those who were led to their deaths in the ghettos and concentration camps. The audience is extremely attentive during these scenes, some humming the melody along with the violin. In interviews, the Bobover identify the hardships of the heroes in the plays with their own experiences.

As was shown in the course of the second part of the chapter, the themes, the images, and the vocabulary of the sacred text of *Tzayt in Farnumen Poyland* and the Play of Daniel place the Bobover piremshpiyln within a large and older corpus of literary and artistic materials in which throughout history Jews have responded to catastrophes in their lives. Literary materials replete with the divine wrath and human lamentation have been written in different generations as a response to forced conversions, the auto-da-fes, pogroms, and most recently the Holocaust. According to David Roskies, who focuses on this genre in his monumental work *Against the Apocalypse: Response to Catastrophes in Modern Jewish Culture* (1984), this literature reflects the "ability, in the midst of and in the wake of the apocalypse, to know the apocalypse, express it, mourn it, and transcend it" (Roskies 1984:310).

CONCLUDING *REMARKS*

The multivocal quality of Purim and it's ability to have different meanings for different people allowed the Bobover to create their own traditions and meanings for the holiday. The Bobover, who do not have their own commemorative events for the Holocaust, have combined in a folk drama in Yiddish elements of Purim and Yom Kippur to create a ritual transcending the Holocaust.

Through a series of inversions and reversals, from the frivolous to the serious and vice versa, the piremshpiyl provides them with the opportunity to confront and come to terms with the abyss, their own experience with the Holocaust.

The Bobover piremshpiyl as a key event in the Bobover calendar for Purim refutes Gila Ramras-Rauch's assertion (1985:3) that "Holocaust literature" is a contradiction in terms. According to her "there is no way to link a life-affirming enterprise such as literature with a death-bound phenomenon of such magnitude" (Ramras-Rauch and Michman-Melkman 1985:3). As a cultural performance for the Holocaust, in their yearly production of the piremshpiyl, the Bobover Hasidim show that for them there is no contradiction in terms.

With the continuation of the piremshpiyl as their key event for Purim, the Bobover "say yes to life," "affirm[ing] life and gaiety despite the facts of failure and death" (Cox 1969:23). The annual performance of the Bobover piremshpiyl illustrates Harvey Cox's notion that "to celebrate with real abandon is most often found among people who are no strangers to pain and oppression" (Cox 1969:25).

NOTES

1. This is in Bobover Yiddish, which is a subvariant of Central Yiddish.

2. On the history of the purimshpil, including many extant versions, see Chone Shmeruk (1979).

3. Literally meaning "The Biography of Aharon,"referring to R. Aharon Roth, the founder of the sect.

4. See Bakon (1986:88–181) for an article on the history of the Bobover Hasidim and their founders, written by a Bobover Hasid.

5. For more detailed information of the event, including the elements of the preproduction (the selection of the themes and the texts), the production itself (the personnel, the rehearsals, the selection of costumes and props, the physical setting, and the music), and the performance (the interaction between the actors and the audience), see Shifra Epstein (1987).

6. See Doniach (1933:125–167) for a survey of these activities in different countries.

7. For examples of these studies, see Victor Turner (1969) and Beverly Stoeltje (1989).

8. I will refer to this play in the course of the paper as the *Daniel Shpiyl*, "The Play of Daniel."

9. See Doniach (1933:125–167) for a survey of these activities in different countries.

10. See *Sefer Tikkune haZohar*, with Commentary by *Ba'al haSulam* (Jerusalem: Yeshivat Kol Yehudah, 1970), vol. 2, ch. 21.

11. One of the earlier Hasidic sages who provides us with the Hasidic inversion of Purim/Kippurim is R. Yaakov Yitzkhak of Pshischah (1766–1813), the originator of Pshischah Hasidim. See *Sefer Niflaot haYehudi* (1908), pp. 35–36.

12. See Sharot (1980), for a discussion of the main Hasidic dynasties today and their beliefs and practices.

13. See *Sefer Tiferet MaHaRel* (1912:38–53) of an account about R. Arye Leib (d. 1811) of Shpola, Russia, a popular Hasidic sage and miracle-worker, known as the Shpoler Zeide (the Grandfather from Shpola). According to the account, he saved a Jew from Kishinev called Mendel from a false accusation by performing a play on Purim.

14. In a recent publication in Hebrew, *Kuntras Divrei Drisha Vehitoterut* (1984), a collection of laments for the victims of the Holocaust written by distinguished rebbes. They are recommended to be recited on the *Tishah b'Av* in memory of those who perished in Europe in 1939–1945).

15. Referring here to hard labor at various camps, or concentration camps.

16. The guidelines for martyrology appear in *Talmud Bavli*, Tractate *Sanhedrin* 74a–b. According to this source, a person should die rather than commit idolatry, adultery, or bloodshed. See also Urback (1960) for a discussion on martyrdom literature in the first and second century B.C.E.

17. Yerushalmi (1982:45) views selihot as "the single most important religious and literary response to the historical catastrophes."

18. See Schindler (1990) for the Hasidic attitude towards those who died in the Holocaust.

19. See *Sefer Arze ha-Levanon* (1964:170–78).

20. See *Sefer Arze ha-Levanon* (1964:170–78).

21. See Schindler (1990).

22. See Spiegel (1967:17–27) for the possible origin of the prayer.

REFERENCES

Sources in English (Arranged in Alphebetical Order by Author)

Babcock, B., ed. 1978. *The reversible world: Symbolic inversion in art and society.* Ithaca: Cornell Univiversity Press.

Bakon, H. 1986. The history of R. Shlomo Halberstam (1847–1905). In *Kerem haHasidut,* vol. 3, 88–181. [In Hebrew.]

Blum-Dobkin, T. 1979. The Landsberg carnival: Purim in a displaced person center. In *Purim: The face and the mask: Essays and catalogue of an exhibition at the Yeshiva University Museum,* 52–58. New York: Yeshiva University.

Cox, H. 1969. *The feast of fools.* New York: Harper and Row.

Doniach, N. 1933. *Purim: Or the feast of Esther.* Philadelphia: Jewish Publication Society of America.

Epstein, S. 1987. The Bobover Hasidic piremshpiyl. In *Judaism from within and without,* ed. Harvey Goldberg, 195–219. New York: SUNY Press.

Huizinga, J. 1972. *Homo ludens: A study of the play element in culture.* Boston: Beacon Press.

Ortner, S. B. 1978. *Sherpas through their rituals.* Cambridge: Cambridge University Press.

Ramras-Rauch, G., and J. Michman-Melkman. 1985. *Facing the Holocaust: Selected Israeli fiction.* Philadelphia: Jewish Publication Society in America. [In Hebrew.]

Roskies, D. 1984. *Against the apocalypse: Responses to catastrophes in modern Jewish culture.* Cambridge: Harvard University Press.

Sharot, S. 1980. Hasidim and the routinization of charisma. *Journal of the Scientific View of Religion* 19(4):325–326.

Schindler, P. 1990. *Hasidic responses to the Holocaust in the light of Hasidic thought.* Hoboken, NJ: Ktav Publication House, Inc.

Shmeruk, C. 1979. *Mahazot Miqra'iyyim beYiddish: 1697–1750.* Jerusalem: The Israeli Academy. [In Hebrew.]

Spiegel, S. 1967. *The last trial: On the legends and lore of the command to Abraham to offer Isaac as a sacrifice: The Akedah.* New York: Pantheon.

Stoeltje, B. 1989. Festivals. In *International encyclopedia of communication,* ed Erik Barnouw, 161–166. New York: Oxford University Press.

Victor, T. 1969. *The ritual process: Structure and anti-structure.* Chicago: Aldine.

Urback, E. 1960. Ascetician and suffering in talmudic and midrashic source. In *Yitzhak F. Baer Jubilee Volume.* Jerusalem: *hakhevrah haHistorit.* [In Hebrew.]

Yerushalmi, Y. H. 1982. *Zakhor: Jewish history and Jewish memory.* Seattle: University of Washington Press.

Hasidic Sources in Hebrew (Arranged in Alphabetical Order by Title)

Kuntras Divrei Drisha Vehitoterut. 1984. Brooklyn, NY: Vaad Lzecher Kdoshei Europe.

Sefer Arze haLevanon. 1964. Compiled by R. Elimelekh E. Ehrenberg. It is a history of the Bobover Hasidic dynasty in the twentieth century, including sections devoted to Ben Zion Halbertam and Shlomo Halberstam. Jerusalem.

Sefer Niflaot haYehudi. 1908. Commentary by R. Yaakov Yitzkhak of Pshischah (1766–1813). Peyetrekow.

Sefer Tiferet MaHaRel. 1912. A collection of the miraculous deeds of R. Arye Leib of Shpola. By Yehuda Rosenberg.

Sefer Tikkune haZohar. 1970. Commentary by *Ba'al haSulan.* Jerusalem: Yeshivat Kol Yehudah Vol. II.

CHAPTER 10

The Charismatic Leader of the Hasidic Community: The Zaddiq, the Rebbe

Solomon Poll

Hasidism is maintained and preserved by the community's charismatic leader—the Rebbe. The term *charisma*, as used in this article, refers to the qualities and characteristics that are assigned by the followers of a rebbe to their rebbe. The rebbe's devotees believe their leader to be a *zaddiq*—a righteous person—and as such, has extraordinary intellect and ability. Moreover, they believe that he has Heavenly guidance in directing and regulating their lives. Hasidism, in point of fact, is the relationship between the rebbe and his Hasidim—the subscription to the specific doctrines taught by the rebbe and the acting out of these doctrines in systematized ritual that elaborate this association.

The critical issue for Hasidism after the Second World War was its existence and continuity. With the destruction of the Jewish communities in Europe, the absence of the "holy spark" and the spirit of holy men and women created an enormous vacuum. The faith of the Jews were shaken as the great rabbis, the holy men, the righteous people, the community leaders, the holy congregations, and the pious communities were destroyed.

Hasidic Jews who came to America after World War II cried: "We remained *katzon b'li roeh,* as sheep without a shepherd." The answer came from various sources: "*lo almon Yisroel*—The people of Israel [the Jews]—is not a widow," meaning, "God is alive and will not allow the Jews to be vanished and destroyed."

God will retain the "spiritual marriage" between Himself and the People of Israel. The Hasidim said: "We are not neglected, we are not deserted, there are among us leaders who can get at the helm, who can direct us and lead us *al derech Yisroel sabbah*—according to the ways of Israel, our forefather."

A great number of Hasidic rebbes came to America from Hungary, Poland, Rumania, and Russia. The Rebbes are known and distinguished by the European towns or cities of their origin: for example, the Lubavitcher (from the city of Lubavitch, Russia), the Satmarer (from the city of Satmar, Rumania), the Tasher (from the city of Tash, Hungary), the Bobover (from the city of Bobov, Poland). These rebbes established communities with their own particular personal and cultural characteristics. The members of these communities considered the rebbes their charismatic leaders. They believed that these rebbes had the capacity to comfort, to advise, to bless, to console, to assure the followers that the world of their fathers and mothers would not come to an end. "On the contrary," the rebbes said, "in this land, which was heretofore considered a *treyf medinah*—a country not eligible for holiness— we will plant *kedushah* (holiness), *zedakah* (charity), *torah* (learning), and *mitzvot* (the observance of the commandments).

Hasidic Jews who survived the Holocaust needed and developed the ability to trust their rebbe and attach themselves to him. Once Hasidic Jews follow their rebbe, "nothing can go wrong," they feel. The rebbe is with them at moments of gladness, at moments of sadness, at births, at weddings, at funerals, and during casual contacts. The rebbe blesses them, wishes them success, good health, good livelihood, good children, "and a whole generation of God-fearing Jews, who will follow in the footsteps of their fathers and grandfathers and together they will go to welcome Messiah, who is sure to come."

Whether or not followers are fully aware of the meaning of the rebbe's particular conduct or mannerism, or whether or not followers are familiar with the Hasidic theoretical principles is of no significance. There is a great amount of literature that deals with Hasidism and the role of the rebbe. Hasidic Jews read this literature and associate it with reality.

Some of the literature—for example, *Or Ha'hayim, Hovat Halevavot, Hatam Sofer, Ta'amei Hamitzvot, Kisvei Ho'ari, Mesilat Yesharim, Noam Elimelech, Kav Hayashar, Kedushat Levi, Meor V'shemesh, Sheloh Hakadosh, Benei Yisoschar,*

Toldot Yacov Josef, Orchas Zaddiqim, Shevet Musar, Reshit Chochmah, is accepted by most of the Hasidic communities. Other literature, for example, the *Tanya* is studied mainly by the Lubavitcher community. *Va'yoel Moshe* is studied in the Satmar community. *S'fas Emes* is studied by the Gerer community. *Imre Josef* is studied by the Spinker community. Each community emphasizes the greatness of their own spiritual leaders in lighter material, such as children's reading and Yiddish articles as well. This literature is constantly quoted by the rebbes and the Hasidim at every occasion when appropriate.

In this chapter I shall present the following:

1. The rebbe as an exemplar of charismatic leadership.
2. The relationship among rebbes and ideological divisions among Hasidic groups.
4. The spiritual attributes of the rebbe as systematized in the writings of Rabbi Elimelech of Lyzhansk.
5. The perception of the rebbe in the Hasidic community.

THE CHARISMATIC LEADER

In his discussion of charisma, Edward Shills defines the concept as "a quality which is imputed to persons . . . because of their presumed connection with the 'ultimate,' 'fundamental,' 'vital' order-determining powers" (1968:386). He further states that "the propensity to impute charisma . . . and to seek contact with transcendental powers . . . is rooted in the neural constitution of the organism" (ibid.). Shils' treatment owes much to Max Weber's discussion of charisma (1957:358–363) "as a propriety attributed to great innovating personalities who disrupt traditionally and rational-legally legitimated systems of authority . . . claiming to be legitimated by the direct experience of divine grace."

The early Hasidic leaders have been portrayed as charismatic figures—innovating personalities who disrupted the normative system of rabbinical authority and claimed to be legitimated by divine grace (Horodetzki 1953, vols. 2–5). Today's leaders of Hasidism are also regarded as creative, innovating personalities to whom divine grace is imputed by their followers (though in order not to appear immodest, contemporary rebbes do not openly claim to possess divine grace). To illustrate, recently I was visiting a famous Hasidic rebbe. Outside, one of his followers whom I met previously wanted to know my impressions of the rebbe. "I recognize that the Rebbe is a great man," I said, "but I cannot see his spiritual powers in healing people and I do not think that his advice holds any more substance than any other intelligent person would give."

"You have to admit that there is a spiritual life in this world," he tried to explain, "and there exists a spirit that has great affect upon our lives. Once you believe that there is spiritual existence, you must admit and believe that there is an individual who has influence and control of this spiritual existence.

"In the Rebbe's advice," he further explained, "in the mere words that the Rebbe utters, there are implications and far reaching meanings. Even if one does not understand the full meaning of the Rebbe's words, one must believe that those words contain the power and spirituality through which help must come."[1]

In the Hasidic community, charisma is a spiritual quality attributed to a rebbe who is believed to have connections with the upper worlds and uses these connections for the benefit of his followers. Hasidic Jews view their rebbe as a visionary, as a man to whom God appears, as a man who is attached to God, "as a man who is full of spirituality, a man who is familiar in the *nigleh* 'open' and the *nister* 'hidden' meanings and mysteries of the Torah, the Jewish law and learning" (Horodetzki 1953: vol. 1, pp.vii–lii). Members of the community believe that he "travels in the upper worlds" and that he has connections with the "ultimate," the "fundamental," and the "vital order-determining" forces. Many Hasidic stories attest to this quality. It is told that the former Satmarer Rebbe used to doze off while he was delivering his *d'var Torah* (Biblical explanation), during the Third Meal Ceremony on the Sabbath. One of the Hasidim who sat at the table in awe related: "The Rebbe is not sleeping, God forbid. During the presentation of his Torah, his soul travels in *olomot elyonim* (the upper worlds) and there he becomes bound together with other *zaddiqim* (righteous persons). It takes him great effort to return."[2]

Another rebbe stands in prayer a long time during the Eighteen Benedictions. He continues praying long after the congregation is through. During this time the congregation waits for the Rebbe in order for the services to continue. "What is the Rebbe doing so long during these prayers? Everybody is done, why does it take him such a long time?" I asked one of the Hasidim. "Oh," he casually replied, "he is traveling in olomot elyonim."[3]

The community attributes to the rebbe supernatural powers and all sorts of miraculous performances. As one Hasid related "I go to the Rebbe where I can hear the prayers the way the prayers must be said." Another Hasid said: "At the Rebbe's I get soaked with holiness." Still another Hasid said, "When I pray with the Rebbe, my prayers connect onto the prayers of the Rebbe, and together our prayers reach Heaven." Almost every aspect of the central figure, the rebbe's behavior, conveys deep, inner emotional attachment to God, and in his mere countenance, this feeling shines through. In the activities and pronouncements of the rebbe, the followers perceive hidden meanings, holy implications, and spiritual intentions. One Hasid remarked, "When I come to the Rebbe's *tish* (ceremonial meal), I just look at him and observe as godliness rests upon his face." Another Hasid said, "I feel spiritually elevated in the presence of the Rebbe." Hasidim also ascribe to their rebbes talent, skill, competence, and knowledge. As one Hasid stated: "I go to the Rebbe to discuss with him all my business activities. I ask him advice on the *shiduch* (marriage) of my children. I seek his consent on the future marriage partners of my children and the future in-laws."[4]

Hence, the rebbe is recognized as the authority of *Yiddishkeit*—everything pertaining to Judaism. He is recognized for his extraordinary qualities, but above all, the rebbe is trusted, obeyed, and revered because the followers believe in his charisma. As Max Weber stated, "In the case of charismatic authority, it is the charismatically qualified leader as such who is obeyed by virtue of personal trust in him and his revelation, his heroism or his exemplary qualities so far as they fall within the scope of the individual's belief in his charisma" (Weber 1947:324–336).

THE RELATIONSHIP AMONG REBBES AND IDEOLOGICAL DIVISIONS AMONG HASIDIC GROUPS

The community tolerates the emergence of other relatively younger, less prominent charismatic leaders, in addition to the eminent and distinguished rebbes, provided that (1) the emerging rebbe remains relatively unimportant and does not seek to control a large element of the community, and (2) this new charismatic leader subscribes to the basic principles, ideologies, and behavior pattern of the major rebbe.

If a relatively obscure rebbe "becomes too big," meaning he obtains substantial followers and resources with which he builds synagogues, schools, and other community service programs, he is not tolerated, for he competes in membership and economic resources. Oftentimes the antagonism between the groups is so great that members of one group will be prohibited to marry a member of the other group, or prohibited to eat the food produced by the other. If, however, he subscribes to the major central figure, the dominant rebbe, in ideology, or better yet, in personal subordination, the community tolerates him. Thus, Hasidim who appear to be uniform in patterns of behavior, in external appearance, in religious ideology, and subscription to Hasidism are divided on the basis of their particular adherence to a specific Hasidic rebbe.

There is a great deal of diversity among Hasidim and among Hasidic rebbes. Some rebbes emphasize the importance of Torah study while others focus on the importance of proper prayers. While certain rebbes are known for their extraordinary charitable activities, others are known for their hidden piety. Some rebbes are politically active, while certain ones prohibit their followers to become involved in politics.

Every Hasidic community and each rebbe has a particular and unique quality and pattern of behavior which distinguish them from any other groups and rebbes. As Reb Zalmen told me, "There is an old adage among the Hasidim which says, '*Yeder rebbe hot zein derech un yeder derech hot zein rebbe*' (Every rebbe has his pattern and every pattern has its rebbe)."

Some of the more consequential and critical ideological divisions among Hasidim and Hasidic rebbes are related to the recognition of the modern State of Israel. The following are the divisions:

1. Subscribe to *Eretz Yisroel*—the Land of Israel. All Hasidim subscribe to ancient *Eretz Yisroel*. In as much as it is believed that God "promised" the Land of Israel to the Jews, the land is inherently holy. Many of the commandments in the Torah can be observed only in connection with the Holy Land. All Hasidic Jews pray three times a day for the return of Zion and Jerusalem.

2. Oppose Israel. Many Hasidim, particularly the Satmar community, reject modern Israel due to the fact that Israel is a secular state, led by secular Jews. Since Israel was not established by God "through His holy Messiah, *eretz hakdoshah*, the Holy Land, was desecrated." Any personal relationship or official involvement with the government of Israel, which may resemble a recognition, is discouraged. Any emotional fervor or expression thereof is prohibited. These groups are vocal and openly express hostility about governmental actions and decisions, particularly those that relate to religion.

The antagonism against Israel is so great that even the Satmarer Rebbe's son, who married the daughter of the famous Vishnitzer Rebbe from Israel, is not fully accepted by the Satmarer Hasidim because his wife is from Israel. That the wife is from Israel and speaks modern Hebrew disqualifies the husband from becoming a full-fledged and recognized Hasidic rebbe in the Satmarer community. Reb Dovid, a Hasidic Jew whose religious views are pro-Israel, said during an interview, "Imagine—a Satmarer Hasid said to me in my own house: 'We pray three times a day for the destruction of the Israeli government.'"[5]

3. Oppose Israel in moderation. There are some groups among the Hasidim who still reject the secular government of Israel. They are, however, less vocal and less critical. They do not publish nor express openly negative opinions and rejections of the Israeli government. They only ideologically subscribe to anti-Israeli sentiment, but do not try to embarrass Israel openly.

4. Supporters of Israel. There are groups among the Hasidim who recognize Israel and its government openly. They maintain a strong tie with its people and leadership and have strong contacts with Israeli organizations. Many of them even maintain an Israeli branch of their special type of Hasidism.

It seems that between those groups that oppose Israel and those groups that support Israel there is a great amount of antagonism (and limited interaction between them). Often their hostilities and antagonisms are contested in public—on the streets and in newspapers. Despite the fact that the relationship between groups that tolerate Israel and those that support Israel is somewhat strained and limited, there is an understanding and open interaction between those groups that oppose Israel and those groups that tolerate Israel since they do not express their views in public.

THE SPIRITUAL ATTRIBUTES OF THE HASIDIC REBBE
AS SYSTEMATIZED IN THE WORK OF
RABBI ELIMELECH OF LYZHANSK

To present the whole spectrum of the spiritual attributes of the rebbe is beyond the scope of this chapter. In this chapter I report on ten random concepts exemplifying the attributes of the rebbe in the Hasidic community. These attributes are some of the components of the conceptual framework of charisma. It will be pointed out that the qualities reflect Hasidic concepts in the literature and are practiced in daily life. Since it is believed that the rebbe has control and influence over all that is necessary for a fulfilled life, followers seek the advice and the blessing of the rebbe. It is in the interest of the followers to attach to the rebbe otherworldly qualities—charisma—because he is the key to their happiness. The more highly the community thinks of the rebbe, the more he is capable of doing for them. As the established values and attitudes are unquestionably followed, the dominance of the charisma is strengthened.

This analysis is based on the teachings of Rabbi Elimelech of Lyzhansk. Rabbi Elimelech of Lyzhansk (1717–1787), the famous *zaddiq* and Hasidic rebbe, was in the third generation of Hasidim from the Besht, the founder of Hasidism (Kahana, 1922:17–99) and the disciple of Dov Ber, the Maggid of Mezeritch (ibid.:141–68). Rabbi Elimelech is considered the theoretician and creator of Practical Zaddiqism—the prescription of the behavior and the theoretical conception of the Hasidic rebbe.

Rabbi Elimelech wrote a book, the *Noam Elimelech*, published by his son in Lvov in 1787, one year after he died. In this book Rabbi Elimelech formulated the major doctrine of the zaddiq—the proper behavior, conduct, and thought processes of the rebbe. According to Rabbi Elimelech, the zaddiq possesses the highest spiritual status in the world, and is the foundation of the universe. The zaddiq has powers that can influence God. Angels are created from the mere utterances of the zaddiq.[6]

To indicate the enormous influence Rabbi Elimelech had on the Hasidic world, one should consider the stature of his disciples—the great giants of Hasidism. The most outstanding ones are Rabbi Abraham Joshua Heschel of Apt (Marcus 1980:125, 162–166); Rabbi Jacob Isaac Horowitz, "Ha-Chozeh"—the Seer of Lublin (ibid.:30, 60, 107); Rabbi Kalonymus Kalman Epstein of

Cracow (ibid.:124, 160, 169); the author of *Maor Va'Shemesh*, Rabbi Menachem Mendel of Rymanow (ibid.:116, 121, 124); and Rabbi Moses Leib of Sasov (ibid.:80, 103, 158). These rebbes, and their dynasties that followed, constituted the bulk of mainstream Hasidism.

Rabbi Elimelech's teaching was selected for analysis because it is the most systematic, consistent, daring, and outspoken work on the power of the rebbe. The following ten attributes are considered in this chapter: (1) *kesher*—tie, connection or bond; (2) *achdut*—unity or oneness; (3) *devekut*—attachment or devotion; (4) *nitzutz*—spark or glimmer; (5) *hirhur*—thought or perception; (6) *hamshoche*—draw or pull; (7) *hashpoeh*—influence or bequeath; (8) *yetzer horah*—evil inclination or evil tendency; (9) *shoresh*—root or source; (10) *mevatel dinim*—cancel or annul judgment.

1. *Kesher*—Tie. The rebbe is considered a spiritual leader who has strong connections with the upper world. Even during his physical and earthly existence, he is tied up with Heaven. Rabbi Elimelech: "The *Zaddiq* ties himself into the high heavens of eternal life. Even while he is in this world, he attains the happiness of the upper world, because all his activities are done in holiness, purity, devotion, love, and awe" (Elimelech: 2a).

2. *Achdut*—Unity. For the zaddiq the upper world is not necessarily a place that he visits, it is an entity with which he is completely united. Rabbi Elimelech: "The *Zaddiq* must be in complete unity with the upper world" (ibid.).

3. *Devekut*—Attachment. It is perceived that the zaddiq is completely attached to God. It is for this reason that he can help others.

Rabbi Elimelech: "It is the *Zaddiq's* desire to walk in the paths of the Lord. As God has spoken in holiness, purity and attachment to [Himself], the same way is the *Zaddiq* who performs the Lord's commandments" (ibid.:6a).

4. *Nitzotz*—Spark. It is believed that everything in the world contains a holy spark, since nothing can exist without this holy spark. The zaddiq has the ability to elevate this holy spark into the upper worlds. Rabbi Elimelech: "God, blessed be His name, desires the service of the *Zaddiqim* because it is they who elevate the holy sparks into the upper world. The world cannot exist without the *Zaddiqim* because they must elevate the spiritual sparks into the upper world" (ibid.:2a).

5. *Hirhur*—Thought. The zaddiq must have pure thoughts even when he is involved in earthly and physical activities. Rabbi Elimelech: "This is the way of a true *Zaddiq*: He has no thoughts and physical desires, not even for his wife. Even during close relationship with her, the *Zaddiq's* thoughts must be in the upper world" (ibid.).

6. *Hamshoche*—Draw. It is believed that God's presence is everywhere. His main domain, however, is considered to be in Heaven. To establish a closer relationship with God, the community must feel God's presence in this world. It is the zaddiq who, through his holiness, draws God's presence into the world. Rabbi Elimelech: "The *Zaddiq* through his holy actions draws the Creator, blessed be His name, into this world. The *Zaddiq* thereby performs a favor for his generation by causing God's presence to be with them" (ibid.).

7. *Hashpoeh*—Influence. It is the zaddiq who causes and maintains the continuity and the flow of goodness and blessing into the world. Rabbi Elimelech: "The perfect *Zaddiq*, who is in constant unity with God, causes the flow of goodness and blessing upon all the people of Israel" (ibid.:3a).

8. *Yetzer Horah*—Evil Inclination. Regardless of how great and spiritual a zaddiq might be, he must constantly guard against his own evil inclination that make him susceptible to sin. Rabbi Elimelech: "The *Zaddiq* even in his most elevated position must guard against the Evil Inclination that might cause him to sin, God forbid" (ibid.:6a). (It may be said that there are two reasons why such a zaddiq is associated with an inclination to sin: (1) Regardless of how great and spiritual a person might be, he is still a human being and there is always the possibility for him to err; (2) Spiritual greatness is shown by the fact, that despite one's basic potentialities to sin, still attains spirituality.)

9. *Shoresh*—Root. Everything, particularly good deeds and Godly commandments, have their base or origin in heaven, from where they stem forth. It is the responsibility of the zaddiq to direct his activities to their roots and their pure essence. Rabbi Elimelech: "As there are many branches of a tree, and all those branches are attached to the main tree, the same is true with the commandments. All commandments have their roots and origins in the Upper Heavenly Tree. A person must understand and recognize the root, the source, and the essence of each commandment" (ibid.:6a).

10. *Mevatel Hadinim*—Cancel Judgments. It is believed that individuals and their behavior are judged in heaven. Judgments and sentences are pronounced upon individuals concerning their health, well being, sufferings, and the number of years they are to live. The rebbe who relates all actions to their source and their origin, has the ability to cancel and annul in heaven the sentence and judgment placed upon an individual. Rabbi Elimelech: "The *Zaddiq* abrogates the judgments by lifting them to their source where they become nullified" (ibid.:3b). These are some of the many concepts that prevail in the Hasidic community about the spiritual man, the charismatic leader, the zaddiq, the rebbe.

Members of the community believe that their rebbe can do all that is necessary for their physical and spiritual well-being. Followers are not always aware of these attributes. It is not even necessary to be aware of them. The mere fact that these ideas are part of the community's religion and that members act in accordance with these religious beliefs indicates that these ideas and actions are the Hasidic experience. They are fully integrated into the Hasidic psyche and the community's daily existence.

THE PERCEPTION OF THE REBBE IN THE HASIDIC COMMUNITY

These theoretical attributes are translated into the real world, into a real person, onto a rebbe. The rebbe may be tied (*kesher*) to heaven, but his advice is down to earth. Or the perception is that due to rebbe's upper world connections, his advise and his blessings are Heavenly powered. The rebbe may be in unity (*achdut/devekut*) with Heaven, but he is approachable as a human being. The rebbe may elevate the holy spark (*nitzotz*) into Heaven, but he also elevates the spirits of his followers. The rebbe may have only pure thoughts (*Hirhur*), but he understands human needs. The rebbe may draw (*hamshoche*) man up to God, but he also brings God down to the people. The rebbe may cause the flow of blessing (*hamshoche*) into the world, but he is real enough to recognize that the flow of blessing is closely related to livelihood. The rebbe may guard himself against evil (*yetzer horah*), but he recognizes the frailties of his followers. The rebbe may direct everything to the source (*shoresh*) in heaven, but he also relates the heavenly source to social relations. The rebbe may annul the harsh judgment (*mevatel dinim*) in heaven, at the same time he comforts his followers about their health concerns.

The followers automatically accept the rebbe's behavior as "other worldly", having spiritual significance. Even though the individuals do not understand a specific behavior, conduct, demeanor, or action, they believe that the rebbe's physical movements and gestures have great significance and meaning. The rebbe's words are holy and his blessings are accepted by God. When I asked Hasidim to explain a certain behavior of the rebbe, the answer was invariably: "*Dos is Kabole*" (This is Kabbalah), or, "*Dos zeinen tife zachen*" (These are deep matters), or "*Noch a reben fregt men nit*" (One does not ask into the conduct of a rebbe).

In practical life the rebbe advises in business, assures long life, comforts in matters of child births, provides confidence to the sick and destitute, and gives blessing to those in need. The following examples will illustrate most of the points:

The rebbe advises in business: "When business was very bad I was contemplating to go to another line of business activity. I thought before I do anything I will go to see the Rebbe and ask his advice. I told the Rebbe that business is very slow and I am thinking of going into a different occupation. The Rebbe told me not to go into any other business, I should stay with the business in which I am. Of course, I did what the Rebbe told me. I stayed with the business. Thank God the business picked up and I am very glad that I stayed with it."[7]

The rebbe assures long life: "My father was ill. Even after he recuperated he still did not feel completely well. He decided to go to Skverer Rebbe. During the visit with the Rebbe my father complained to him about his health. The Rebbe told him in these words, '*Ihr wet noch tantzen of eire ur-einiklach chasene*—you will dance at your great-grand children's wedding.' My father is reaching ninety and he did dance at his great-grand-children's wedding."[8]

The rebbe is a miracle healer: "This is a miracle that I myself have witnessed. My friend whose father was in the hospital, in a coma, asked me to go to the Bobover Rebbe for a blessing for his father. I came to the Rebbe's house and told the attendant that I came to see the Rebbe with an important request. I was allowed to see the Rebbe immediately. I came into the dining room where the Rebbe was sitting with his family in the middle of the Shabbat meal. He recognized that I was a stranger, whom he has never seen before, and asked what I wanted. I told the Rebbe that I was sent by my friend, whose name he recognized, who asked me to ask the Rebbe for a blessing for his father who is in the hospital in a coma. The Rebbe said, 'They should not be concerned because *alte mentchen dreien sich araus fun dem*—old people pull themselves out of this.' 'But Rebbe,' I said in amazement, 'he is in a hospital in a coma.' The Rebbe calmly repeated what he said before, 'Old people pull themselves out of this.' I went back to the my friend and his family and told them what the Rebbe said. They demonstrated great happiness because to them the Rebbe's words were an assurance that everything will be all right with their father. Within a few days the old man got better and left the hospital. He is still around, living a normal life."[9]

The rebbe comforts in matters of child birth: "My wife had great difficulties during her pregnancy. The family was worried that she may not carry the baby for the full length of nine months. The doctor was not very encouraging. When her due date came my wife's parents and I worried that she may have extraordinary labor pains. I went to see the Skverer Rebbe and told him about our fright and apprehension. The Rebbe told me, 'The delivery will be as easy as you pull out a hair from a glass of milk.' I was even astonished at the Rebbe's characterization of the situation. A few days later she had a perfect delivery."[10]

The rebbe's blessings secure positive results: (1) "My second daughter was a beautiful baby. Each time my wife took her to the street for a walk, people always admired the child. My wife and I noticed that each time the child was taken out for fresh air, she became sick with a cold and low fever. Upon my visit to the Rebbe, I mentioned to him that my child is sick each time she is taken out. The Rebbe said, 'An evil eye will not hurt her.' Ever since that time my child was all right." [Do you think that your child's well-being is related to the Rebbe's assurances?] Somewhat annoyed: "Well, what do you think helped the child if not the Rebbe's assurances?" ["Maybe it was coincidental?"] More annoyed and antagonized: "What is the matter with you? Of course it was the Rebbe's blessing. A man who goes every morning to the ritual bath to purify himself, learns Torah all day, prays all day, and is involved in holiness all day, is a holy man. The blessing of such a holy person has a definite effect."[11]

(2) "When I was young my father used to take me to the Ratzferter *Zaddiq*, Rebbe Sholem Eliezer. In his time he was considered the greatest among all the Hasidic rebbes because he was the son of the Zanzer Rebbe, Chayim Zanzer. During the war I was hiding from the Nazis. I went to see Rebbe Sholem Eliezer, in Ratzfert, Rumania (not occupied by the Nazis at this time), to give me a blessing. Due to the awe and reverence his persona commanded, I did not know how to approach him. Thus, I followed him around in the house of prayer. When he noticed that I was around him too much, he asked me, 'Who are you?' I told him that I am the grandson of Feivel Zimmerman. 'Oh, you are the grandson of Feivel Zimmerman?' he asked, as he recognized the name of my grandfather. 'What do you want?' he asked. I told him that I am hiding from the Nazis and I want the Rebbe to bless me. The Rebbe closed his eyes for several seconds, he put his hand on my head and muttered something that I did not understand, after which he said, 'Now you can go!' During the entire war I was hiding from the Nazis and met many policemen and not even once was I asked for my identification. As I was running from the Nazis, I traveled from one city to another where the opportunity to hide looked better. As I and two companions bought tickets at a railroad station, the ticket clerk recognized that we were Jews and called the police. I asked the clerk if I may leave my bags here and is there any place where I could wash. He told me that I may leave the bags and in the woods, not far from the station, I could wash. I went to the forest and hid myself. I left my bags in the station. The police came and my two companions were arrested. The police were looking for me in the woods but did not find me. A Rumanian peasant found me and offered to help. I was frightened. He told me that he helped other Jews also. After paying the price and much physical difficulties he took me to the city where I wanted to go. After the war I found out that my two companions were arrested and kept in prison during the entire war. The Rebbe's blessing helped me to be free during all that time."[12]

The Hasidic community is replete with stories of the rebbe that attest to his charisma. Everyone has an anecdote, a personal experience, a legend to tell. In spite of their ubiquity, these stories are far from being the only signifiers of the rebbes' abilities. A cursory review of the daily speech patterns and writings of Hasidim also discloses community sentiment toward the rebbe. The following are some of the titles and honorary expressions, used in conversation and in print by Hasidim to refer to the rebbe :

Used in the Presence of the Rebbe

1. *Adonenu*—Our master;
2. *Morenu*—Our teacher;
3. *Rabbenu*—Our rabbi;
4. *Zaddiq*—Righteous.

Used in Writing and in Print

5. *Zaddiq hador*—The zaddiq of the generation;
6. *Amud esh*—Pillar of fire;
7. *Amud Hatorah v'hayirah v'hachesed*—The pillar of Torah, of God fearing, and of loving kindness;
8. *Rabban shel kol b'nei hagola*—The rabbi of all the people of the Diaspora;
9. *Meor hagola*—The light of the Diaspora.

Used after the Rebbe's Death

10. *Ish Elokim*—Man of God;
11. *Kadosh Hakodoshim*—Holy of holies;
12. *Rabban shel Yisroel*—The recognized rabbi of all the people of Israel.

Used in the Funeral Oration

13. *Hu hoish asher yolichenu likras Melech Hamoshiach*—He is the man who was to lead us to welcome King Messiah;
14. *Avihem shel Yisroel*—The father of the Children of Israel;
15. *Hu hagever asher hevi es kol ho-olom kulo lechaye olam haba*—He is the man who brings the entire world to everlasting life;
16. *Hu hagever asher hitzis es hoamuna hatzrofa beatzmaos hayeveshos bedorenu*—He is the man who has ignited the fire in the dried bones in our generation;

17. *Melitz yosher far klal Yisroel*—A pleader [before the Heavenly Court] for the entire House of Israel.

In order to discover what a community thinks about the Hasidic rebbe during his lifetime and after his death, one should consider the book, *The Sun Set*.[13] Rabbi Joel Teitelbaum, the illustrious Satmarer Rebbe, died on August 1979. In 1980 *The Sun Set* was published in his memory. The book contains 223 articles and eulogies. Seventy three of these articles are collected from the English press, 14 articles from non-English press, 101 articles in Hebrew and Yiddish about his life and death, and the full text of 35 eulogies in Hebrew.

I would like to conclude this section with an example of charisma that is taken from the Lubavitcher Hasidim. Lubavitchers held their late rebbe in such high esteem that many regarded him as the Messiah himself. In the very least, Lubavitcher Hasidim believed that their Rebbe's prophecies herald the messianic age: They assert that in 1951 when the late Lubavitcher Rebbe formally became the Rebbe, he "clearly stated [his] goal of bringing the Moshiach."[14]

An advertisement by the Lubavitcher Hasidim about the ninetieth birthday of the Rebbe, reads:

> Rebbe, in April 1987 you stated that Soviet Jews will soon be free to leave the Soviet Union and you called upon Israel to prepare for them.
>
> In the Summer of 1989 you declared that the upcoming Jewish year will be a Year of Miracle.
>
> That year we witnessed the beginning of the exodus of Soviet Jewry. The Iron Curtain fell throughout Eastern Europe in revolutions that were virtually bloodless—a phenomena unparalleled in history.
>
> In May 1990 you predicted that the year to come would be a year of yet greater and more openly revealed miracles.
>
> From November through February 1991 you repeatedly assured a frightened people that the impending war in the Gulf will not harm the people of Israel. Your promise that there is nothing to fear, no need for gas masks and that Divine protection is certain was fulfilled in every detail.
>
> This year you told us that it will be a year of miracles and wonders in everything.
>
> The Soviet Union and the communist regime collapsed, again through astonishingly peaceful means.

Jews converge upon the land of Israel from undreamed of locations, echoing the Biblical promise, 'Behold I shall bring them [to Israel] from the land of the north and from the ends of the earth.

You have explained that all this indicates the we are now standing on the threshold of the Messianic age.

Your message today reverberates around the world: The era of Moshiach [the Messiah] is upon us. World peace, universal Godly enlightenment and a final end to all suffering—is only a moment away.

Dear Rebbe, as we approach your ninetieth birthday, the world awaits expectantly the fulfillment of your ultimate prophecy. In perfect health you will lead us into this blessed age, with everlasting joy and celebration.[15]

CONCLUSION: THE REBBE PROVIDES THE FORCE THAT HELPS THE COMMUNITY TO ENDURE SOCIAL LIFE

Questions may be asked: Are the members of the community aware of the upper world connections of the rebbe? Do members of the community believe that the rebbe has upper-world connections? If they believe that he has, what is their perception of the upper world? These questions are totally irrelevant. Hasidic Jews do not confront themselves with these questions. Nor are Hasidic Jews ever challenged to answer whether or not they believe in the rebbe's upper-world activities, for they simply never doubt in the rebbe's abilities. Because Hasidim perceive the rebbe to be endowed with charisma, the Hasid–rebbe relationship is one that works.

The Hasidic beliefs and patterns of behavior and their relationship with the rebbe are not individually confronted, confirmed, or defended. Religious beliefs are part of the culture of the group that are deeply rooted in the thoughts and actions of the community. They are constantly acted out as if all the participants fully adhere to the group's religious belief system.

Christians, for example, do not prove, confirm, or defend that Christ was immaculately conceived. Jews do not prove, confirm, or defend that Moses stood at Mount Sinai with the two tablets of stone. Muslims do not prove, confirm, or defend that Mohammed ascended to Heaven. It is sufficient that members of these groups behave as if those events took place. Hasidic Jews do not prove, confirm, or defend that their rebbe is a Godly man. They in fact behave towards him as if he is.

Durkheim argues (Parsons, 1961:677) that "the real function of religion is . . . to make us act, to aid us to live. The believer . . . feels within him more force, either to endure the trials of existence or to conquer them. It is as though he were raised above the miseries of the world, . . . he believes that he is saved from evil, under whatever form he may conceive this evil."

As Durkheim stated, the function of religion is to aid individuals and communities in coping with life. This function is personified in the rebbe who helps individuals manage the vagaries of their existence and to ultimately prevail. While religion raises individuals above the miseries of the world, it is the rebbe that makes this into a factual experience. Though religion saves the followers from evil, it is the rebbe, the artful practitioner, who restores the spirit from decline. In the final analysis, the rebbe can accomplish these tasks because the community attributes to him the qualities of a charismatic leader.

NOTES

1. Interview, S. L. 1991.
2. Interview, S. Y. 1989.
3. Interview, D. H. 1991.
4. Interview, G. L. 1990.
5. Interview, R. D. 1991.
6. "Elimelech of Lyzhansk," Encyclopedia Judaica, vol. 6, pp. 661–663.
7. Interview, L. G. 1992.
8. Interview, G. E. 1992.
9. Interview, Zelzer 1992.
10. Interview, L. L.
11. Interview, G. L. 1992.
12. Interview, P. R. 1992.
13. *The Sun Set* (1980) Brooklyn, NY: Gross Bros. Printing Co. The English title page reads: The Sun Set / Memoirs / of the holy Grand Rabbi / of Satmar and Jerusalem / Rebbe Joel Teitelbaum / of sainted memory. The translation of the Hebrew title page reads: The Sun Set / Memorial Book / of his honorable holiness, our master, our teacher, our rabbi, holy of holies / Rebbe Joel Teitelbaum, to remember the zaddiq and the holy for blessing and for heaven / the Head of the Rabbinical

Court of Satmar and the Head of the Rabbinical Court of the holy city of Jerusalem.

14. The Jewish Press, April 10, 1992.
15. Ibid.

REFERENCES

Durkheim, E. 1961. Religion and society. In *Theories of society* Vol. 1, ed. Talcott Parsons et al., 677–682. New York: The Free Press.

Elimelech of Lyzhansk. 1977. *Noam Elimelech*. Brooklyn: Moriah Offset Co. [Hebrew.]

Horodetzki, S. A. 1953. *Hahasidut V'hahasidim*. Tel Aviv: D'vir Co. [Hebrew.]

Kahana, A. 1922. *Sefer Hahasidut*. Warsaw, Poland: Die Welt. [Hebrew.]

Marcus, A. 1980. *Hahasidut*. Translated from German into Hebrew by Moshe Schonfeld. B'nei Berak, Israel: Nezach. [Hebrew.]

Shils, E. 1968. Charisma. In *International encyclopedia of social sciences*. New York: Collier-Macmillan and Free Press.

Teitelbaum, Joel. 1980. *The sun set*. Brooklyn, NY: Gross Bros. Printing Co.

Weber, M. 1947. *The theory of social and economic organizations*. Trans. A. M. Henderson and Talcott Parsons, ed. Talcott Parsons. Glencoe, IL: Free Press.

———. 1957. *The theory of social and economic organization*. Ed. Talcott Parsons. Glencoe, IL: Free Press.

CONTRIBUTORS

Janet Belcove-Shalin is a senior research associate at the Southwestern Social Science Research Center at the University of Nevada, Las Vegas. She has conducted ethnography in Hasidic communities of Brooklyn, Boston, and Las Vegas. Her chief areas of interest include religious fundamentalism, the anthropology of religion, and the interface of humanistic and social scientific knowledge of Hasidic life. She has published on the methodological issues of ethnographic work and modes of sanctification among Hasidim, and is currently serving as a consultant to a NIH funded documentary film project on Hasidic life in America.

Lynn Davidman is the Dorot Assistant Professor of Judaic Studies and Sociology at Brown University. Her first book, *Tradition in a Rootless World: Women Turn to Orthodox Judaism* (University of California Press, 1991), won the 1992 National Jewish Book Award in the category of Contemporary Jewish Life. Her second book, coedited with Shelly Tenenbaum, is called *Feminist Perspectives On Jewish Studies* and is due out from Yale Press in 1994. In addition, she has written several articles and review essays on gender and religion.

Shifra Epstein is an assistant professor in the Department of Near Eastern and Judaic Languages and Literatures at Emory University, Atlanta, Georgia. She has conducted research among Hasidim in New York and among Israeli Jews of Middle Eastern origin. Her research and publications are in the area of Jewish folklore and ethnology, with special interest in Jewish and Hasidic celebrations, festivals, pilgrimages, and material culture. She also produced two documentary films, the most recent one being *Pilgrimage of Remembrance: The Jews of Poland Today*. She is currently completing a monograph entitled *Performing for Survival: The Bobover Hasidim and the Celebration of Purim*.

277

Samuel Heilman is the Harold Porshansky Professor of Jewish Studies and Sociology on the faculty of the Graduate Center and Queens College of the City University of New York. He is the author of numerous articles and reviews as well as six books: *Synagogue Life; The People of the Book; the Gate Behind the Wall, A Walker in Jerusalem; Cosmopolitans and Parochials: Modern Orthodox Jews in America* (co-authored with Steven M. Cohen); and most recently *Defenders of the Faith: Inside Ultra-Orthodox Jewry.* He has also been the Scheinbrum Visiting Professor of Sociology at the Hebrew University in Jerusalem, visiting professor of social anthropology at Tel Aviv University, and a Fulbright visiting professor at the Universities of New South Wales and Melbourne in Australia. In 1993 he gave the Samuel and Althea Stroum Lectures at the University of Washington. His Stroum Lectures will be published by the University of Washington Press in 1994 as *Choosing to be Jews: A Sociological Reflection on American Jewry since 1950.*

Debra Renee Kaufman is a professor of sociology, the former Klein Lecturer and founder and coordinator of Women's Studies at Northeastern University. She is the author of numerous articles and chapters on women, work, the family, feminist methodology, and theory. Her most recent book, *Rachel's Daughters: Newly Orthodox Jewish Women* (Rutgers University Press, 1991), explores the relationship between fundamentalist Religious-Right women and feminism during the final decades of this century. She is currently working on identity politics and concepts of the Other as she analyzes the data she collected during her semester stay as a visiting scholar at Brigham Young University, where she interviewed both Mormon and Jewish feminists.

Ellen Koskoff is an associate professor of ethnomusicology at the University of Rochester's Eastman School of Music. She is the editor of *Women and Music in Cross-Cultural Perspective,* and the author of numerous articles on music within the context of Hasidic life. Her book, *Heel, Head, and Heart: Music and Spirituality Among Lubavitcher Hasidim,* is forthcoming.

George Gershon Kranzler is a professor emeritus in the Department of Sociology of Towson State University, and lecturer at Johns Hopkins University in Baltimore, Maryland. He received a

Ph.D. in philosophy and education from the University of Wurzburg, Germany, and a Ph.D. in sociology from Columbia University. The first of four volumes of his longitudinal study of the Jewish community of Williamsburg in Brooklyn, New York, *Williamsburg: A Jewish Community in Transition* (New York, 1960), is cited in many books and encyclopedias. The last volume, *Hasidic Williamsburg: A Contemporary American Hasidic Community*, is being readied for publication. He has contributed numerous articles on the American Orthodox Jewish and Hasidic community to books and magazines. (He is also the author of over twenty books of nonfiction and fiction for juveniles.)

Laurence D. Loeb received his Ph.D. in anthropology from Columbia University. He served as chair of the Anthropology Department at the University of Utah, where he is currently an associate professor. He has chaired the Jewish Ethnology Network and currently co-chairs the Committee on the Anthropology of Jews and Judaism of the American Anthropologoical Association. His research on Jewish communities includes extensive fieldwork in Iran and Israel. He is presently completing a manuscript on Jews in South Yemen in the nineteenth and twentieth centuries.

Bonnie Morris received her Ph.D. in women's history from SUNY-Binghamton after completing her doctoral dissertation on Lubavitcher women. She went on to teach at Dartmouth, Harvard Divinity School, Northeastern, and St. Lawrence Universities, and in Fall 1993 served as women's studies professor for "Semester at Sea"—a global voyage for 500 students and faculty. Her work has appeared in over a dozen anthologies and, in summer, she performs one-woman theatre at women's music festivals.

Solomon Poll is a professor emeritus of sociology at the University of New Hampshire and a former dean of social sciences at Bar Ilan University, Ramat Gan, Israel. He has written numerous articles on Orthodox Judaism, Hasidim, social linguistics, and Yiddish. He is the author of two books: *The Hasidic Community of Williamsburg* and *Ancient Thoughts in Modern Perspective*. His current research includes the study of charisma in Hasidism, religious zealotry, and the Neturei Karta.

William Shaffir is a professor of sociology at McMaster University in Hamilton, Canada. His chief areas of interest include the sociology of religious transformation, professional socialization, and field research methods. His current research includes studies of Montreal's Hasidic community, the processes of defection from the ultra-Orthodox fold in Israel, and a social psychological study of the Lubavitcher Hasidim's messianic proselytization.

Janet Stocks is currently finishing a Ph.D. in sociology at the University of Pittsburgh. Her dissertation is an ethnographic, comparative case-study of two small evangelical Christian groups in which feminist challenges are currently occurring. She is also involved in a qualitative study of an innovative math program that has been developed for teaching math in elementary schools. She holds a B.A. in philosophy and an M.A. in sociology from Oberlin College.

INDEX